Diálogos Series

KRIS LANE, Series Editor

Understanding Latin America demands dialogue, deep exploration, and frank discussion of key topics. Founded by Lyman L. Johnson in 1992 and edited since 2013 by Kris Lane, the Diálogos Series focuses on innovative scholarship in Latin American history and related fields. The series, the most successful of its type, includes specialist works accessible to a wide readership and a variety of thematic titles, all ideally suited for classroom adoption by university and college teachers.

Also available in the Diálogos Series:

Driving Terror: Labor, Violence, and Justice in Cold War Argentina by Karen Robert
Anti-Catholicism in the Mexican Revolution, 1913–1940 edited by Jürgen Buchenau and David S. Dalton
The Struggle for Natural Resources: Findings from Bolivian History edited by Carmen Soliz and Rossana Barragán
Viceroy Güemes's Mexico: Rituals, Religion, and Revenue by Christoph Rosenmüller
At the Heart of the Borderlands: Africans and Afro-Descendants on the Edges of Colonial Spanish America edited by Cameron D. Jones and Jay T. Harrison
The Age of Dissent: Revolution and the Power of Communication in Chile, 1780–1833 by Martín Bowen
From Sea-Bathing to Beach-Going: A Social History of the Beach in Rio de Janeiro, Brazil by B.J. Barickman
Gamboa's World: Justice, Silver Mining, and Imperial Reform in New Spain by Christopher Albi
The Conquest of the Desert: Argentina's Indigenous Peoples and the Battle for History edited by Carolyne R. Larson
From the Galleons to the Highlands: Slave Trade Routes in the Spanish Americas edited by Alex Borucki, David Eltis, and David Wheat

For additional titles in the Diálogos Series, please visit unmpress.com.

Frontier

Justice

State, Law, and Society in Patagonia, 1880–1940

JAVIER CIKOTA

UNIVERSITY OF NEW MEXICO PRESS — ALBUQUERQUE

Library of Congress Cataloging-in-Publication Data
Names: Cikota, Javier, 1983– author.
Title: Frontier justice: state, law, and society in Patagonia, 1880–
    1940 / Javier Cikota.
Other titles: Diálogos (Albuquerque, N.M.)
Description: Albuquerque: University of New Mexico Press, 2025. |
    Series: Diálogos series | Includes bibliographical references and
    index.
Identifiers: LCCN 2024024801 (print) | LCCN 2024024802 (ebook) |
    ISBN 9780826367501 (cloth) | ISBN 9780826367518 (paperback) |
    ISBN 9780826367525 (epub) | ISBN 9780826367532 (pdf)
Subjects: LCSH: Frontier and pioneer life—Argentina—Comahue
    Region. | Police, State—Argentina—Comahue Region. |
    Comahue Region (Argentina)—History—20th century. |
    Comahue Region (Argentina)—Social life and customs—20th
    century. | Comahue Region (Argentina)—Social conditions—
    20th century. | Comahue Region (Argentina)—Politics and
    government—20th century.
Classification: LCC F2936 .C535 2025 (print) | LCC F2936 (ebook) |
    DDC 982.7—dc23/eng/20240624

LC record available at https://lccn.loc.gov/2024024801

LC ebook record available at https://lccn.loc.gov/2024024802

Founded in 1889, the University of New Mexico sits on the
    traditional homelands of the Pueblo of Sandia. The original
    peoples of New Mexico—Pueblo, Navajo, and Apache—since
    time immemorial have deep connections to the land and have
    made significant contributions to the broader community
    statewide. We honor the land itself and those who remain
    stewards of this land throughout the generations and also
    acknowledge our committed relationship to Indigenous peoples.
    We gratefully recognize our history.

Cover image: Gauchos resolviendo una discusión; El Duelo Criollo,
    1939 courtesy of Archivo General de la Nación in Argentina.
Designed by Isaac Morris
Composed in BC Parlament, Katari, and Minion pro.

*To my parents, Denise and Victor, who
taught me the importance of climbing "muy
tranquilo la colina de la vida"*

Contents

Illustrations

Maps

Acknowledgments

Writing a book, much like raising children, takes a village. At least this book took a village to bring to life. It took the work, love, patience, insight, and interest of a lot of people, who left their marks on these pages. I wanted to thank the individuals and institutions that made this work possible and absolve them from any shortcomings in the book—those are all my own.

This book is indebted to everyone in Argentina who helped me collect the data. The book would not exist without all the hard work put in to keep the archives alive. At the Archivo Histórico Provincial Río Negro (AHP-RN) in Viedma I want to thank its director, Rebeca Pajón, as well as the relentless staff members Lourdes and Fernanda. They have kept the collection open against impossible odds, taught me patiently how to use their collection, and tirelessly brought out documents for me to read. I am especially indebted to Jorge Calvo who always had a warm *mate* ready to share in the early hours of the cold gray winter mornings. Professor Graciela Suárez showed me the ropes in the AHP-RN and pointed me in the direction of relevant historiography. Professor Pilar Pérez is a role model of how to be a true scholar.

In Neuquén, I am profoundly indebted to Enrique Masés, who kindly allowed me access to court cases housed in the Grupo de Estudios de la Historia Social (GEHiSo) archive, and Gabriel Rafart, who entertained my endless questions. The faculty and staff of the GEHiSo are a testament to the historical practice borne out of love. The archive they constructed and maintained in a library basement inspired my research and nurtured the academic careers of countless students. Francisco Camino Vela warmly opened his home, sharing his kindness and wisdom. In Buenos Aires, the staff at the Archivo General de la Nación–Archivo Intermedio was a tireless resource, painstakingly caring for the recent past and allowing researchers to learn from it. Christine Mathias met with me in San Telmo and taught me ropes during her own research at the AGN. Hanz Schultz met me early in my research process in a café in Bariloche and shared what he knew and what he thought needed to be done. The legendary antiquarian and collector of stories Ricardo Vallmitjana shared his shop and his expertise, reminding me of the stories that don't make it to the archives.

Books take time and money. Time to write and think was generously provided by my colleagues and institutional homes through the years. At Bowdoin College my colleagues in the History Department and throughout the college helped shield me from service and advising as much as possible. I want to thank David Gordon, David Hecht, Page Herrlinger, Dallas Denery, Patrick Rael, Rachel Sturman, Connie Chang, Brian Purnell, Matt Klingle, and Meghan Roberts, who have been exemplary senior colleagues. Sakura Christmas, Salar Mohandesi, and Strother Roberts blazed a path ahead of me and shared kindness and resources generously as well. Outside the History Department, Willi Lampert, Adanna Jones, Aretha Aoki, Nadia Celis, Krista Van Vleet, Margaret Boyle, Maron Sorensen, Jeff Salinger, and Sebastian Urli, among many others, offered advice, encouragement, and know-how since arriving at Bowdoin. Funding from Bowdoin College helped cover some of the costs related to the production of the manuscript, and a generous junior sabbatical allowed me to complete it in a timely manner. During graduate school at the University of California, Berkeley, funding from the Cota-Robles Fellowship, the Berkeley-Connect Fellowship, and the History Department's Dissertation Completion Fellowship help fund the travel to the archives and the time away from teaching to go over the files, write, and think. I remain grateful for the mentorship of Margaret Chowning, Brian Delay, Mark Healey, Laura Enriquez, Robin Einhorn, John Connelly, Victoria Frede, Elena Schneider, Beth Berry, Joe Bohlin, David Beecher, and Linda Lewin, to name a few. Too many fellow graduate students to adequately list here helped make Dwinelle Hall less daunting.

Before I realized what this book was, Mark Healey changed the way I think about history, challenged me to consider which questions are worth asking and whose stories are worth telling. I am forever indebted to him for encouraging me to study "the interior" and to think broadly about inquiries that engage academics both in the United States and in Argentina. Despite the distances his advice, encouragement, and good spirits always made him feel closer. Margaret Chowning has been an incredible mentor. Her relentless optimism and constructive criticisms made this project infinitely better. Brian DeLay's kind, steady advice made me think of Patagonia comparatively, reminding me of what is unique about this frontier and what it can contribute to our understanding of other frontiers. Laura Enriquez, who knows how to ask disarmingly simple questions that force you to reconsider fundamental ways in which you approach a particular problem, was a constant reminder of the value of kindness in academia.

I was lucky to have my interest in history nurtured throughout my life. Mr. Stephen Cohen organized a history club for a few of us in high school after hours, and his incisive questions those afternoons have continued to resonate with me as the decades passed. As an undergraduate, in a time of confusion and disappointment, Jonathan Brown rekindled my interest in history and forced me to become a better writer. Robert Abzug, Susan Deans-Smith, Jorge Cañizares-Esguerra, Seth Garfield, and Virginia Garrard-Burnet shepherded me through the unknown world of American universities and mentored me in ways big and small. Julie Hardwick introduced me to court cases and the fascinating stories they hold, and she taught that the study of women, families, and everyday life was worthwhile. She also modeled, before I fully understood it, how to be a real person to my students.

Many people read chapters of this book throughout the years. Bianca Premo, Ashley Kerr, Julie Hardwick, Kris Lane, and Carrie Ryan read parts of the entire manuscript and enriched it with pointed critiques and generous advice. Thank you, each and every one of you. I want to thank the New Borderlands History Working Group for offering incisive advice and for helping me think through our shared interests. I am particularly indebted to Kyle Harvey, Maria de los Angeles Picone, Sarah Sarzynski, Sarah Foss, Geraldine Davies Lenoble, Hannah Greenwald, and Christine Mathias for their careful reading of chapter 4 when it was freshly written. The interdisciplinary working group of Latin Americanists at Bowdoin, Bates, and Colby offered vigorous feedback and a keen reminder of the multiple audiences of my manuscript. I want to particularly thank Stephanie Pridgeon, Ana Almeyda-Cohen, and Ben Fallaw for their sharp criticism of chapter 2. I was fortunate to have brilliant colleagues like Sylvia Sellers-García, Ryan Edwards, Rwany Sibaja, Jeff Erbig, Juandrea Bates, Pilar Herr, Josh Savala, Lily Balloffet, Jennifer Adair, Steven Hyland, and Nicolas Sillitti comment on my work during conference panels and shape the project in their own ways. The student-run Berkeley Latin American History working group (BLAH) was an invaluable resource in the early years of this project. It is a cherished tradition, passed down from generation to generation of graduate students in the program, and I was honored to be a part of it. Its members read and commented on several early chapters. Within the working group, but also in countless seminars, my extended cohort of *latinoamericanistas*—Sarah Selvidge, Sara Hines, Pablo Palomino, German Vergara, Lynsay Skiba, Alberto García Maldonado, Rebecca Herman, and David

Tamayo—shaped the ways in which I understood Latin America and helped me articulate what was unique about my own perspective. Gracias, compañeros.

The editorial team at the University of New Mexico Press have been absolutely delightful to work with this entire time. Michael Millman was my point of contact as the acquisitions editor and shepherded me through the whole process. Thanks also to the production team, including James Ayers, Isaac Morris, Anna Pohlod, and Min Marcus. The index was compiled by Michael Goldstein. Zubin Meer painstakingly went through the manuscript and offered incisive copyediting advice. As series editor, Kris Lane encouraged and nurtured this project, and his tireless feedback made the final text better than it had any right to be. Thank you to everyone who made this book possible.

A group of friends, near and far, kept me sane between chapters. In Maine, I want to thank Meghan and Strother, Sakura and John, Allison and Kevin, Nadia and Brian, Carolyn and Dimitri, Willi and Anna, Maggie and Morten, and Dan and Heather for their friendship, companionship, and help navigating everything from housing to childcare and beyond. In California, Kristie and Emily shared their love, humor, and intellect freely and eagerly in end-of-semester wine tastings. They have been role models of how to be a supportive, loving couple. Miguel Nolla brightens an entire room with a smile and has the uncanny ability to contextualize any problem, making it seem manageable. In Berkeley, Jenelle and James, Mia and Zach, Molly and Paul, and Megan and Joe punctuated the rhythms of graduate life with their unparalleled culinary prowess, timely happy hours, and contagious good spirits. Alberto García Maldonado became an instant friend, sharing with me thunderous laughter during office hours and offering comfort in times of distress. ¡Gracias, Primo! In Argentina, Tomás Moller Poulsen offered not only a healthy dose of hedonistic nihilism, but he also patiently explained to me how the Argentine judiciary *actually* works and discovered several hidden gems in my files that I had overlooked. Francisco Suárez gave me shelter in the storm, always offering kindness and wisdom since childhood.

My family provided the foundation upon which everything else in life was built, including this book. My grandparents, Olga and Mario Cikota, and Herminia and Antonio Jakubauskas, humored my questions about how things were "back then," helping me imagine a time long gone and making me want to make sense of the worlds they had lived in as immigrants. My great-aunts, Nelida and Liliana Burba, made the family's history come alive. My in-laws, Gelu and

Tamara Popescu, have been an endless source of compassion, love, and comfort through trying times. Their love of good food and wine is infectious. My brothers Daniel and Andrés always listened to my rambling explanations of things that they were only marginally interested in with a patient smile. They expanded my world by sharing their passions with me and remain my role models in more ways than one. Sarah and Heather, who chose to join this family, added bright delights, levity, and love. My father, Victor, kept the family's history alive for us as children with nightly stories involving people we knew and some we did not. Some of his impossible work ethic, resolve, and determination might have rubbed off on me. My mother, Denise, inculcated the love of reading at a young age and encouraged my curiosity. She always made space for me to be weird and myself. She also played a critical role in this project, by constructing a searchable database of cases and proofreading each chapter—several times, in fact—over the years. ¡Gracias eternas, Ma!

Irina Popescu's name should have been in every single paragraph in these acknowledgements. She has been my best friend, my sharpest critic, my dearest colleague, a steadfast supporter, and partner in daily adventures, real or imagined, from Texas to California, and then Maine. She introduced me to the idea of a life in academia and kept my resolve high when it began to falter. She bravely weathered the loneliness, cold, and boredom of provincial archives with me, and made the research not just bearable but enjoyable. Her passion, curiosity, and kindness are unbound. Thank you.

And to Mateo and Lucca, who came into my life at the end of this project, threatened to derail it, but ended up giving it meaning. I cannot wait to see who you will each become.

Finding the Seams of the State
at the Edge of the World

That's the way it is in Patagonia. There are no people there. . . . In Patagonia,
there is nothing. It's not the Sahara, but it is the most similar thing to it that
can be found in Argentina. No, in Patagonia, there is nothing.
—Jorge Luis Borges, in the late 1970s.[1]

Make sure to befriend the judge / and don't give him reason to complain / it is
always good to have a tree to scratch your back.
—Martín Fierro, "Consejos del Viejo Vizcacha."[2]

I n an isolated meadow near the banks of the Limay River, a few days before
Christmas, on 21 December 1921, eighteen-year-old Pedro Gómez waited for
the sun to set before riding his horse to Juana Huenchual's home, a compound
of mud huts. Gómez asked Huenchual, whom he knew from his time as a police
officer, for a few *mates* (yerba mate sipped from a gourd) before nightfall and the
widow agreed, asking her daughters to entertain the traveler in their kitchen. After
a few rounds of the warming, shared beverage, Gómez broached the subject that
had brought him to Huenchual's hut: he wanted to marry her oldest daughter,
fifteen-year-old Rosa Mena. Huenchual refused flatly and asked him to leave, only
for Gómez to strike her violently with his *rebenque* (riding crop) twice, caving
in her orbital bone and cheek. Huenchual's youngest daughter, thirteen-year-old
María Mena was also struck and fell hard to the ground. Terrified, Rosa Mena
fled outside and attempted to get help. Gómez pursued her, tied her hands tightly
behind her back with blue stockings, covered her eyes with a handkerchief, and
drove her about a half mile on horseback to the shores of the Limay River, where
he raped her repeatedly. When he had "satisfied his carnal desires" he attempted

to hoist her back onto the horse, but the teen ran away and jumped into the river to get away from him.

Frustrated, Gómez returned to Huenchual's hut and rifled through their belongings, stealing a knife, a bag with money, and other valuables. In an effort to cover his tracks he tossed a burning match on the hut's straw roof, causing the kitchen to go up in flames. Maria Mena watched all this happen from a nearby wheat field, where she had crawled after being struck by Gómez earlier. The next morning, the young teen sought the help of a neighbor, who together with Huenchual's oldest son, seventeen-year-old Fermin Mena, proceeded to contact the police and dig out the charred remains from the burnt hut. For two weeks Fermin Mena and the neighbors searched for Rosa Mena, who they presumed to have survived her plunge into the river. An unidentified child found her severely decomposed remains two weeks later about a hundred miles downriver. To challenge Gómez's allegations that the teen had jumped into the river before he raped her, the police charged a medical examiner with autopsying the body where it was found—which took an additional week, as the examiner had to travel to the remote area. Confronted by María Mena's visceral testimony of his crimes, Pedro Gómez confessed and went on to spend a quarter century in Argentina's most notorious prison, in the furthest reaches of Patagonia, near Ushuaia.[3]

At first glance this brutal murder case might seem to fit a frontier space like northern Patagonia: it took place in an isolated agricultural outpost left vulnerable, and it involved a transient figure wreaking havoc, a ghastly reminder of the entrenched lawlessness and senseless violence of frontier life. Contemporaries shared that view. In 1946, twenty-five years after Pedro Gómez was found guilty of double murder, battery, arson, robbery, kidnapping, and rape, President Juan Domingo Perón commuted his sentence. As part of the process, the state reviewed Gómez's appeal to be released on parole (*liberación condicional*), crafting a long assessment in response to his request. The report characterized Gómez's upbringing in stark terms, shedding light on how dire frontier life seemed a short quarter century earlier.

The state's report explained that Gómez had had fifteen siblings and experienced the loss of his mother, who died of liver failure when he was just sixteen. Six of his siblings had died before adulthood, with another infant having drowned. His father worked odd jobs and money was always tight, resulting in a "very modest" home. Gómez attended a year of primary school when he was "four or five" but

FIGURE 1. "Piedra del Águila, Neuquén, undated" (AGN-Ddf, Caja 947, Inventario # 77849). Rosa Mena's body was found near this settlement.

when the family moved deep into the Patagonian plateau his formal education ended. From a young age he worked as a farmhand, a shepherd, and after turning eighteen he served as a police officer for a few months, before committing the crimes that defined his life. This book contextualizes Gómez's crimes by placing these "dark ages" of the northern Patagonian frontier under a different light. I do not see this region as a barbaric redoubt awaiting the civilizing force of the state, but rather as a place where a wide variety of people, including indigenous residents, immigrants, and their offspring, painstakingly built up the practices and norms that allowed frontier society to flourish.

Gómez's case file offers a lens through which to view how this peculiar frontier society emerged, what kind of interpersonal dynamics shaped it, and how state power was deployed and legitimized there. Asking hard questions of dramatic cases like this one helps us to reconstruct the world in which this crime took place. For example, consider that Pedro Gómez had been a police officer in the area for a few months before abandoning his post to return to his father's land to help with seasonal work. How professionalized was the police force in northern Patagonia, and how typical was it for a rural constable to be effectively homeless?

Ostensibly, Gómez had returned to the Limay River basin to collect back pay owed to him by Juan Jones, the area's largest landowner. Jones also served as the justice of the peace, the top civilian authority for that district. How was local government constituted in northern Patagonia, and how were conflicts of interest resolved when top officials were also prominent merchants and landowners?

Juana Huenchual and her family were known in the area as "the Chehuelches" in reference to their indigenous background. How did indigenous people survive the military occupation of their homeland between 1879 and 1885, a period that scholars have characterized as genocidal? The neighbors in the area of the Limay River basin were all white settlers from Argentina or abroad, and they rallied together to capture Gómez and even to support Huenchual's orphaned children. What role did the Huenchual family's indigeneity play in the state's response to the crimes committed against them?

Juana Huenchual managed a large household as a widow, exercising authority even over her adult son. How was patriarchy established and negotiated on the frontier? Gómez's visit went from neighborly to criminal when Huenchual rebuffed his advances toward Rosa, prompting him to assault the widow and kidnap the teen. What was the significance of kidnapping prospective brides? How much power did teenage girls have in choosing their intimate partners? What were courtships usually like on the frontier?

While the police were called right away and they began preparing an investigation, the search for Rosa was led by her brother and their neighbors. What role did neighbors, and civil society in general, play in the establishment and maintenance of order in the frontier? What were the consequences of such a close relationship between neighbors and police? Although Gómez confessed to the crime, his lawyer's defense centered on delegitimizing the medical examiner who helped identify Mena's and Huenchual's remains, exposing him as a quack. Why did the police rely on unlicensed physicians to perform duties usually reserved for medical doctors? Why did the medical examiner take so long to perform the autopsies?

How else was legitimacy contested on the frontier? In frontier spaces where the reach of the state was weak and its power contested, struggles over race, gender, reputation, and legitimacy were laid bare and made explicit. In other words, power relations between individuals, manipulation of government institutions by different stakeholders, and the compromises that allowed everyday life to prosper despite chronic violence, neglect, and scarcity became not only tangible but evident.

Prominent settlers in northern Patagonia were especially successful at drawing from their reputation within their communities to achieve political prominence at the local level. In other words, successful elites gained political power in small towns by heading orderly families, avoiding scandals, assisting in the lodging of vulnerable members of the community, and supporting social and cultural institutions. This book argues that the incomplete and uneven incorporation of Patagonia into Argentina between 1880 and 1940 resulted in the emergence of a strong locally based sense of community, a kind of citizenship developing despite the lack of formal political structures or institutions in the region.

The Puzzle: Situating *Frontier Justice*

This book takes part in three broad intellectual conversations. First, it contributes to studies of state formation and nation building in frontier spaces. Second, it also contributes to a vast and complicated literature on the nature of citizenship and belonging in liberal Argentina. The third conversation this book engages with is the "new" social history of legal culture. Each chapter also draws from its own set of intellectual discussions on the nature of Argentine rule in Patagonia, on the history of indigenous people in Argentina, on patriarchy and spousal abuse, on elopement and teen sexuality, on citizenship, and on the illegal practice of medicine.

Showcasing small community dramas and struggles in rural towns in northern Patagonia, a rugged expanse characterized by windswept plateaus and jagged Andean peaks, might seem like an unusual way to try to piece together how legitimacy and political power are constructed. But in northern Patagonia, the state (or, more specifically, the state system of government practices and institutions) arrived and developed alongside settler society.

This is fairly unusual. States have often "come into being as the structuration of political practices" or as military impositions. If, as Philip Abrams proposed, "the state is not the reality which stands behind the mask of political practice . . . it is itself the mask . . . it is the mind of a mindless world, the purpose of purposeless conditions, the opium of the citizen . . . the ideological device in terms of which the political institutionalization of power is legitimized," then communal conflicts in small Patagonian towns allow us to see how the mask took form, how the power struggles in rural communities became legitimized in the shape of the state.[4]

As Pilar Pérez noted, the weakness and instability of the state on a frontier like northern Patagonia is not merely a characteristic of its development but an essential feature that is easiest to spot at the edges, where state order is never able to impose itself.[5] In other words, the state in northern Patagonia was underdeveloped not in the sense that it was on its way to *being* developed, but rather its underdevelopment was an intrinsic aspect of its being—the frontier state was weak by design. Understanding how power relations—patriarchal, white supremacist, capitalist, and otherwise—become institutionalized as the abstract entity we call "the state" remains a puzzle central to political science, sociology, and history.[6]

This book contributes to the work done to understand the nature of the state in Argentina by treating the institutions and practices of the government on the frontier as illustrative of broader patterns and practices in the country as a whole. Liminal spaces—frontiers, borderlands, settler-colonial spaces—remain particularly rich settings in which to study power. As Pekka Hämäläinen and Samuel Truett argue, in liminal spaces "face-to-face relationships could trump centrist power and orthodoxies . . . family ties, patron-client relations, and local alliances [that] often determined membership and power" in idiosyncratic and unexpected ways.[7]

Frontier studies proliferated after Frederick Jackson Turner, historian of the American West, proposed his "frontier thesis" suggesting that the engine of American history lay not on the coasts but in the ever-advancing frontier across the continent. In an imprecise yet provocative 1893 essay, he argued that "to the frontier the American intellect owes its striking characteristics" of inventiveness, practicality, inquisitiveness, restlessness, optimism, and individuality. Scholars of Latin America, starting with Herbert Eugene Bolton (a student of Turner), have tried to articulate the ways their own frontiers affected national histories.

Scholars of Latin American frontiers have found a less decisively positive impact of frontiers on national histories. While Mexico's northern frontier before 1846 (California, Texas, and the high deserts and plains in between) certainly "seemed to be the guardian of liberty" during the tumultuous post-Independence decades, it was also "a refuge for political despots" who thrived far from the reaches of the central government. Hal Langfur, a historian of Brazilian frontiers, has argued that the *fronteira* in Brazilian history had a similarly maligned connotation, being described as "a source of exploitation and injustice." In his own way, the great Argentine intellectual, later president, Domingo Faustino Sarmiento articulated a negative "frontier thesis" for Argentina—namely, that it was in the vast expanses of the hinterlands, the "interior," where warlords ruled and knowledge was cowled, that Argentina was *unmade*.[8]

Frontier Justice builds on this literature on the importance of frontier spaces for national histories, splitting the difference between Turner and Sarmiento. In northern Patagonia, the frontier was clearly a space of dynamic social experimentation, a testing ground for national citizenship. Yet it was also a capricious place prone to violence, despotism, and exploitation. How settlers navigated this paradox is the subject of this book.

The way northern Patagonia was incorporated into Argentina is remarkably distinct compared with other, more studied, frontiers. Scholars have identified two broad ways in which frontiers have been administered by advancing states. Some states imposed hegemonic rule over a native population that they transformed into vassals. Others "followed" their own subjects as they sought to settle new territory, effectively legitimizing expansion.

The North American territories of New Mexico and Arizona were examples of the first type of frontier administration, as the large proportion of indigenous, Mexican, and Mexican American residents made national elites nervous about the low "Anglo" population level, ultimately delaying admission of these territories into the Union as full states.[9] Similar patterns can be seen in Boer colonialism in South Africa, Mexican rule over Yucatan, or Russian rule over Arctic nomads and central Asian Muslims.[10]

The trans-Mississippi frontier, by contrast, offers a classic example of the second type of state expansion. Here European-born settlers encroached on indigenous lands, forcing the native groups to retaliate, which then dragged the government into these frontier conflicts to manage settlement and dispossession.[11] Similarly, the occupation and annexation of the New Mexico Territory during the Mexican-American War followed merchant inroads and a small occupation force to topple Mexican rule.[12]

In Patagonia, two factors shaped how Argentine rule unfolded. The first was the implementation of a temporary wartime arrangement, the 1878 law establishing a military governorship for all of Patagonia, as a long-term governing framework, which was identified by contemporaries as inadequate but never reformed. The second was the composition of northern Patagonia as a foreign population, made up of immigrants, indigenous people, and second-generation settlers. This combination of temporary institutions used as a long-term occupation force makes the Patagonian example unique and highlights the grassroots efforts by a *colonial* population to exercise citizenship.

Citizenship comprises more than institutionalized political processes such as voting. It is the expression of a "specific social culture," based on a wide array of activities (not always political), which result in specific institutions, attitudes, values, and ideas that make up a typical citizen.[13] In recent years, Argentine scholars have attempted to understand the construction of citizenship beyond a simplified teleological model that saw the expansion of rights as an orderly progression: civic rights following the mid-nineteenth-century constitution, political rights coming after the 1912 electoral reform, and social rights following the rise of Perón to power in 1945.[14] Recent scholarship has instead found rights won and lost in piecemeal, idiosyncratic ways. Political rights might contract as economic rights expand. Or the rights of some ethnic groups may seem to gel, while those of others evaporated.[15]

Contemporary scholarship on Brazil, Mexico, the United States, and Latin America more broadly has similarly sought to understand the acquisition of some rights, the restrictions of others, and the exclusion of particular individuals from formal citizenship in innovative, dynamic ways.[16] This nuanced, complex interplay between expanded rights in some spheres and contracted rights in others underscores how citizenship was constructed through contestation, and trial and error, rather than wholesale "granting" of rights at particular turning points. This process becomes tangible when looking at how settlers became stakeholders in implementing the Argentine national project on the frontier.

Northern Patagonia also serves as a prism that reflects, or refracts, how the Argentine elites envisioned the progress of the country. Patagonia was seen as a model testing ground for the Argentine elite's political experiment. Could a restrictive, exclusionary republic "teach" its citizens civic virtue, gradually expanding their political rights as they "learned" democracy? The Patagonian experiment, however, was never fully completed. After the area was annexed following the so-called "Conquest of the Desert," as the 1878–1885 military campaign against the independent indigenous peoples came to be known, the elite's revolutionary zeal dissipated.[17] Indeed, the enterprise of turning a mélange of "Indians," immigrants, and settlers into Argentine citizens faltered as soon as it was conceived.

Unwilling to extend full political rights to Patagonians, Argentina's national government administered the region in an almost colonial fashion, deploying two types of federal appointees: governors and judges. Projecting mostly symbolic power, Patagonian governors tended to prioritize creating an orderly, stable society, often at the expense of the rule of law. Judges by contrast, were charged with upholding the rule of law, yet they often found creative solutions to avoid upending the established social order. As a result of this paradox, the judicial system had a dismal conviction rate: few people accused of breaking the law ended up in jail, and those who did soon found their way back to freedom (and sometimes even joined the police force). To some observers, frontier justice was injustice—as the case of Pedro Gómez and his victims, the Huenchual family, may suggest.

There were other factors besides federal-level ambivalence limiting national integration. The proximity of Chile tied many Patagonian ranchers and farmers to foreign merchants, rather than to the trading houses in Buenos Aires, part of a long-standing east–west commercial integration that worried Argentine nationalists. The paucity of state infrastructure in Patagonia continued to embarrass national authorities and critics alike, at least until the conservative governments of the 1930s began to invest in major projects throughout the region. Before this time, the territory largely lacked police stations, postal offices, and government buildings, to say nothing of bridges, roads, and railroads. Political institutions never matured, and what were labeled national territories failed to become formal provinces.

Picking up Eugene Weber's provocation that nation building in rural France during the Third Empire looked conspicuously like the colonial enterprise in Corsica or Algiers, *Frontier Justice* emphasizes the ways in which Argentina's own modernization of northern Patagonia took on a colonial patina.[18] Government officials continued to treat Patagonia's diverse residents as little more than colonial subjects. Contemporary accounts of Argentine rule in the district focused on these shortcomings. Signs of failure, neglect, or injustice empowered journalists, reformers, and travelers to make demands on the national government to live up to the lofty goals it had set out for the region, or to complete, as it were, the "Conquest of the Desert."

Since the late 1990s, scholars have echoed this narrative, highlighting how claims that the state was powerful papered over problems and chronic short-comings.[19] Although that story remains mostly true, it misses a series of important hidden developments. *Frontier Justice* tells these stories. One might expect full state failure and devolution into caudillo-style clientelism or judicial tyranny, but thriving in the shadow of the elite's failed project were a variety of resilient, local social networks, tied loosely to regional and national ones. Competing networks working at cross-purposes made this arrangement dynamic. While members of one network would attempt to mobilize state agents to investigate a complaint, representatives of a different network would try to stall the investigation and derail it. For example, popular faith healers could call on patients, neighbors, and colleagues to fend off and neutralize an investigation launched against them by a new doctor and his police allies, despite laws against the unlicensed practice of medicine.

Patagonia's diverse array of competing social networks included people of different socioeconomic backgrounds, broadening the avenues available to plebeian settlers to access justice, and making the institutionally undemocratic government in Patagonia surprisingly accessible. Without electoral means to translate social and economic power into political power, locals found other ways to solidify their social standing, consolidate power or wealth, and, for those with a civic streak, assist their humbler neighbors in resolving their grievances. Positioning themselves as *vecinos*, or active citizens, Patagonian elites grew to dominate local municipal life and helped to establish "good governance" in their communities.

In contrast to other scholars who see only a void of central authority in "the backlands," I argue that northern Patagonia's settlers and indigenous peoples developed a vibrant and dynamic civil society in their communities because they lived under a semicolonial, porous set of state institutions. This peculiar Patagonian type of citizen sought to reap the cultural and material benefits of the state that they themselves strove to build (and of which they saw themselves as stewards) on the frontier. Not everyone agreed on how this might be done, but I argue that it was a shared project.

Legal history has recently incorporated practices and methods from social history, infusing a human element to the study of how regimes of law incorporate subaltern responses. Incorporating the kind of attention to detail typical of microhistories, some recent studies have used a single court case to reconstruct the lived experience of pre-Independence Guatemala, including the ways in which they brought ideas of the sacred into an expanding secular state.[20] In part due to the "newness" of the state in northern Patagonia, litigants seemed keener than their counterparts in Mexico, Guatemala, and elsewhere, to seek extralegal remedies once the legal process had brought attention to their complaints. Even studies of criminality more narrowly defined, have taken the study of the law in unexpected directions, piecing together the ways in which criminal behavior and criminalized subjects were constructed and reconstructed through the decades.[21] *Frontier Justice* shares a genealogy with these works not only because it relies primarily on legal documents to reconstruct everyday life in northern Patagonia. Like that growing literature, this book places common litigants (daughters, husbands, healers, traders) at the heart of the story about legal regimes, showing how the overlapping structures of social domination were built by common people making cumulative decisions on everyday matters.

Geographic and Temporal Boundaries

The term *Patagonia* conjures up images of majestic mountains, immense arid deserts, and windswept coastlines. Charles Darwin famously labeled it as a "cursed place."[22] In this view, Patagonia is an idea as much as a region. In Argentina, the term refers to an area bounded in the north by the Colorado River and in the south by the island of Tierra del Fuego, with the Andes Mountain range as its western boundary and the Atlantic Ocean as its eastern one. Covering almost 800,000 square kilometers and making up about a third of all of Argentina's continental landmass, Patagonia's surface area is comparable in size to the combined US Pacific coast states of Washington, Oregon, and California. Travelers' and explorers' imaginations have flattened the region, combining its features into a geographically uniform whole. However, Patagonia's distinct subregions, with their different climates, geographies, and physiologies, have shaped human settlement patterns in significant ways.

Frontier Justice focuses on northern Patagonia, often called the Comahue region, which means "carved by waters" in the Mapudungun language. It comprises the present-day provinces of Neuquén and Río Negro. This region's proximity to areas of older settlement, the Pampas region (La Pampa and Buenos Aires, to the northeast) and the Cuyo region (Mendoza and San Luis, to the northwest), led to a markedly different development than in southern Patagonia. The "far south" developed a rapacious economy based on large-scale sheep-ranching and oil extraction in an "enclave model," making it almost an "autonomous economic zone" that some scholars equate to neocolonialism.[23] Northern Patagonia developed a much more mixed economy: family farms in the Andean valleys and the Río Negro valley, large-scale cattle ranching on the plateau, and smaller sheep-raising outfits in the Andean foothills. Livestock raising—in particular sheep—was the main source of income.

Map 1. Patagonia in relation to the rest of South America.

This study focuses on the period between 1880 and 1940. This periodization is unusual, but there are good reasons for retaining it. Although direct federal administration of the northern Patagonian territories of Neuquén and Río Negro lasted until 1956, the last decade and a half (c. 1940–1956) witnessed emergence of a fundamentally different sociopolitical arrangement, with the institutions and structures that made Patagonian citizenship possible changing dramatically. Other scholars have studied discreet periods individually: the years in which indigenous society was besieged (1875–1890), or the decades of active municipal life in the area of old white settlements in the lower Río Negro valley (1890–1905), separately from the years following the repression of the labor strikes in the far south (1916–1930). The effects of the "Infamous Decade" of the 1930s (the series of military-civilian governments during the Great Depression) on Patagonian society and institutions have not received much scholarly attention. This is strange, since they represented a dramatic shift in how the region was administered and how citizenship was practiced. The period between 1930 and 1940 saw increased state presence in the form of heavy investment in infrastructure, which included the creation of national parks, the exploitation of new oil fields, and the construction of new roadways. All this coincided with an expansion of nationalist sentiment on the frontier, a new generation of settlers, and a professionalization of the police force. *Frontier Justice* considers the period between 1880 and 1940 as a whole to emphasize the ways in which the people, their practices, and the institutions themselves changed and adapted to the shifting historical moments.

Sources and Book Structure

This book uses federal court cases to reconstruct how social relationships in Patagonia were built, maintained, and used by a wide array of social actors (including doctors, merchants, indigenous subjects, heads of households, and runaway daughters, as well as police officers, prosecutors, and defense attorneys). The court cases came from two large judicial archives in the northern Patagonian capitals of Viedma (maintained by the state in a regional archive) and Neuquén (preserved by a group of researchers in Patagonia's first public university). Additionally, the Archivo General de la Nación in Buenos Aires houses a valuable trove of reports from state officials (governors, inspectors, and ministerial staffers).

The process for selecting court cases was threefold. First, I scoured the indexes (when available) to identify the kind of investigations that would likely yield

Map 2. The broader Comahue region (northern Patagonia) with neighboring provinces.

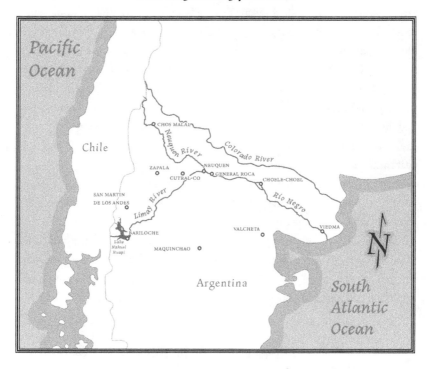

open-ended queries into everyday Patagonians' gripes, concerns, and priorities. I singled out several sets of cases early on: prosecution of "illegal doctors" and midwives, cases of runaway daughters and wives, and complaints against state officials. I read and digitized those cases for later reference. Additionally, I analyzed hundreds of cases in other categories—mainly complaints over workplace injuries, gambling, cattle rustling, assaults, rapes, and murders, as well corruption of minors, all to provide context (what kind of crimes did Patagonian officials and settlers care about?) and to establish the parameters of "normal" jurisprudence (how long were suspects usually held before a deposition? How many character witnesses did poor Patagonians need? How many officers were involved in the search for a fugitive?).

Previous studies of court cases in the frontier justice system have focused particularly on violent crimes as a way to understand how criminality and marginality were constructed by government officials and elites. My work builds on this tradition but expands the body of sources, focusing on nonviolent crimes and civil complaints, which shows more mundane ways in which settlers invoked the state apparatus to resolve conflicts in their private and public lives. In this sense, the opening story of Pedro Gómez's violent attack on the Huenchual family is illustrative of how court cases can shed light on deeper social dynamics.

Frontier Justice contains six chapters, each focusing on a different dimension of political life in northern Patagonia. Chapter 1, "A Fictional Government," discusses the establishment of Argentine rule in Patagonia, contrasting how elites imagined government function with the actual deployment of a scarce state presence that relied almost exclusively on police and judges. Chapter 2, "Civilization's Embrace," centers on the fate of the indigenous population in the first years of Argentine control of the area. This chapter argues that the Argentine response to indigenous people in northern Patagonia followed a process of displacement, disarticulation, and indigenous persistence. Moreover, it shows how indigenous responses to these processes shaped the way Patagonian institutions developed.

Chapter 3, "Public and Notorious," deals with the relationship between the state and family life, focusing particularly on the constraints placed on patriarchal violence. Abused women and children used the reputation of the abusers in the community to inflect the state's response, underscoring how someone's standing in the community dictated their access to justice. Chapter 4, "Suspicious Virginities," further explores the link between family life and public reputation by looking at how runaway teens followed an elopement script to force their parents into consenting to their partner choices by running away from home. This chapter highlights how public arguments over virginity, as a proxy for chastity, served as ways to expand or limit the power of teenage girls to control their own lives.

Chapter 5, "The Most Respectable Neighbors," builds on the relationship between reputation and power in small towns by looking at the figure of the "vecino," the self-styled local elite in small towns throughout northern Patagonia—who funded police forces, developed tense, contested relationships with local authorities, and learned to mobilize collectively to defray the cost of resistance. Building on their reputations, vecinos coalitions articulated concerns in terms of good governance and social harmony, painting themselves as the paladins of "culture" on the frontier. Their authority did not go unchallenged, however, and over time they became less effective. Established vecinos were increasingly labeled as troublesome "gringos" (foreigners) by a new generation of more nationalistic settlers.

Chapter 6, "A Trusted Doctor," explores the ways in which locally based sources of legitimacy survived the arrival of new settlers and the expansion of a more professional state apparatus in the 1930s. To get at the tension between the legitimacy of the new "outsiders"—armed with titles and backed by a more institutional state—and the legitimacy stemming from the reputation of the "first settlers," this chapter looks at conflicts over the practice of medicine. The ways in which "illegal" folk healers, pharmacists, unlicensed doctors, and other medical professionals were able to offer a social constraint on state power suggests an active, ongoing social dimension to the development of a settler-colonial regime in Patagonia and ultimately underscores the contingent nature of state formation.

A brief personal note on my own subjectivity

I grew up in northern Patagonia, not far from where Pedro Gómez committed his crimes. In the early decades of the twentieth century, my great grandparents, immigrants to Argentina from Lithuania, turned some of the profits from their textile factory in Buenos Aires into marginal, useless land on the side of a mountain in an Andean valley. Their children and grandchildren would return to the area over the following decades until my grandparents set up a general store in one of the larger towns in the area, Bariloche, in the late 1970s. My own parents moved there in the early 1980s when I was a newborn, building a cinderblock house on

FIGURE 2. "Vista del Nahuel Huapi desde el Cerro Otto cubierto de nieve" (AGN-Ddf, Inventario, #183054).

the edge of the town, in an underdeveloped neighborhood dominated by rutted gravel roads and vacant, forested lots. The road leading out of the town, dubbed "Pioneers' Avenue," ended just a few blocks from our house. To my folks it felt like the edge of the civilized world, and they liked it that way.

I grew up as part of settler society on what had for millennia been indigenous land—most recently Mapuche, but before that belonging to the Puelche, Poya, Tehuelche, and Pehuenche peoples. We used a reverent euphemism—*pobladores originales*, or "the original settlers"—to describe anyone who had lived in the area before the mid-twentieth century. In a collapsing of categories and decades, the Jones family, the Vereertbrugghen family, the Frey family, and the many nameless denizens of rickety huts at the edges of marshes or tucked into ravines were all people who had been part of the town of Bariloche since its inception. Rhetorically, all of them were equally and unproblematically "the founders."

When I went back to the area during graduate school in search of a research topic, I began to see not only Bariloche but also northern Patagonia anew, as something more than what I had always naturally assumed it was. Historical conflicts dotted the landscape, with rivers borrowing indigenous names pouring their waters into lakes commemorating missionaries, and peaks bearing the names of explorers covered in orange flowers bearing the name of mythical indigenous princesses. Conflicts over resources and land were also much more evident to me than they had been, or that I remembered them being, in my youth. It has taken me a long time to unlearn these childhood and "original settler" lessons. I am still (un)learning.

In this book I have tried to decenter my own privileged position within settler society, within the patriarchy, and within the North American academy. When possible, I have used the preferred name for indigenous and immigrant groups. But when a source used a derogatory term—calling Middle Eastern immigrants *Arabs*, for example, or indigenous people *Indios*—I have left those labels intact not out of insensitivity but for accuracy.

I considered replacing the names of all the people in the book for pseudonyms, in response to recent discussions by feminist historians about the duty to prevent further harm to victims of violent and sexual crimes by anonymizing their experiences. But I ultimately decided against it. As much as I want to minimize the damage to people's privacy and their reputation in their communities, the cases are publicly available and their stories were sometimes paraded in local newspapers. Finding suitable pseudonym for immigrant and indigenous names posed its own risk of harm by my own ignorance. I left everyone's names as they appeared in the documents, noting when different people spelled names differently.

Similarly, I have tried to present individual choices people made in the context of their own times, without attaching a present-minded moral value to their actions. I doubt that I have fully succeeded in neutral representation, but I hope to have honored the experiences of the people that I found in the archive.

"A Fictional Government"

Building a State on the Frontier

It is true that the Rio Negro Territory has remained uncivilized; the state has
never done anything to help it . . . nothing was done to spur the progress of
that rich area of the republic, and whatever progress it has reached, *is solely
due to the isolated efforts of its residents.*
—*La Nueva Era* (Viedma), May 27, 1906.[1]

The Law has placed me as a guardian of all of humankind.
—Luis B. Guiñazú, *comisario* of the hamlet of Rucachoray, in the Territory
of Neuquén, attempting to defend his heavy-handed and tendentious
interrogations.[2]

A small crisis engulfed the town of General Roca in 1898, forcing regional
authorities to grapple with the gulf between how the region was supposed
to be governed and how it was actually being governed. The town, built
around a military base established in 1880 as part of the campaign to forcibly
incorporate Patagonia into the nation, had quickly developed into the frontier's
main urban center. General Roca enjoyed a vibrant economy. The town was
connected to the rest of the country by railroad, and it even boasted one of the
few elected municipal councils in all the recently annexed territories—a clear
mark of its "progress" under Argentine rule.

The president of the municipal council, Alberto Lizarriaga, sent a somber note
to the federal judge presiding in the nearby capital of Viedma, a somewhat older
town, asking him to intercede in a conflict between the council and the justice
of the peace, Fermín Viera. Lizarriaga explained that despite Viera's repeated
and well-documented abuses, he remained in office, threatening the "civility

and dignity" of the community. Further, Lizarriaga asked the judge to discipline Viera, remove him from his post, and name a temporary replacement since the municipal council of General Roca did not have the "legal force" to discipline a rogue justice of the peace.[3]

The scant details of this crisis that emerge from the documents—a short collection of complaints against Viera, forwarded to the judge—might lead a curious reader to formulate some follow-up questions. How were municipal councils and justices of the peace supposed to share power in small frontier towns? Why did the municipal council frame its request in terms of "civility and dignity"? Were federal judges often called upon to deal with staffing issues at the municipal level? Did such conflicts steer the development of municipal institutions? Answers to these questions may help us reconstruct what the Argentine government looked like in northern Patagonia soon after the military annexation of the region.

Argentina's liberal statesmen felt it was their political project to make citizens out of immigrants, rural peons, and indigenous peoples, and Patagonia was an ideal laboratory. After a turbulent nineteenth century characterized by civil strife, broad political participation, and a concentration of rural political power in the wake of the wars for independence (1810–1820), a generation of liberal thinkers argued that the government ought to "educate the sovereign"—that is, to train the citizenry to assume their proper political role. Facing challenges from warlords in the western mountains, from immigrants and workers in the cities, and later from the urban middle class, Argentina's liberal elites turned their hopes to territories recently annexed in Patagonia to the southwest and the Gran Chaco to the northwest.

It was in these newly designated national territories, "frontiers" devoid of political institutions, and with populations made up of immigrants and recent arrivals, that the liberal elite deployed the institutions and practices they hoped would create citizens worthy of the country they imagined. It was not a smooth deployment. The introduction of formal democratic institutions (elected city councils, elected justices of the peace, local legislatures, elected congressional representatives, and ultimately self-rule) stalled. It was then abruptly reversed as factionalism and squabbles eroded institutional and individual legitimacy.

State authorities, mostly judges, governors, and police officers, adapted to these structural limitations, focusing on providing "nothing more than justice and heavy policing."[4] Patagonia continued to feel remote to national elites, and it was not solely the vast distances separating it from the rest of the country. This relative remoteness stemmed from what Hugo Casullo and Joaquín Perren call "the precariousness of the state's reach" into it.[5] The region remained a frontier space, a borderland where national authority was fragmentary and contested.

Scarcity and poverty hampered the functioning of all state agencies in Patagonia. The governors complained that they headed "a fictional government . . . without prestige or the efficiency to do anything."[6] The transient and underfunded police built strong ties with their communities, often relying on vecinos (both "citizens" and "neighbors") for their own survival and strengthening the relationship between state and society in concrete ways. Ironically, the very high level of complaints against bad police in the files—which others have pointed to as signs of its dysfunction—shows a social body growing impatient and demanding of the state, and confident that it could remedy those irregularities.

The courts, charged with establishing and maintaining the rule of law, were mocked by contemporaries for the "awesome majesty" of their precarious institutions and the high number of cases that were started but not resolved.[7] The abysmally low conviction rate troubled contemporaries—who feared chaos on the frontier—and intrigued scholars.[8] This chapter argues that the state representatives in northern Patagonia operated creatively, and that in their haphazard approach to governance they created a resilient and flexible administration. In other words, the Argentine project to incorporate Patagonia to the nation succeeded not only despite its shortcomings but also because of them.

This chapter unfolds in two sections. The first section looks at the theoretical and legal underpinnings of what became the "skeletal state" on the frontier. Emerging from mid-nineteenth-century debates about how best to develop republican values, the policy toward national territories envisioned them as incubators for those values. Low-stakes local elections would prepare the growing population of northern Patagonia for eventual higher-stake elections, testing whether Argentina's population could be cured of its proclivity toward demagoguery by only introducing democracy once the population had been taught how to behave democratically.

The second section outlines how the state actually operated in practice once the municipal-level republican ideas failed to take off and the expansion of political rights stalled. Both of the top administrators in each territory—governor and judge—were outsiders appointed to limited terms, who managed uneven human and financial resources. The police force, a staple of each small village and town, and the justices of the peace, drawn from the local elite, served as the main representatives of the state in most communities. The police were caught in a bind: their intimate ties with the rural population ameliorated the lack of financial resources and exacerbated the national elites' distrust.

A Semicolonial Administration: The National Territories

When Mayor Lizarriaga worried that General Roca's municipal council did not have "the legal force under Art. 10 of the national territory law" to remove the justice of the peace, he was highlighting a key dynamic in how northern Patagonia was administered. Municipal politics were at the center of the Argentine project for the frontier, but the region as a whole was administered in an exclusionary, somewhat colonial manner. The result was a temporary arrangement, racked by contradictions and resting on inconsistent assumptions about the region and its inhabitants.

In his complaint, Lizarriaga alluded to the Ley N° 1532 de Organización de los Territorios Nacionales (known simply as Ley 1532), the legal and administrative framework approved in 1884 to administer northern Patagonia, which established the national territories. Ley 1532 was intended as a temporary measure until each individual national territory was mature enough to be admitted to the nation as an autonomous province. It was a modification to the law that had created a "military governorship" over Patagonia in 1878 as the Argentine military prepared to invade the region. The main articles of the law were inspired by a similar piece of legislation governing national territories in the United States: the 1787 Northwest Ordinance, which had pioneered a three-tiered system of incremental political rights to transition territories into states.[9] Like its North American counterpart, Ley 1532 proscribed the political rights of Patagonian residents by restricting their participation in national elections.

In practice, the national territories were administered as colonies: they could not convene legislatures or elect governors, nor have representation in the national congress. According to historian Martha Ruffini, the goal was to avoid the emergence of individuals or factions with "independent power" beyond the control of the national government.[10] Ley 1532 limited all political activity to the municipal level, which helps explain Lizarriaga's hesitancy to act in defiance of the law in a seemingly small matter: local conflicts were central to the political life of northern Patagonia and the only way for residents to show their worthiness for expanded political rights.

The was an unresolved philosophical paradox at the heart of Ley 1532. On the one hand, the law sought to limit political participation to the relative low stakes of local elections. This was an extension of the belief that the state had to "educate the sovereign" before it was allowed the responsibility of governing. Historian

FIGURE 3. "Viedma. Edificio de la cárcel y comisaria de la capital, 1918" (AGN-
Ddf, Inventario #155690). Notice the cannons out front, a relic from the
military campaigns against indigenous groups.

Hilda Sábato explains the elites did "all that was possible to keep the creole and
immigrant people away from political life" while the population trained to be
part of the "True Republic."[11] That period of restricted popular participation was
known at the national level as the "Possible Republic." On the other hand, Ley 1532
automatically expanded political rights as the population increased, regardless of
any qualifications. After reaching 60,000 residents, each territory could petition
Congress to receive admittance into the nation as a province. When a territory
reached 30,000 residents, they could seek permission to convene a legislature and
elect a governor. The paradox reflected the divergent views of Domingo Faustino
Sarmiento and Juan Bautista Alberdi, Argentina's foremost liberal thinkers in the
nineteenth century.

   At its most idealistic, Argentine liberalism held that mass education could
overcome the "barbarizing" effects of the countryside. Domingo Faustino Sarmiento,
who served as president between 1868 and 1874 and popularized the idea of

Table 1. Population in northern Patagonia						
Year	1886	1895	1905	1914	1920	1931
Río Negro	6,980	9,241	20,220	42,242	42,652	115,380
Neuquén	n/a	14,517	n/a	28,866	29,784	42,241
Northern Patagonia	>6,980	23,758	>34,737	71,108	72,436	157,621

"educating the sovereign," believed that the emptiness of the countryside had a corrupting effect on people. Sarmiento argued that Argentina had an eschatological choice between "civilization or barbarism," and he believed that rural folk had abandoned civic duty and became beholden to dictators and tyrants during the civil wars that followed independence (1810–1853). Low-stake elections of municipal councils and justices of the peace, who served short, staggered terms, would allow for elections every year and serve as the schoolyard of democracy. In other words, the residents of the national territories would become better citizens by being better neighbors who participated yearly in local elections.

The other, less idealistic current of liberalism, believed that good republican practices could not be taught and had to come from abroad. Juan Bautista Alberdi, who framed Argentina's 1853 liberal Constitution, argued that "take the building blocks of our popular masses, the *roto*, the *cholo*, or the *gaucho*, and give them the best education possible, not even in a hundred years will they turn into British workers."[12] Civilization, Alberdi declared, did not "grow from seeds, but rather, like a vine, takes hold from a branch cutting."[13] Following Alberdi's pessimism toward the local population, the 1853 Constitution explicitly encouraged immigration into the country.[14] Alberdi famously argued that to "govern was to populate" implying that the entire country was bereft of people—a desert in wait for a nation. The assumption that Patagonia was "absolutely depopulated," as Ramón Cárcano qualified it when proposing Ley 1532 in Congress, underscored the need to fill it with people already holding republican values.[15]

A shared belief that the national territories had inhabitants rather than citizens justified the imposition of a highly centralized colonial administration with Ley 1532.[16] Governors, judges, and other officials were appointed by the executive branch and remained loyal to them rather than any local constituencies. Additionally, different appointees responded to different ministers in the national government, resulting in competing and overlapping jurisdictions. For example, the president himself appointed governors, but they reported to the Minister of the Interior and his deputy, the General Director of National Territories. The federal judges, on the other hand, were appointed by the Minister of Justice, and were tasked with overseeing the work of the police. The police in turn received their pay from the governor.[17] Despite the awkwardness of this arrangement, in which governors and judges governed as equals, Law 1532 proved hard to modify.

The shortcomings of Law 1532 were evident to contemporaries, but meaningful changes never materialized. Within the executive branch, efforts to reform and streamline how the national territories were administered faced pushback from cabinet members weary of diminishing their own power to control appointment and direct policy.[18] For example, attempts to create a unified "Minister for National Territories" in 1911 faced collective opposition from the ministers of the Interior, Agriculture, Public Works, and Education, since it would weaken their own power.

Congress similarly failed to reform a system that it acknowledged was not working. A 1911 congressional commission considering a wholesale change to the arrangement called Ley 1532 "antiquated" and "denaturalized," but failed to pass meaningful reforms.[19] Between 1916 and 1930, at least seventeen laws were introduced to deal with the "political issue" of the national territories, though none of them passed or were even voted on.[20] For example, when President Hipólito Yrigoyen (1916–1922) introduced a law to provincialize two national territories in 1919, conservatives blocked the measure out of fear that the new provinces would likely elect pro-Yrigoyen representatives. Although both Río Negro and Neuquén had reached the demographic benchmarks necessary to acquire greater political rights (see table 1) by 1919, Conservatives argued that the population was not ready.[21]

Beyond the political rivalries of the period, national elites agreed that northern Patagonia needed to be made more Argentine before it could have increased political rights. In the mid-1920s, congressman Belisario Albarracín highlighted the lack of national affinity in the population of the frontier. He worried that northern Patagonia would be "a piece of soil with an Argentine flag, but with a foreign spirit, tied to Chile economically and socially."[22] Faced with the opposition from the presidency, the legislature, and nationalist sectors, the national territories waited until 1956 to become full-fledged provinces.

The administration of national territories evolved into something different from what the framers of Ley 1532 had intended. At times it resembled a colonial administration, as the political restrictions, the centralization of power, and heterogeneity of the population led to a series of ad hoc arrangements that seemed to replicate the institutions and practices of Spanish rule in the Americas. The temporary, "overly uniform," centralized, and bitterly divided administrative arrangement would stagger along for seventy years, cementing an exclusionary political system even as citizenship expanded nationally. As the dysfunction was institutionalized, it created stability and predictability, which the settlers quickly learned how to navigate.

"Guardians of all humankind": Municipal Councils, Judges, Governors, and Police

This section describes the institutional roles and characters that made up the colonial administration of northern Patagonia. These were the people, like Comisario Luis Guiñazú in the epigraph, who believed in their messianic role on the frontier where the law had made them "guardians of all humankind." They found creative ways to exercise that mandate within a system that followed three organizing principles. First, as we have discussed, it emerged from precarity and scarcity. Second, institutionally, there was a reactionary tendency to the maintenance of order above all else. And last, there was an expectation to maintain the outward appearance of liberal republicanism.

Municipal Councils and Local Elections

Municipal councils in northern Patagonia, which Ley 1532 envisioned as the spaces where electoral politics would take hold, did not offer national elites much assurance that their project was working. Municipal citizenship was universal for men over the age of eighteen; the only requirement for them to vote in municipal elections was "residence in the jurisdiction," allowing poor people, renters, rural workers, and immigrants to join in the democratic process. Despite this radically inclusive approach, many municipal politics quickly became hotbeds of dysfunction.

Statesmen considered municipal politics the "schoolyard of democracy" because elections were held yearly and were open to all male adults. Any town with at least a thousand residents could elect a municipal council. For towns that had not reached the population threshold, governors could appoint councilmen and justices of the peace.[23] The five councilmen would serve two-year terms, with half of the council up for re-election any given year. Those towns could also elect justices of the peace (*Jueces de Paz*) to two-year terms, which meant that on a yearly basis, residents of north Patagonian towns would hold elections to cover three local posts, giving them a "practical experience" of democracy.[24] Despite their inclusiveness, municipal councils failed to establish and sustain political life. After some early excitement, turnout for most municipal elections hovered around half of all eligible voters in the early years and dropped dramatically after that. Political participation became reserved to a few well-connected individuals and their political parties, who zealously curated the voter rolls.[25]

Political elites in the provincial capitals colluded with one another and with the governors to shape the scope of political participation. For example, in a 1905 private communication between Carlos Bouquet Roldán, the governor of Neuquén, and Miguel Mango, the leader of one of the local political parties, the Unión Popular, the pair discussed allowing only "serious and honorable people" with the "required capacity for civic life" to be in the electoral rolls.[26] Elites also complained of irregularities when enrollment for elections was open to self-registration. For example, Abel Cháneton, twice president of Neuquén's city council and editor of the *Neuquén* newspaper, used the pages of his publication in 1915 to allege that the opposition party, the Liga de Vecinos Independientes, had sent farm workers to the polls. Cháneton complained that the mostly illiterate workers did not "know the candidates, but had been told by the *patrón* [meaning both "boss" and "patron"] which way to vote."[27] These rudimentary political machines were denounced in the local press, especially by political rivals without access to similar resources.[28]

By the first decade of the twentieth century, lawmakers' faith in municipal politics had eroded. The few local political parties that emerged were personalist factions formed around particularly powerful neighbors, and their factionalism threatened the continued existence of the municipal councils.[29] For example, in 1901 the municipal council in General Roca had two presidents simultaneously since the outgoing one refused to yield his post, requiring an intervention by the governor to forcefully remove both and suspend the council until the situation was normalized. In 1899, the Interior Minister Felipe Yofré complained loudly to Congress that "the experience so far in the municipal regimes makes me fear that wider self-governance will only lead to frequent disruptions, engulfing the territories in ceaseless conflict." Soon after, he recommended Congress that his office continue the "complete administration" of Patagonia.[30]

Councils fell into a self-perpetuating cycle of futility in the early years: a fearful national government gave the councils limited powers, and without control of their budget or police force the councils were wracked with conflict, which often required intervention from the governors, which in turn further eroded the state's trust in the elected councils.[31] The consequences were dramatic. For example, Río Negro had seven towns with elected municipal councils in the early 1890s, but by 1907 internal dissent and apathy had resulted in the dissolution of all but one (in Viedma), while seven other towns had downgraded theirs to unelected municipal councils stocked by local elites (*comisiones de fomento*, which translates to "development committees"). In the Territory of Neuquén, the situation was equally bleak. The town of Neuquén reached the population threshold for an elected council in 1905 and held its first elections in March 1906, only to collapse by the end of that year following an open conflict with the governor and the police. In 1907, a new governor decided to appoint a council—rather than hold elections—which did not last long either. Only in 1911 was the body reconstituted and continued to operate for the rest of the decade.[32]

The opening of the political arena at the national level following the 1912 electoral reform (the "Ley Sáenz Peña" made national elections compulsory, secret, and universal for adult males) resulted in a renaissance for elected councils, but it proved to be short-lived. For example, by 1922, only two of the five municipal councils that operated in Río Negro in the midteens remained active (in Viedma and General Roca). The other three had been dissolved by the governor or faced the mass resignation of all elected members, leaving the administration of the town in the hands of the *comisario* (a police deputy in charge of a county or town). Unelected councils were preferred by governors because it placed the comisarios at the center of local politics.[33] During most of the 1920s, the trend in northern

FIGURE 4. (*opposite*) "Amargueando en la puerta del toldito, Patagonia 1938" (AGN-Ddf, Inventario #161061). Rural dwellers, like the one in this picture, caused local elites to attempt to curtail their voting rights, in part because of their poverty.

Patagonia was to create comisiones de fomento instead of municipal councils since that allowed the governor to appoint trusted confidants and allies.

So why did the municipal council in General Roca signal to the regional authorities that it found itself in distress in 1898? Part of the answer is that justice Viera's political trajectory in General Roca was emblematic of the narrow pool of participants in local politics. Fermín Viera was born in 1836, and having participated in the "Conquest of the Desert" he settled in General Roca after the campaign ended, like many other military men.[34] In Roca he served as a councilman in 1889, in 1890, and again in 1892, during a period in which Roca's municipal activity was anomalously stable (remember that Roca's municipal council was intervened by the governor in 1901, and by 1905 it had been turned into an unelected council following infighting and instability).[35] Viera would go on to serve as the justice of the peace for General Roca between 1898 and 1899—when his tenure was questioned by the municipal council—and again between 1901 and 1904. However, when Viera clashed with the municipal council in 1898, the council happened to also find itself in conflict with the governor. That same year Governor Eugenio Tello, citing how the president of Roca's municipal council had established a "caudillo-style dictatorship," urged the Interior Minister to further restrict municipal politics in the entire Río Negro Territory, using Lizarriaga as a cautionary tale.

The conflict with the governor forced Lizarriaga and the municipal council to seek the assistance of a different federal appointee: the federal judge. After the council's initial complaint to the judge, Viera responded by arresting the president of the municipal council, labeling him a "dangerous charlatan." He also sent an undertaker to the house of the former municipal president, a schoolteacher by the name of Santiago Ghiglia, with a corpse and an order to bury the body immediately. When Ghiglia refused, Viera berated and loudly insulted him in the middle of the street, damaging the "dignity and decorum" of the council itself. In short, in frontier towns electoral politics failed to decisively take root in the first few decades after the military annexation of northern Patagonia, signaling to prominent neighbors that they should try to cultivate informal ways to wield political power.

Unable to rely on the governor and fearful of passing a resolution of uncertain legitimacy, the council decided to place the matter before the federal judge directly so that "he could decide on its gravity and on how justice [should be] served in this community." Since judges and governors ended up playing an outsized role in local politics, to them we now turn.

A "Judicial Dictatorship": Judges and Justices of the Peace

In his note to the judge listing the "almost daily" complaints against Viera, Lizarriaga outlined his reasoning for involving the head of the judiciary in the conflict. Without much subtlety, the councilman urged the judge to intervene in a municipal discord not because it was his constitutional prerogative, but because he might want to protect the judiciary as an institution. Lizarriaga argued that Viera operated "autonomously" with "little or no understanding of the law" since he was "almost illiterate" and was following the counsel of "advisers who also operate as his proxies." He tried to paint Viera as an embarrassment to the law itself.

The administration of justice was seen as a linchpin of state order in northern Patagonia. Under the stipulations of Ley 1532, two types of officials administered justice in the region: a presiding federal judge for each territory (*Juez Letrado*), and each county or town had justices of the peace (*Jueces de Paz*). Scholars have noted that throughout Argentina courts played an important role as "battlefields of citizenship," which made the appointment of judges an issue of utmost importance in elite debates.[36]

In northern Patagonia, judges not only presided over these critical battlefields, but they also shared in the day-to-day administration of the region with the governors, often working at cross-purposes with one another. According to the Minister of Justice, already by 1891 "the incidents continued to mount and threaten the coexistence of judicial and administrative authority . . . the judges complain that their decisions were not being heeded, while the governors oppose the establishment of a *judicial dictatorship*."[37] The federal judge received a salary that eclipsed the governor's, an uncomfortable slight that compounded conflicts over ill-defined jurisdictions. They were usually career jurists, trained in Buenos Aires, and appointed directly by the Minister of Justice to three-year tenures, without input from the community. In some cases, they were promoted from within, elevated from prosecutors or alternates into full judgeships.[38]

Judges presided over a cumbersome judicial apparatus. Each case left behind extensive paper records, documenting initial complaints, depositions, investigations, correspondence, summaries, and legal opinions. Usually, a case would start with a complaint filed with the police, who would then assign an officer as the investigator. The initial investigation had an outsized role in how a case developed, and police diligence in deposing witnesses, gathering evidence, and pursuing leads went a long way in determining the outcome of any case. If the investigator found enough probable cause to elevate the case to the court, they could detain the suspect, adding another instance in which they wielded justice fairly autonomously.

Once a case (including depositions, evidence, the testimony from the suspect, and a free-form "assessment" from the investigator) made it to the court, the *fiscal* (prosecutor) would evaluate the evidence and determine whether the state wanted to pursue the case. If the prosecutor deemed the case was strong enough to take to trial, he would interrogate the suspect again, and book them into the territorial prison (one in Viedma and one in Neuquén). At this point a suspect could spend weeks deprived of their freedom, transported to a far-off prison to await judgment based only on a complaint, a malicious investigation, and an overworked prosecutor.

The power of the judicial process to "punish" settlers before any sentence was passed became an integral part of how different stakeholders in northern Patagonia tried to use the process to fight rivals, scare competitors, and break through established patronage arrangements. This contrasts dramatically with the US frontier, which was provided with "weak and ineffective courts" by the national lawmakers—in fact, while in the United States "the territorial judiciary was one of the 'weakest' parts of [the] jerry-rigged government" in the frontier, it was the strongest state institution in northern Patagonia.[39] While the suspect awaited judgment, the prosecutor and the defense evaluated the evidence and produced summaries of their interpretation of the evidence and recommendations for action to present to the judge.

The judge, armed with the two competing interpretations, had three courses of action available: he could accept the recommendation of the prosecutor and convict; he could suspend the case (*sobreseimiento provisional*) until more information was gathered; or he could close the case for good, exonerating the accused (*sobreseimiento definitivo*). Judges were constrained by the letter of the law, but they still sought creative ways to apply the law in ways that ensured that justice was served. For example, they could suspend a case until new evidence appeared without *actually* requesting any additional investigations, avoiding having to rule on the case at all.

Evidence from the court records suggests that settlers interpreted this flexibility as an exercise of personal power by the judges. For example, in early 1930, Carlos Vivoni, a self-described "humble worker" from the agricultural town of Villa Regina, thirty miles downriver from General Roca, contacted the judge imploring him to intervene on his behalf against the justice of the peace, Bartolomé Porro.[40] Vivoni had been owed money by an employer, Leopoldo Zapata, and he had complained to Porro in order to force Zapata to pay him. But even after an arrangement had been struck, the payment had not materialized. Vivoni believed that the justice of the peace was colluding with the employer and had only pretended to arrange a payment to appease him, similarly to how authorities in small towns throughout the region would resolve issues in a dually informal and formal manner. The judge in Viedma intervened by asking the authorities in General Roca for further information, as was routine.

A few weeks later, Vivoni sent another telegram to the judge, thanking him for resolving the issue. He claimed that his complaint "has been swiftly resolved to my uttermost happiness, thanks solely and exclusively to your valuable intervention." He went on to assert that the intervention had "once again filled [him] with faith and trust in national justice, and . . . convinced [him] that *there is still a good judge, even for the humble folk*." The details in the file do not allow us to ascertain exactly how the judge compelled Porro to expedite the worker's claim, or if the timing of both events was merely coincidental. As far as Vivoni could tell, though, the judge had cared enough about him personally to break through the local arrangements to redress his situation. In other words, settlers believed that the highest regional authorities were personally accessible to them and that they could be persuaded to act on their behalf, bypassing local arrangements.

Federal judges had to oversee and review the work of myriad justices of the peace. Like the examples of Fermín Viera in General Roca and Bartolomé Porro in Villa Regina suggest, the justices' lack of formal training, penchant for extralegal arrangements, and allegiance to the governor complicated their relationships. Making things thornier, though justices were expected to "assist" the judge with investigations, their budgets were controlled by the governor. Additionally, except in the few towns large enough to elect justices of the peace, the governor appointed prominent vecinos to the position. Like all other governor's appointees, these justices were expected to report to him personally.

Judges resented having to oversee legally untrained justices, whose only qualification was residence in the district and basic literacy. While the judges had jurisdiction over most criminal, civil, and commercial cases, the justices of the peace were charged with settling "small local conflicts" and violations of the rural code that did not exceed a fine of three hundred pesos. The justices of the peace also maintained the *Registro Civil* for their district, registering births and deaths, as well as issuing transit permits for hides and cattle.[41] In some cases, the judges handled cases brought against justices of the peace, resulting in condescending reprimands for their illegal rulings, lack of competency, and ignorance of their duties.[42]

The justices of the peace's local roots often turned them into powerbrokers. They were the linchpins of a makeshift rural social order, which historian Gabriel Rafart labels a "web of firm loyalties."[43] The connections that the justices of the peace had to the local police, prominent merchants, and the governor sustained the "web of firm loyalties," which they used to avoid open conflicts and channel social conflict into informal solutions. These arrangements mirrored, in a distorted way, similar arrangements in rural counties in southern Buenos Aires province, where justices of the peace cobbled together a flexible and resilient way to ameliorate social conflict by adjudicating local complaints in creative ways.[44] The core of this social order was not the dispensation of justice but the maintenance of "order" and "peace." How each town created its own network of loyalties tying local merchants, justices of the peace, and the police force is the subject of much of this book, but the entire structure of interlocking relationships existed only insofar as it could graft on to the sturdy, deliberate, arcane system of federal justice.

The judges, on the other hand, tended to eschew social peace in favor of strengthening the rule of law. Historian Maria Elba Argeri highlights their outlook as pursuing "equality before the law" over anything else.[45] The judges were considered to be outsiders: city dwellers who came to the frontier bearing their university diplomas, meddling in the political life of the territories. Their lack of a local support base, which the governors sometimes had in the elites in the territorial capitals and the justices of the peace almost always had in their communities, meant that in many cases the local and regional press singled judges out particularly.[46] These divergent goals, allegiances, and methods created a surprisingly dynamic system of balances and counterbalances within the rigid structures laid out in Ley 1532. The isolation of the judges proved to be instrumental in keeping local alliances from capturing the functioning of the frontier state. In other words, the "judicial dictatorship" prevented the emergence of any other powerful coalition in the region.

Perhaps, then, Lazarriaga turned to the judge for help in dealing with Viera not because of the latter's interest in good justice, but because he perceived him as a possible ally or mediator.

FIGURE 5. "Regino Velázques, juez de paz de Choele Choel, noviembre 1910"
(AGN-Ddf, Inventario #403938).

A "Fictional Government": Governors and Political Administration

In his note pleading with the judge to assume the "supervisory" responsibility of removing Viera, Lazarriaga hinted at his frustrations with the governor's unresponsiveness. He bemoaned that "given the lack of quick and easy communications" the municipal council "was forced to abandon its rights" to appeal to the governor and turn instead to the judge. Although Ley 1532 made the governor's office potentially powerful, it soon became clear that it was mostly a ceremonial position. The law stipulated that governors, appointed by the president for three-year terms, would be in charge of all legislation for their territory and of administering the police. In practice, with limited fiscal resources most of their initiatives devolved into pleas for funding, directed at supervisors and residents. Lack of vocation, absenteeism, and budget constraints limited the effectiveness of governors in the frontier.

In the first years after the military annexation of the region, the governors of Río Negro and Neuquén were career military men and their appointments reflected recognition of their capabilities in the battlefield rather than any ability or vocation to rule.[47] Once the threat of continued armed struggle against indigenous groups ended and the border conflict with Chile was settled in 1893, governorships became résumé fillers for career politicians with little desire to transform the territories to which they had been appointed.

By the early twentieth century, the position of governor was defined for some by a lack of ability to govern, for others by a lack of commitment, and for those who did try, by a lack of effective power. This was similar to the situation in the North American West where "territorial appointees after 1865 were political hacks, defeated congressmen and cabinet members . . . [and] . . . owed their loyalty neither to the territory nor to the branch of the government they served."[48] Unlike the American context, however, northern Patagonian appointees could not expect to get rich by "controlling federal expenditure in their territories" as budgets were always lacking.

The role of the governors in the Patagonian territories, as described by Río Negro's first civilian governor, José Eugenio Tello, was a fairly limited and frustrating one:

> With the exception of the police force, no other government departments report to me, given the decentralized law [Ley 1532] which has created

a fictional government here, without prestige or the efficiency to do anything but police, making it subservient to the judges and other state agents demanding his services. The governor is constrained in such a way that anyone can personally disrespect him without fearing that he could punish them.[49]

As Martha Ruffini shows, the power of the governors was "corseted" by federal authorities to maintain internal stability. In effect their power was mostly symbolic, and their role was primarily to prevent dissent, fueling the perception that they were malleable and inconsistent.[50]

The governors had limited authority over territorial employees like school inspectors or public health providers, who often reported directly to authorities in Buenos Aires, much to the governors' chagrin.[51] Governors also lacked the power to control the territory's budget, which neutered many of their initiatives and plans. For example, efforts to open a second prison for Río Negro in 1914 had faltered by 1919 due to the impossibility of securing funding for the staff.[52] Bridges and irrigation canals lagged behind, especially in more remote areas, despite continued pleas and complaints by governors in their yearly reports.[53]

Absenteeism contributed to the governors' lack of effective power. They were required to live in the capital of the territory that they had been appointed to, but they sought to find ways to avoid having to spend time in the frontier. As early as 1894, the national government decreed stricter limits on vacations and licenses for appointed governors, attempting to compel governors to live in the frontier.[54] As a workaround, some governors held other government posts elsewhere in the country, suggesting that they considered the post as little more than a ceremonial appointment. For example, Carlos Rafael Gallardo continued to serve as a member of the national legislature representing his home province of Santiago del Estero while he was a "special envoy" to Patagonia (1901–1906) and later governor of Río Negro (1906–1910).[55] Similarly, Victor M. Molina served as governor of Río Negro between 1920 and 1924 while also serving as Finance Minister for President Marcelo T. de Alvear after 1923.

Most governors seemed to treat the post as a temporary assignment, often returning to their hometowns once their appointment ended. Even governors who proved transformative for their territories did not stay there long. For example, Col. Manuel Olascoaga, who presided over Neuquén between 1885 and 1891, produced a detailed survey of the Andean foothills while in the military, and as governor he brought the first printing press to Neuquén and used it to help establish a robust territorial newspaper. Despite these bonds, he retired to his native Mendoza when his appointment ended. The notable exception was José Eugenio Tello, who was governor of Río Negro between 1898 and 1905, and settled in a winery in the middle Río Negro valley after his term.[56]

Governors ruled by edicts and decrees, changing tax codes and setting policy on their own often without feedback, or pushback, from the population affected by those measures, and without contending with legislatures or facing electoral repercussions for their policies.[57] Because of the lack of institutional pathways to influence state policy in northern Patagonia, and because they often shared similar elite social circles, settlers in the capitals expected to have access to governors and tried creative ways to have their opinions and complaints heard by them.[58] In the regional capitals of Viedma and Neuquén, vecinos often jockeyed for political power with the governors and their entourages, using conventional avenues like political parties, newspapers, and municipal councils to exert influence on the workings of the colonial administration.

Away from the capital cities, in remote rural districts settlers also imagined their relationship with the governor in very personal ways, operating under the assumption that he deployed his power capriciously. Consider the case of José Lerman, a merchant from the remote Andean hamlet of Curi Leuvú in the northern district of Chos Malal, under the imposing Tromen volcano.[59] In a criminal complaint against the governor of Neuquén in 1922, Lerman claimed that the governor had ordered the local police to break into his business to close it down, using unpaid taxes and expired operating licenses as a pretense. The merchant had earlier traveled to the capital to discuss the legality of the governor's most recent tax decree, but despite staking out both of their offices for a week neither the governor nor the chief of police met with him.

The merchant's complaint was dismissed by the judge immediately, as the police swiftly documented the new taxes decreed by the governor the previous year as well as and the telegram from the governor to the police ordering the closure of all businesses with unpaid taxes, including Lerman's. The merchant understood his relationship with the governor in personal terms, assuming that the governor not only knew him but had chosen to target him. Although the judge ruled against him, Lerman's complaint succeeded in one point: he received an explanation for the taxes, which was his original intention when he unsuccessfully staked out the governor's office. Even though he was a lowly merchant in a backwater of a remote district in a frontier territory, Lerman seemed to *expect* an audience with the governor to discuss tax policy.

Settlers relied on direct appeals to the governor to break through local arrangements designed to keep them from accessing state power. Petitions and complaints became an effective way to appeal to governors, especially in conjunction with demands through newspapers and traditional patronage networks. Unlike those other methods, though, petitions were available to all the settlers in the territories, providing an avenue for political participation for non-elites. This is not unlike what historian Brodie Fischer finds for how poor Brazilians understood their relationship to President Getúlio Vargas in the 1930s and 1940s. Fischer uses letters written by "poor Cariocas" (the residents of Rio de Janiero's sprawling shantytowns) to Vargas to personally petition for his help in enrolling children in schools, reinstating dismissed workers, or for stipends to support their children.

Like Lerman and Vivoni, who wrote to the judge with personal appeals, the Carioca letter writers "sought to apply [his] words to their own life experiences" repurposing the elite's preferred rhetoric to convey their concrete demands. Indeed, the striking quality of these relationships is "the assumption—and the expectation that [the authorities] might take a personal interest in the smallest and most private of troubles."[60] Although Patagonian governors did not court popular participation like the Brazilian populist leader would, settlers still perceived them as proximate and responsive, and imagined themselves as the kind of stakeholders that could appeal to them in their times of need. In other words, settlers believed that the highest regional authorities were accessible to them and that they could be persuaded to act on their behalf, bypassing local arrangements.

Governors ultimately made the state in the frontier more responsive to complaints against its agents' abuses, in particular when the number of police officers roaming the countryside ballooned in the mid-1920s, leading to increased settler unhappiness.

Policing the Frontier: An Impossible Symbiosis

The job of policing northern Patagonia proved complicated. Statesmen in Buenos Aires believed that the government need only establish order and discipline in the territories for economic and social development to follow. Governors, however, constantly complained of the lack of funding, making dramatic appeals for an increased police budget in their yearly reports.[61] The three main problems for northern Patagonian police stemmed from this shortage of funding. First, it made it hard to reform, train, and retain qualified personnel. Second, the short tenure of those in command robbed the institution of stability and know-how as well as a coherent set of policies. Last, the police had a tense relationship with *vecinos* (prominent neighbors), who were vocal in their demands for good police but had few avenues to demand change.

Attempts to train, reform, or retain police personnel were hindered by two mutually reinforcing systemic issues.[62] The first arose from the difficulties in recruiting and retaining rank-and-file police officers. The initial police force of northern Patagonia was drawn mostly from the veterans of the military occupation, and as such it proved quick to violence and lacked community-building skills. With police departments perpetually understaffed, authorities relaxed already lax selection criteria in order to widen the pool of applicants, allowing recruits with criminal records, those unable to read or write, prone to violence, and simply incompetent to be added to the police force out of necessity. The result was an overworked, underfunded, and untrained police force made up partially of subjects with unsavory pasts.

The criminal background of some of the recruits tainted the whole force in the eyes of many settlers. A survey of Patagonian newspaper accounts in the first decade of the twentieth century revealed some of the descriptions used for the local police force: "inefficient, incompetent, biased, incapable, unfit for service, irresponsible, uncultured, untrained in their duties, unsuitable, and with a tendency to brutality."[63] The national press agreed, describing the territories' police forces as not only "bad" but also "scarce."[64]

The scarcity was exacerbated by uneven geographical distribution. The few police that were hired were concentrated in the urban areas. For example, in the Neuquén Territory, about a third of the police force worked in the capital city even though the population as late as 1924 was around 75 percent rural.[65] Notoriously, rural agents would abandon their posts to pick up additional pay as farmhands and peons when that work became available in the spring and summer.[66] For many of the officers, joining the police force was a stepping stone into the labor market, an avenue out of marginality, as the post of *vigilante* (watchman) in late nineteenth-century Buenos Aires had been for recent immigrants.[67]

The police commanders, the local elite, the representatives of the national state, and the population at large continually complained there were insufficient police. These complaints obscured the fact that there were more police officers every decade (see table 2).[68] As part of a series of reforms aimed to increase the quality rather than quantity of police officers in the mid-1920s, the government introduced a series of penalties against absenteeism as well as improved pay and more comprehensive benefits.[69] The result, by the mid-1930s, was a more professional and better-equipped police force with substantially fewer officers per capita (see table 3).

The second systemic issue blocking meaningful reform was the difficulty of recruiting commanders, from the chief of police to regional comisarios and detectives. Initially they were drawn from two very different groups of people. The majority were veterans of the military campaign against the indigenous groups, with little experience managing jails or police stations. Others were political appointees with distinguished reformist credentials, steeped in cutting-edge positivist thinking, but with little, if any, policing experience.[70]

Neither group was particularly well suited to making the unstable and ill-trained police force worthy of the public's trust. For example, between 1890 and 1930, seventy-two different individuals were appointed chief of police for the Neuquén Territory. The appointment was supposed to last two years, but only one chief achieved that benchmark. Instead, a new police chief was appointed every eight months, on average. This made it almost impossible to design, implement, and enforce any meaningful reforms.[71] However, by the early 1930s the efforts seemed to have borne some fruits, as contemporaries began to note the increased professionalization of senior management ("integrity" and "competence" were adjectives commonly used in the press to describe the commanders) while continuing to lament the ineptitude and apathy of the rank and file.[72]

The relationship between these "inept and apathetic" police forces and the settlers veered from contentious to symbiotic, depending on local circumstances. In the capitals, where the public outrage over bad police reached the national press more quickly and damagingly, the police actively courted the population. For example, some governors in the early twentieth century began naming prominent vecinos as comisarios, in an attempt to co-opt the emerging local elite into joining the police. In some cases, where capable comisarios already existed, vecinos were instead appointed as "honorary *sub-comisarios*," a made-up position characterized by short tenures and ineffectiveness.[73] The state attempted to ingratiate the police force to the population by attaching volunteers to each police station, which for years failed to lower crime rates and had mixed results.[74]

In remote rural districts, the relationship between local elite and police was less formal, often relying on reciprocal arrangements characteristic of patronage

Table 2. Number of police officers in Northern Patagonia.

Year	1902	1914	1924	1934
Neuquén	150	300	440	364
Río Negro	>150	~300	500	410

Table 3. Police officers per 1,000 residents.

Year	1914	1920	1934
Río Negro	7.1	11.7	3.6
Neuquén	10.4	14.8	8.6

networks based on loyalties.[75] For example, when payments fell behind, local merchants would extend credit to the local commanders to use as salary advances, guaranteeing themselves a captive clientele in the police force. Similarly, when the police found itself without adequate weapons, horses, or even without headquarters, affluent neighbors would offer their own, turning them into de facto patrons of certain police detachments.[76] In some cases, the police would act as informal attachés of prominent neighbors, using the implicit weight of their office to coerce other neighbors.[77] Both formally and informally, the underfunding of the state in the frontier turned settlers into active patrons of the police.

Despite the goals of Ley 1532, most local administrations in northern Patagonia fell outside of the control of the residents. Regional authorities were appointed directly by the executive in Buenos Aires, with only minimal need to court local elites, whose lack of effective political power curbed their ability to interfere. In turn, those federal appointees themselves appointed local authorities in most towns, rendering the "schoolyard of democracy" a cruel mirage: judges, governors, and police officers were the main institutional staples of the state in Patagonia. This helps us understand how, when the municipal council in General Roca clashed with Viera, a prominent neighbor turned justice of the peace, it felt compelled to act according to the prescriptions of Ley 1532, only to find itself without legitimacy to act and stifled by inaction from the governor and attempting a clever Hail Mary by involving the judge. In other words, fraught with internal contradictions, unclear jurisdictions, and constant scarcity, the state representatives of Argentine rule in Patagonia made virtue out of necessity, creating a stable and responsive institutional scaffolding on to which civil society could begin to develop in the frontier.

Conclusion

Argentina's newly incorporated southern territories received only minimal state attention between 1884, when their administration passed to civilian authorities, and the 1930s, when their administration was overhauled. During that period, the management of the frontier space relied exclusively on an ill-supported skeleton crew of governors, judges, and policemen. The poverty of these institutions contrasted sharply with lofty designs for Patagonia as a testing ground for a republican pedagogy. In short, expediency and political turmoil made a temporary administration into a permanent arrangement. The cornerstone of the republican pedagogy—municipal autonomy as training ground in electoral politics—never really gained traction. Early disappointments and contention left national authorities wary of increasing local power beyond a certain threshold.

Ruled locally by unelected councils, comisarios, and appointed justices, settlers found unlikely allies in the dual administration of the national territories: governors and judges. Yet caught between the settlers, the judges, and the governors were the police, who struggled to become a well-trained and well-funded repository of public trust. A variety of arrangements, both formal and informal, tied the Patagonian police to the local elite, complicating a relationship otherwise characterized by violence and material scarcity. Ultimately, the national state remained a remote (but still accessible) presence in the frontier until the transformations of the late 1930s. Meanwhile the local presence of the state was both intimately felt and constantly challenged by the settlers.

This chapter outlined how the state in the frontier came to operate as a space of contestation. Settlers learned to use the state by using petitions, complaints, investigations, and allegations against one another and against state agents in an effort to establish and modify social order in their communities. The following chapters will examine how settlers *forced* the government into action by taking its claim to be the guarantor of order in the region seriously, and how the state agents in turn shaped the contours of the institutions they staffed with their own priorities, expectations, and prejudices.

CHAPTER TWO

Civilization's Embrace

"Indios" and the Frontier State

> Let us morally destroy the Indian race, annihilating their political organizations and networks, dismembering the tribes, and, if need be, breaking families apart. Once broken and dispersed, this race will finally embrace civilization.
>
> —*La Prensa* (Buenos Aires), on March 1st, 1878, channeling Julio Argentino Roca's rationale for the military campaign against the indigenous population of northern Patagonia.[1]

> Barbarism is damned, and in the desert nothing remains, not even the carcasses of their dead.
>
> —Estanislao Zeballos, 1880.[2]

In 1890 Alejandro Nahuelcheo, a resident of the hamlet of Segunda Angostura in the lower Río Negro valley, complained to the police in nearby Viedma that his wife had been kidnapped by don José Pazos.[3] Nahuelcheo and his wife, Juana Legipán, had grown up as subjects of the independent indigenous state known as the "País de las Manzanas" in the Andean valleys of northwestern Patagonia, before they were attacked by their erstwhile allies, the Argentine army. Finding this case in the archives was very unexpected—not because of the crime being investigated but because of the story that emerged from the information in the file. Since the time of the military annexation of Patagonia in the late nineteenth century, a consensus was built that Argentina had disappeared all of its indigenous population. Scholars have recently begun challenging this "myth of a white Argentina," but it remains deeply entrenched.

Nahuelcheo's story in the state archives not only testifies to the survival of indigenous people in towns not far from major Patagonian settlements, but it also allows one to begin to sketch out the ways in which strands of indigenous culture survived, adapted to, and even shaped Argentine rule. This story of Juana Legipán's displacement to the opposite side of Patagonia, her "lawful marriage" to Alejandro Nahuelcheo, her "theft" (kidnapping) by Pazos, and her eventual reconciliation illustrates the often-overlooked complexity typical of relationships between the surviving indigenous people of Patagonia and the Argentine state.

The details in the case suggest that some indigenous people quickly learned how to use the language, laws, and practices of the new rules to their advantage while maintaining their own language, practices, and even unwritten rules. Nahuelcheo appealed to his status as an "indigenous subject" to demand swift and decisive action by the state. He argued that "offenses of this magnitude deserve the full punishment of the law, *especially* in this case, since the offended party is an *indígena*, submitted and subjected to the dispositions of civilized societies as well as observing Christian law, having lawfully married . . . and living peacefully while working hard . . . and forming a serene home, which was all taken away in an instant by a bold and daring thief."[4] He juxtaposed his own "lawful Christian marriage" to the "bold and daring theft" of his wife by José Pazos, drawing a sharp distinction between someone that had embraced Argentine law (himself), and someone who seemed to undermine it (Pazos). In other words, Nahuelcheo offered his own marriage as a testament of his assimilation, while painting Pazos as behaving outside of "civilized" conventions.

Nahuelcheo's framing of the "theft" of his wife was a political appeal: he presented himself as someone who had recently, consciously, and actively chosen to live under Argentine law. Appealing to his rights as a patriarch, Nahuelcheo asked the police to not only arrest Pazos—whose behavior he characterized as "illegal, against the rights of husbands"—but to also detain his wife whenever they found them. Although Pazos escaped custody while in transit to Viedma, Legipán was placed under the care of the Colegio de las Hermanas de la Caridad, a religious institution used to house and educate young girls. Eventually, Nahuelcheo requested her release "considering that she has expressed regret toward how the events unfolded, [and] that she has sworn faithfulness," but also because his "young children miss her."

This case introduces the subtle way in which indigenous people exercised citizenship under Argentina's colonial rule in Patagonia, while also laying out this chapter's three main arguments. First, Nahuelcheo's exodus from the País de las Manzanas to the lower Río Negro valley was part of a badly coordinated and brutal, but ultimately successful, effort by the Argentine government to disperse the indigenous population after the military campaign. This displacement was instrumental in making indigenous people "invisible" by subsuming them in settler society.

Second, almost as soon as the military campaign ended, the job of disarticulating and disciplining indigenous people fell to the local representatives of the state (governors, judges, police officers) as well as some nongovernmental agents, like the Colegio de Hermanas, which undertook their "civilizing mission" in a haphazard and piecemeal fashion. As scholars like Pilar Pérez and Hannah Greenwald emphasize, this chaotic approach was intentional: disorganization and bad records were a feature of the state's policy, not an unintended consequence.[5]

Finally, Nahuelcheo's characterization of his wife's infidelity as an act outside the parameters of civilized society (that is, as an "indigenous" act) suggests the degree to which indigenous cultural practices persisted—or at least people behaved *as if they persisted* in their dealings with the courts. In fact, a compact of practices and traditions that operated outside of the Argentine authorities' control came to be known colloquially as the "Ley de Indios." This Ley de Indios was not as well articulated as customary law in other colonial contexts, but it was used nonetheless by indigenous and settler litigants to challenge how Argentine authority was enforced.

Finding "Indians" in the archive: A brief note on methods and sources

Studies of Patagonia follow a somewhat paradoxical pattern: they tend to focus on indigenous people before the military occupation of 1878–1885, and on settler society after 1885. Why was this break so pronounced? One possibility was that indigenous people had simply "disappeared." In memoirs and government reports, statesmen insisted that "Indians" had disappeared after the military invasion, even as their accounts noted with disdain how many indigenous individuals engrossed the rural population in northern Patagonia.[6] This paradox—the survival of indigenous people, but the disappearance of "Indians" in official records—turned out to be part of a broader process of erasing nonwhite people from the nation. Because of this effort to remove racial markers in government records, finding indigenous people in court cases became a matter of luck and persistence.

Indigenous people were hiding in plain sight, but finding them required some careful delimiting of the archival record without superimposing modern preconceptions on who might be indigenous based on their last name, on where they lived, or which kind of crimes they were most likely to commit. Eventually, using strategies pioneered by social and legal historians of the colonial period in Latin America as well as of the early modern period in Europe, I was able to read the archive "against the grain"—that is, finding ways to decode the small pieces of evidence available to us, as well as the absence of evidence, to reconstruct the experiences of indigenous people under Argentine rule.

The first step to determine how likely it would be to find indigenous people in the archives was to ascertain how many indigenous people lived in northern Patagonia after the military invasion. Since the national census of 1895 and 1914 did not have a category for indigenous people—as far as they were counted, they were simply labeled as either Argentine or Chilean, depending on which side of the Andes they had been born—I needed to find other sources. An array of offhand observations, local surveys, and a "territorial census" in 1886 painted a picture of the size and dispersal of Patagonia's indigenous population.

By some estimates, in 1886 indigenous people made up as much as 40 percent of the *total* population of the Territory of Río Negro.[7] This number is both surprisingly high and tragically low. It is high considering the prevailing narrative of "indigenous disappearance" after the military annexation, showing the degree to which the military campaign dispersed rather than destroyed indigenous communities. It is low considering how quickly settlers moved into northern Patagonia behind the military, and how even without infrastructure or established urban areas they were already replacing indigenous people. Of course, the mere presence of indigenous people did not guarantee that they would appear in the archive; they would need to have interacted with state agents to appear in state records.

The next step was to identify areas where a high proportion of the population was indigenous, which would suggest that documents from those districts would be *more likely* to involve indigenous people either as subjects or as authors. From the same documents that confirm the survival of indigenous people in northern Patagonia, we can also gather that the distribution of indigenous people in the territory was uneven. The disbandment of the camps after 1885 led to the settlement of indigenous people in marginal areas, the *tierras fiscales* that the state had not managed to sell. The majority of these state-owned lands were in the central plateau, and along the rugged southern shores of the Limay River (the present-day counties of El Cuy, 9 de Julio, and 25 de Mayo). In those districts, the indigenous population represented most of the total population for decades afterwards. For example, the entire population of 25 de Mayo County was considered to be indigenous in 1886.

Even after the arrival of a large number of immigrants and Argentine settlers, some counties remained significantly indigenous; for example, in El Cuy County "Indians" still represented as much as 30 percent of the total population as late as 1920 and made up half of all "productive units" in that county. Along the more fertile areas of Río Negro valley, indigenous people made up about one-third of the population of General Roca County and one-fifth of the population in Avellaneda County in 1886, while as late as 1920 indigenous residents made up almost 20 percent of the arid areas south of the middle Río Negro valley.[8] In counties surrounding Viedma, along the lower Río Negro valley where Nahuelcheo and his family had settled, the indigenous population represented a bit less than 15 percent of the total. Indigenous people lived throughout northern Patagonia, but they were concentrated in rural districts, in arid marginal lands, and away from the railroads.

After identifying areas where indigenous people were more likely to have lived, and more likely to have encountered state agents and their fastidious record-keeping, the next step was to determine what kind of behavior would capture the attention of the record-keepers. For example, scholars have previously zeroed in on the important role played by the judicial system in establishing a private property regime conducive to large-scale agricultural development. In effect, these scholars argue, the courts made "warriors" into "criminals" by outlawing and persecuting behavior they deemed "indigenous" but that was central to how indigenous people derived meaning of life and established their identities. Rustling, for example, was often seen as a particularly indigenous crime, which

FIGURE 6. (*opposite*) "Araucanos y Tehuelches, en Chubut 1896" (AGN-Ddf, Inventario #303579).

the state pursued systematically: groups of indigenous men traveling together on horseback became immediately suspected of rustling cattle, and were treated as guilty until proven innocent by settlers and police officers.[9]

The assumption, as one scholar explained, was that the first step in identifying indigenous subjects in the court records was to look for "indigenous crimes"—that is, to find crimes most likely to have been attributed to indigenous people. This approach has often led to an overemphasis on violence and mobility as proxies for indigeneity; the only indigenous practices that attracted scholarly attention were those that the state considered as dangerous, unintentionally reinforcing a crude caricature of "Indians" as antagonists. It should be no surprise, then, that a search that starts by looking at criminal activity concludes that the main relationship between indigenous subjects and the state was that of legal coercion. Shifting the focus away from criminality, however, allows for more comprehensive inquiry into what indigenous people and "indigeneity" looked like to the people and institutions of the state in Patagonia. This chapter draws from a broader set of documents to present a richer picture of how indigenous people interacted with the colonizing Argentine state.

Just because indigenous people stopped being labeled as such in government documents did not mean that they no longer *thought* of themselves as indigenous, or that they were no longer *treated* as indigenous, or even that the perception of indigeneity did not affect how they navigated the judicial process. Indigeneity—the physiological, behavioral, and cultural traits that combined to mark someone as "Indian"—was a powerful force affecting how much justice people had access to, how that justice was delivered, or even what rights people could expect to have. To illustrate the subtle, but powerful, ways in which indigeneity played a role in legal proceedings, recall Nahuelcheo's request to "show no leniency to his wife" and her companion whenever the police apprehended them. This request might seem extreme considering that the crime was framed as a kidnapping, but the ostensibly forceful removal of women from households had a different meaning in the frontier.

Throughout the nineteenth century, the capture of white and indigenous women had been a contentious issue in frontier society. In fact, the image of the captive woman (the *cautiva* of frontier lore) loomed large in the imagination of writers and statesmen who associated the practice of captive raiding with an "excessive indigenous masculinity," as Ashely Kerr finds.[10] As the historian Kristine Jones explains it, elite families on the frontier found that "an elopement" of a daughter or a wife "could most honorably be explained as a kidnapping, and local justices of the peace [in Buenos Aires] recorded dozens, if not hundreds, of such events" throughout the nineteenth century. On the other hand, for people in the País de las Manzanas as well as in other indigenous groups across the Americas, "marriage traditionally involved mock kidnapping, with the warrior later providing recompense to the woman's family."[11] By framing Pazos's offense (seducing his wife) as part of a longer tradition of suddenly illegal indigenous culture, Nahuelcheo sought to articulate his family's personal tragedy in a coded language that state authorities were unlikely to ignore, while also underscoring his own, unthreatening, "civilized" masculinity.

Once the archive is read this way (what historians call "against the grain") new questions emerge that would otherwise remain not only unanswered but unasked: How exactly did state authorities interact with the surviving indigenous people in the region? How did they relate to those they perceived as "indigenous"? Could the perception of "indigenousness" ever be an asset to individuals as they engaged the state and became entangled in its workings? To what extent were nonstate actors (like the unknown person who helped Nahuelcheo with his complaint, or the convent where Juana Legipán was detained) involved in the process of assimilating indigenous people in northern Patagonia? And, perhaps more crucially for the central question of this book, after they were dispersed and made landless, the indigenous groups of northern Patagonia had an unclear political status: were they prisoners, subjects, citizens, or something else altogether?

The evidence in the cases, and the research done in the last few decades to recover the stories and experiences of indigenous people on the frontier, do not provide a straightforward answer.[12] By dispersing the indigenous population throughout a settler population that had civil rights but no political rights, their status was the same as the rest of the population in northern Patagonia, which is a simple answer but not a satisfying one. As Nahuelcheo put it in his complaint, he had "submitted" to the Argentine state and "subjected" himself to its laws, presenting himself as a subject. But his manipulation of the "civilizing" language used by Argentine statesmen and intellectuals suggests that he chose to present himself as a stakeholder in the effort to make northern Patagonia part of the country. Determining if that choice was an earnest expression of his own political allegiances or a strategic redeployment of official discourses remains beyond the ability of historians. In fact, these kind of uncertainties prompt scholars to speculate, carefully, about the inner lives and motivations of their subjects.

Throughout the book and particularly in this chapter, instances of "scholarly speculation" are presented as transparently as possible, using them as an opportunity to discuss the limitations of the sources and the methodologies that historians use to craft their interpretations. Beyond these conjectures, what stands out from Nahuelcheo's complaint is that the indigenous people of Patagonia used the courts, and their own ambiguous status within the legal framework, to their advantage, continuing a tradition dating back to the colonial period throughout Latin America.[13]

Unpacking the "Conquest(s) of the Desert"

The so-called "Conquest of the Desert," the campaign by the military which solved the "Indian problem" by 1880, has been viewed as a watershed moment in Argentine history. In her introduction to a recent collection of essays on the Conquest of the Desert, Carrie Ryan noted that the year 1880, in particular, was seen as the beginning of a period of "social progress, economic growth, and national unity."[14] The violent campaign to conquer and eradicate indigenous people from Patagonia was full of symbolic meaning, elevating it to something "comparable to the struggle for national independence," as Diana Lenton and her collaborators remind us.[15] Contemporaries imagined Patagonia as a "grandiose amphitheater" that would point Argentina to the future once it had, to borrow Ashley Kerr's phrasing, "neutralized the savagery associated with both the land and the indigenous people who lived there."[16]

Scholars and activists have revised some of the assumptions of this narrative, challenging the way it is remembered, the significance it is given, and the historical conclusions that are drawn from it. This section offers a (brief) unpacking of the main misconceptions surrounding the campaign to eradicate indigenous people from Argentina as a way to help understand why Nahuelcheo and Juana Legipán found themselves hundreds of miles from their home. Their exodus, like that of thousands of others, was the result of a badly coordinated, but ultimately highly successful, effort to disperse and disappear indigenous people from northern Patagonia.

Three myths around the "Conquest of the Desert" need to be dispelled to better understand how the military annexation of northern Patagonia affected indigenous people. The first, foundational, myth was that the area being annexed was a "desert." The region was certainly not a hydrological desert, nor, as the phrase

FIGURE 7. "Familia Tehuelche en el Parque Nacional Nahuel Huapi, undated" (AGN-Ddf, Inventario #114165).

implied, uninhabited. Patagonia had been a fluid, dynamic space for centuries—a borderland between Spanish colonial society and nomadic cattle traders. Before the Andes range became an international boundary in the late nineteenth century, it was porous: skilled herders and warriors adroitly navigated its mountain passes, and control of low-lying passes conferred power over trading networks. Patagonia has also been a space of conflict, as the frontier between creole and indigenous societies advanced and receded during the colonial and early national period.

The century before Patagonia's incorporation into Argentina (roughly between 1776 when Buenos Aires was made a viceregal capital, and 1878 when the military annexation began) saw a shifting frontier line, increased competition for dwindling resources, and armed conflict. While the Bourbon administrators had attempted to normalize relations in the southern frontier of the Spanish Empire through increased trade (establishing trading posts), advanced fortifications (*fortines*), and political autonomy, those arrangements were interrupted by independence struggles and ensuing civil wars. After the wars for independence, the southern frontier fell under the jurisdiction of Buenos Aires, whose elite remained committed to the expansion of cattle ranching, and encouraged the continued colonization of the plains, pushing the frontier south beyond the Salado River in central Buenos Aires province.[17]

The conflict between nomad herders and cattle ranchers was temporarily resolved by a compromise between 1829 and 1852, known as Pax Rosista, after Juan Manuel de Rosas, the Buenos Aires governor that instituted it. On the one hand, this arrangement offered preferential treatment to "allied" indigenous groups, which received allotments of cattle and goods in exchange for giving up raiding, and for providing the frontier settlements with salt, clothing, and military assistance. On the other hand, the Buenos Aires government (and its newly acquired indigenous allies) pursued punitive actions against nonallied indigenous groups, sometimes quite asymmetrically, which increased the number of indigenous people living under the allotment system. However, with the fall of Rosas in 1852, frontier life became characterized, once more, by *malones* (Indian raids) and punitive expeditions. An Araucanian leader recently arrived from Chile, Calfucurá, emerged as the head of the indigenous coalition.

Immediately after Rosas's defeat in the Battle of Caseros, Calfucurá's warriors retreated back to their stronghold in the Salinas Grandes and raided Bahía Blanca in southern Buenos Aires, seizing 65,000 head of cattle.[18] In a massive uprising in 1855, his followers and allies raided almost every settlement in Buenos Aires's southern frontier, defeating the provincial army in open battles in Sierra Chica, San Antonio de Iraola, and, decisively, in the swamps of San Jacinto by Tapalque creek.[19] With the provincial armed forces in disarray, Calfucurá's followers sacked Azul, Tandil, Junín, Melincué, Olavarría, and Bahía Blanca, forcing the government in Buenos Aires to resume the allotment system. In the two decades that followed, Calfucurá and his followers put relentless pressure on the ranching frontier to guarantee treaty obligations from the authorities in Buenos Aires.

Rancher encroachment on indigenous territory in the 1860s and early 1870s, coupled with a failure to sustain treaty obligations by Argentine authorities, led to a series of malones that emptied large swaths of the frontier.[20] One wave of raids in 1872 by Calfucurá's followers laid waste to towns throughout Buenos Aires province, effectively pushing the frontier line to the colonial boundary (a mere two hundred miles from the city of Buenos Aires). For example, the population of the town of Veinticinco de Mayo, in central Buenos Aires, dropped from five thousand to only six hundred after "malones took thousands of heads of livestock and several hundred women and children," which were transported through the Andean passes in northern Patagonia to Chile to be sold.[21] After the expansion of the frontier and the stability achieved during the Pax Rosista, the twenty years that followed had managed to "virtually depopulate" Buenos Aires's southern frontier.[22]

Historians have begun to understand the depopulation of a region as a political strategy, a calculated maneuver by nomadic raiders as they attempted to force concessions from settled states.[23] Calfucurá was finally defeated in the battle of San Carlos, late in 1872, by an alliance of Argentine forces (seasoned veterans after the Paraguayan War) and "friendly" indigenous forces (followers of cacique Catriel). This was a turning point in the frontier, as it marked the sudden decline of the once mighty empire of the Pampas, which descended into dynastic scuffling following Calfucurá's death in 1873. In that context, the Argentine government changed its frontier policy rather swiftly during the 1870s, from coexistence to "Indian removal."

President Nicolás Avellaneda (1874–1880) argued that simply defeating the indigenous people would not solve the frontier issue; Argentina needed to *occupy* all their territory, expanding the productive surface of the country. In 1878, the newly appointed Minister of War, Julio Argentino Roca, dismissed earlier gradualist strategies to control the region and revived an eighteenth-century plan to advance the frontier line by taking effective control of the territory north of the Río Negro in one sweeping, overwhelming assault designed to "exterminate or remove the Indians . . . through a war of aggression."[24] The oxymoron of labeling a military operation to "exterminate" people as "Conquest of the Desert" was part of what the scholar of settler colonialism Patrick Wolfe calls the "logic of extermination" that sought to physically and discursively erase the people of northern Patagonia.[25] The military annexation of northern Patagonia was not a steady march into a depopulated steppe; it sought to depopulate it as it advanced.

Determining how many people lived beyond the frontier when Argentina started their military campaign remains an elusive goal. Official figures remain incomplete and partial, but scholars estimate that somewhere around 20,000 people lived in Patagonia beyond the control of the Argentine government before the military campaign commenced in 1878. Without reliable numbers, the figure was arrived at negatively by Enrique Masés and others: they approximate the number by considering that the military campaign left behind about 13,000 indigenous people captured, another 1,500 deceased, and an additional 6,000 displaced throughout Patagonia.[26] Because of the lack of reliable records, we can assume that the total of 20,000 is probably a conservative estimate. Other scholars, particularly anthropologists Walter Delrio and Ana Ramos, argue that the number could be exponentially higher. Delrio and Ramos quote a Salesian missionary who estimated that the Territory of Neuquén *alone* had 20,000 indigenous people in 1880.[27] These figures are in constant revision and refinement by scholars as more information becomes available. As we now know, the Argentine government's actions had genocidal results, even if their means were not always systematic and decisive.

The second myth requiring closer examination is that the "Conquest" was a singular event limited to 1880, as it is often commemorated. It was a decade-long process including planning, "inverted raids," a swift advance, and a series of targeted campaigns until 1885. Leading up to the military campaign, Argentine authorities prepared to administer northern Patagonia once it was occupied. During 1878, Avellaneda secured funding for the campaign by issuing bonds against the land that would be acquired and established the "military governorship of Patagonia" to administer the new territory as it came under Argentine control.[28] Starting in 1878–1879 a series of targeted forays, sometimes called "inverted raids" or *malón winka*, the white man's raid, disrupted frontier life.[29] The Argentine army began mimicking indigenous cattle raids by launching quick and limited assaults on non-combatant targets beyond the frontier, signaling a change in state policy.

Building on the success of those early forays in breaking the military capacity of indigenous people to resist, Roca personally lead a scaled-up campaign starting in April 1879, which advanced swiftly toward the Río Negro. Advancing rapidly southward from Buenos Aires, the military "swept" the retreating indigenous groups, disbanding *tolderías* (encampments), liberating captives, and "recovering" as many as ten thousand heads of cattle. The army claimed a symbolic triumph on the shores of the Río Negro on 25 May 1879, to coincide with the anniversary of Buenos Aires's declaration of independence from Spain. As one of the commanders asserted at the time, "this day . . . inaugurates the dominion of civilization . . . where barbarism had reigned for three centuries."[30] The military took thousands of indigenous prisoners, mostly noncombatants, without having fought any major battles, and the ease of the victory was celebrated back in Buenos Aires with the election of Roca as president in 1880.

The military campaign, however, was not complete, as a new phase began in the summer of 1881 when Col. Conrado Villegas, relying on indigenous informants, led a three-pronged approach on the great Nahuel Huapi Lake to secure the fertile Andean valleys. We do not know as much about this phase because, as a pair of scholars of the indigenous response to the invasion put it, "this was a war of raids rather than of large battles or even massacres . . . the army launched attacks whose actions were rarely documented."[31] The Andean valleys had historically been the most densely populated region in northern Patagonia, and their numbers increased dramatically as refugees from the 1879 "sweeps" settled there. The fighting in the valleys was traumatic, with the military "using constant violence to subdue, evict, or reduce" the indigenous population to "poorer lands."[32] Resistance by indigenous groups was fierce—guerrilla warfare—but it nonetheless resulted in the expulsion of an "important number" of people from their Andean settlements. With the military having "sustained control" of the valleys, agricultural settlers began to trickle in and displace the indigenous population.

Villegas' forces abandoned the fast-paced sweeps and instead switched to a strategy of "effective and sustained" control of the valleys to prevent the dispersed indigenous groups from regrouping. Between 1882 and 1883, Argentina established small military bases along the Andes to prevent the re-entry of indigenous groups from the Chilean side of the mountains. These smaller bases along the valleys allowed the military to combine combat and policing operations by launching expeditions to fight roving bands throughout the mountain range. In many ways, these mixed police-military "pacifying" operations continued into the following decades, as the police forces in both Neuquén and Río Negro drew heavily from the demobilized veterans of the Conquest.

The military spent the next two years pursuing and battling the remaining indigenous groups, using the forts it had established as clearinghouses for the "system of distribution and allocation" of indigenous people. After the defeat of the last two "great caciques," Manuel Namuncurá and Valentín Saygüeque in March 1884 and January 1885, respectively, General Lorenzo Vintter (the military governor of Patagonia at the time) declared the "humiliating internal frontier" finally closed. He proudly notified the president that "the secular war against the Indian, begun in Buenos Aires in 1535, has finally been won."[33] Of the estimated 20,000 people that lived south of the frontier line on the eve of the conquest, 14,500 had been captured or killed, 4,000 were under the military's jurisdiction (either as soldiers, or in concentration camps), and the remaining 1,000 remained scattered throughout Patagonia.

The final myth is related to the figures of deceased, captured, and dispersed indigenous people, which undermine Zeballos's cruel boast that "nothing remained," after the military invasion, "not even the carcasses of their dead." From the onset, the Argentine government lacked a clear policy toward indigenous people after the military invasion of their lands. Initially, the government had hoped to replicate the model developed by the United States in its own western territories. After considering an expensive "reservation system," in 1879 President Nicolás Avellaneda decided to instead pursue a policy of internal redistribution—breaking up indigenous communities, and even families—which was discontinued within a few years, without any other policy taking its place.

As Hannah Greenwald shows, efforts to create "agricultural colonies" to resettle captive indigenous groups, like the followers of Juan José Catriel in the town of General Conesa, were ultimately disbanded after the elite came to find indigenous sovereignty—even acculturated sovereignty—as "undesirable." The agricultural colony in Conesa, for example, was disbanded summarily after three years, when Congress "halted rations . . . granting only enough resources for a onetime payout intended to remove any remaining inhabitants from the territory."[34] This left behind a patchwork of ad hoc arrangements managed by military officials and governors. Without a clear policy for how to handle the defeated indigenous groups, the capture, transportation, and relocation of captives devolved into a haphazard system of internal redistribution and assimilation.[35]

The volume of indigenous removal in the first few years of the invasion was staggering: over 1,800 captives arrived in Buenos Aires in 1878, and 1879 saw an additional 2,400. The process of "redistributing" these captives throughout Argentine society to acculturate them was decentralized. A newspaper advertisement from late 1878 announced that "Indian men and women will be given away on Wednesdays and Fridays to the families of this city, through the Welfare Society," underscoring the role played by religious institutions.[36] The scene at these "Indian giveaways" was harrowing, as "children [were] removed from their

FIGURE 8. (*opposite*) "Marcelino Bustamante, paisano centenario de la Patagonia, 'sargento de la Reconquista,' Neuquén, 1938" (AGN-Ddf, Inventario #163428).

mothers to be given away in front of them, despite the screaming, the wailing and the pleading from the bowed indigenous women, their arms reaching for the sky [. . . and] some cover their faces, other look despondently to the ground, as the mother holds her child—the flesh of her flesh—close to her chest, and the father fruitlessly throws his body in front to protect his family."[37]

The redistribution system was designed as a "civilizing" tool, a way to break families apart and blend them into the urban poor. By 1881 the number of captives arriving in Buenos Aires would be less than fifty, a sharp decline suggesting that captured indigenous people were "dispatched north to ranches, barracks, workshops, sugar plantations, religious missions, wealthy homes, and ships" rather than sending them directly to Buenos Aires.[38] If we take Masés's estimates drawn from the military records (which were most certainly incomplete, as each commander sent captives to Buenos Aires independently), about five thousand people suffered this fate.

The military invasion not only removed thousands of indigenous people from the frontier, it also dispersed several thousand more. When Nahuelcheo made his appeal to the Argentine authorities in 1890, his family had undergone a traumatic decade of dislocation and violence that remains impossible to fully reconstruct. Nahuelcheo claimed to have been part of the País de las Manzanas, a powerful coalition of Tehuelche and Mapuche groups under the leadership of the great cacique Valentín Saygüeque that settled around Lake Nahuel Huapi. Saygüeque and his followers (including, we assume, Alejandro Nahuelcheo and Juana Legipán) had been staunch supporters of the Argentine government and remained allied with the Argentine military as late as 1880.[39] So the question remains, how did Nahuelcheo and Legipán find themselves so far from their homeland in 1890?

One of the main ways the invasion reshuffled indigenous society was by blotting up indigenous people as it advanced. For example, the army added about a thousand indigenous warriors to the infantry (labeled as "auxiliaries" and *indios de lanza* in the government documents). By 1881, indios de lanza represented a third of all military forces in Patagonia, creating a paradoxical occupying force made up of the occupied themselves.[40] For example, Marcelino Bustamante, shown in figure 8, was both a "sergeant in the Reconquest" in allusion to his role in the military occupation of the region, and a "paisano" in reference to his indigenous ancestry.

FIGURE 9. "Rancho Indígena, Chos Malal, Neuquén" (AGN-Ddf, Inventario #140419).

The Argentine military also added a significant number of indigenous "camp followers"—mostly women and children—either as spouses and families of the indios de lanza, or as captives and servants of the commanders. Several forts were set up at strategic points—in Choele Choel and General Roca, along the Río Negro, Confluencia (at the meeting of the Neuquén and Limay rivers), and Chos Malal (at the confluence of the Neuquén and Agrio rivers), to name a few—which would quickly become the first population centers of the newly incorporated territories.

The noncombatant "camp followers" made up the bulk of poor in the newly established towns around the forts.[41] In legal documents, women with indigenous surnames living in Roca, Choele Choel, or Confluencia described their occupation as laundresses, cooks, or simply as caretakers. Had Nahuelcheo been one of these indios de lanza joining the Argentine forces once their victory seemed inevitable?

That seems unlikely, given that Saygüeque was the last of the great chiefs to surrender, in 1885, with a thousand followers. The rest of the *manzaneros*, according to the government's own accounts, had been captured in the 1881–1883 raids led by Col. Villegas.

It is more likely that Nahuelcheo and Legipán had fallen captives to the raiding forces and been removed from the area against their will. The government established several "concentration centers" throughout northern Patagonia—one in Comallo on the western edge of the plateau, another one in Valcheta, in the central plateau, and two along the Río Negro: one near Chichinales, and the other one in Fortín Castro.[42] Scholars are still grappling with the scope and nature of these camps, since their existence at the time was shrouded in mystery, without any explicit mention of them in government records.

Based on accounts from travel narratives, in proselytizing propaganda and bureaucratic footnotes, the picture emerges of an ad hoc, brutal system. The Valcheta camp was mentioned in the travel narrative of a Welsh colonist who recalled with horror seeing an old friend languishing behind a fenced pen. According to the traveler "most of the Patagonian Indians were reduced in this camp . . . enclosed by a high chain link fence . . . their big boney, wind chapped hands reaching through the fence" as they asked him for food.[43] The Chichinales camp, adjacent to the General Roca fort, became famous through Salesian propaganda that highlighted the success the Order had in converting the indigenous people there to Christianity.[44] Military communication in the early 1880s mentioned "256 captives" in Valcheta and 1,547 in Chichinales, but they did not discuss their legal status or if these "captives" were held in the camps themselves, or elsewhere.[45] Additionally, a group of about 1,500 "uncivilized Indians" (the followers of the cacique Catriel) awaited their "eventual fate" somewhere between the Negro and Colorado rivers, according to an 1895 census. This is probably how Nahuelcheo and his family ended up in the lower Río Negro valley, hundreds of miles east of their homeland in the Andean valleys. In fact, his insistence on their Christianization and submission to Argentine law makes it likely that they were part of the groups proselytized by the Salesian missionaries.

No overarching policy was put in place once the military operation officially ended in 1885, despite worries about the destabilizing impact of releasing a large landless population of demobilized and impoverished people into northern Patagonia. Without a clear "Indian policy" to guide state action, and complaining that the national coffers were struggling under the burden of "maintaining, transporting, and placing" the estimated 4,000 indigenous people under the care of the government in Patagonia, the camps were slowly disbanded on a case-by-case approach.[46] Indigenous groups that received land grants to create reservations established them in isolation, often on marginal lands.[47]

Individual families, on the other hand, used a special law designed for immigrant families to settle in the region to obtain small plots at low costs. Despite their preference for European immigrants as a colonizing force, the government hoped this workaround would serve as a "civilizing" process by forcing formerly nomadic people to farm—imitating what the United States had done with its western territories following the Dawes Severalty Act of 1887.[48] Reservations and family holdings, however, were not the norm. A large majority of indigenous people simply settled in state-owned marginal land, without titles, hoping to benefit from the state's apathy and the booming "white gold" of Merino sheep-raising.

Indigenous society and culture as it had existed until 1877 had been eradicated, but the indigenous population, dispersed and hidden in plain sight, remained. Either because the promises of land were not kept or because of the harshness of the marches, individuals, families, and entire communities ended up scattered throughout the plateau in a haphazard manner.[49] For many groups, this exodus from the camps became a foundational moment for their communities, one which they used time and time again to defend their right to occupy that land. However Nahuelcheo and his family ended in the lower Río Negro valley, they had been subsumed in settler society, living in a colony of Argentina, which had entered a "golden age" of "social progress, economic growth, and national unity."[50]

In short, the double "desertification" of the frontier—first by "Indian raids," and later by the Argentine military—created, in the minds of statesmen, a blank canvas without people or institutions in which to attempt to build a "civilized" (modern, liberal, productive) society where before only "barbarism" reigned. The people that remained there, in remote valleys, in protected towns, in detention centers, that moved back and forth through the mountain passes, and who arrived soon after, had to contend with an administrative structure that assumed they were not there, and with administrators who knew very well that they were, but were less sure of how to shape them into a "civilized" population. The colonial institutions that Argentina used to govern Patagonia had been designed to *occupy* the region, and as Nahuelcheo and his family learned when Pazos absconded with Legipán, they proved ill-suited for peacetime administration.

Educating the "Hijos del Pueblo"

When the police finally apprehended Juana Legipán, her husband asked that she be placed in the care of the Colegio de Hermanas de Caridad, which was run by Salesian nuns. Scores of women and children ended up confined to the care of the Salesian schools, which were part of an informal solution to what authorities saw as a simmering social issue: the abandonment of indigenous children. The use of religious institutions for social control had a long history in the time when the Spanish Empire ruled Latin America, ending in the early nineteenth century. It would be tempting to see Legipán's confinement in a religious institution in the late nineteenth century as a *continuation* of colonial-era practices into the national period. But Patagonia did not have any of these colonial institutions and practices, as it remained outside of effective Spanish control. That an avowedly modernizing, liberal, and secular state decided to outsource the housing and education of indigenous people to religious groups deserves some unpacking.

Hamstrung by an assumption at the highest level of government that the "Indian problem" had ended with the military annexation, state-run institutions of social control were scarce and ill-equipped in the early period of Argentine administration. The paucity of state resources beyond "good justice and heavy policing" was staggering. Famously, the prisoners in the Territory of Neuquén's public jail made a difficult pilgrimage through the rugged precordillera when the territorial capital was transferred from Chos Malal to Neuquén in 1904, only to find that the new jail was not completed, and would not be for another eight years. For almost a decade the convicts slept in the police headquarters, and even after that, no fence or wall was built around the jail until the 1920s, making prison breaks in Neuquén a routine event during the 1910s.[51] Other institutions lagged even further behind—the government would not build hospitals, schools, and orphanages until decades later. The civilian governments that succeeded the military invasion of northern Patagonia were ill-suited to rule, but their isolation and centralization of power in governors and judges facilitated the exploration of creative workarounds to the scarcity of the frontier.

The task of housing, educating, and caring for women and children, especially indigenous ones, fell on nonstate actors: the Salesian order. The Salesians were unusual because of their late arrival to the spiritual scene in Latin America. The Salesian Order of Don Bosco and the Sisters of María Auxiliadora first arrived to Argentina from Turin in 1875, and began operating in Viedma in 1879, just

FIGURE 10. "Plaza Huincul, Neuquén. Camión que conduce niños a la escuela, Diciembre 1923" (AGN-Ddf, Inventario# 77851).

as the town became the capital of Patagonia.[52] During the period of the Spanish Empire, several religious orders established secular missions between the sixteenth and eighteenth century, including the Dominicans, Augustinians, Jesuits, and eventually the Franciscans. The crisis of the late colonial period, which included an unpopular order by the crown to expel all the Jesuits from the Americas, reshaped the missions in frontier areas, which continued to decline during the wars of independence.[53]

As Jane Rausch suggests, "philosophically and legally" the new liberal republics were "primed to eliminate the missions." However, as Erick Langer found when studying Franciscan missions in Bolivia, "republican-era missions remained instruments of state frontier policy, just as in colonial times . . . the missions helped significantly in breaking the independence of the native peoples on the frontier." In a few critical ways republican-era missions differed from their antecessors: rather than draw from local elites, or Spanish friars, the missionaries of the nineteenth century were foreigners, mostly from Italy; and more significantly, "power was distributed differently" mainly because anticlerical governments demanded greater oversight and expected the eventual transformation of neophytes into citizens.[54]

Although missionary activity in the nineteenth century was not unusual, it tended to be in areas where it had been interrupted during the early nineteenth century. That is, liberal missionary efforts were restorations of old missions. But northern Patagonia had never experienced sustained religious colonization. The Salesians who arrived there after the military annexation were entering a territory without an established Christian tradition and built the religious infrastructure from the ground up.

As part of their efforts to spread Christianity in the region, Salesian brothers and sisters built churches, schools, and even temporarily housed "malcontent" women and youth.[55] The arrival of Salesian missionaries on the frontier coincided with a moment of heightened tension between the state and the church at the national level: liberal reforms to the civil code reserved for the state the right to record births, marriages, and deaths, to the dismay of the clergy, while the national education reform of 1884 secularized all schools.[56] Despite these tensions, the Salesians established a decisive foothold in northern Patagonia. By 1890 Salesian brothers and sisters had opened four schools in Río Negro: two for boys and two for girls, spread between Viedma and the neighboring town of San Javier, serving the area with the oldest white settlements, which was also the area around one of the detention camps discussed earlier.

According to a report sent to the Interior Minister in 1900, the Territory of Río Negro had 6 state-run primary schools, serving 350 students, and 8 Salesian schools, serving 455 students, underscoring the outsized role of the Order in northern Patagonia in the first few decades after the military annexation.[57] In the Andean valleys, a Chilean group of Salesian brothers established a boy's *colegio* in San Martín de los Andes, in 1896, and Domingo Milanesio, a Salesian brother, established a pair of colegios (one for boys and one for girls) in Junín de los Andes, explicitly to educate indigenous children. The schools, according to a beaming report by one of the administrators in 1890, had at least 90 "boarders" with a significant number of "orphaned indigenous children or minors referred to them by the local authorities."[58]

The process of "referring" children to the schools often fell to the representatives of the judiciary, in particular prosecutors, judges and, in later decades, children's advocates. That practice would become institutionalized in 1894, when a presidential decree made the colegio in Viedma (as well as the rest of the Order's convents and schools) into makeshift public jails for minors and women until the government finished building prisons for women in the national territories, in the 1930s.[59] In a way, the colegio continued the colonial-era juridical practice of *depósitos* and *recogimientos*: serving as a repository for indigenous children removed from their families to acculturate them.[60] As the scholar of colonial society Zeb Tortorici explains it, when women were placed in a recogimiento, the purpose was "both to punish and to protect."[61] During Juana Legipán's short stay at the colegio in 1890, she probably interacted with dozens of other indigenous people confined to the care of the sisters.

Although Nahuelcheo requested that his wife be held in one of the schools, patriarchs and family members had limited say on whether their loved ones ended up under the care of the Salesians. Once a minor was deemed an orphan by the state and placed in religious institutions, the parents or guardians struggled to reclaim their children. Many indigenous parents, who lacked legal proof of parenthood, found it hard to establish their claims on their progeny, and this made internment in a religious institution a one-way trip for many children.[62] Consider a case from 1889, involving Marta Acosta (a twenty-seven-year-old washerwoman) who fought what she came to understand as the abduction of her daughter Carmen by the state, with no success. Acosta was married to a soldier (Luis Rivero, stationed in General Roca with the Seventh Cavalry Regiment) and had decided earlier that year to "cede" her ten-year-old daughter to the family of her husband's supervisor, a military commander simply called Sergeant Cabrera in the court documents.[63] "Ceding" children to the care of elite families was not an unusual practice for impoverished Patagonians. Acosta expected that Carmen would receive an education from her wealthier guardians in exchange for "accompanying" Mrs. Cabrera and helping the family with domestic chores. Her daughter, however, suffered a different fate.

This case poses an interesting challenge. The documents do not directly and explicitly label Marta Acosta as indigenous. As mentioned earlier, deducing indigeneity from the archive can be an exercise in typecasting and educated guesses. In this case, a few clues in the file suggest to us that Marta was indigenous; none of these clues offers enough evidence by themselves, but taken in combination they present a reasonable assumption. For starters, consider that in 1886, an estimated 30 percent of the residents of the county where Marta Acosta lived were identified by government officials as indigenous. Additionally, she was labeled as illiterate in the documents, which was not unusual but definitely a marker of poverty and rurality. The document noted that she worked as a laundress "attached" to a military base, which was a common job for indigenous "camp followers," as detailed earlier.

Another clue that points both to poverty and indigenousness was her inability to produce official documentation of her marriage, the birth of her daughter, or her baptism. Her daughter was ten years old in 1889, meaning she was born at the beginning of the military invasion of northern Patagonia, consistent with the assumption that she was a not-entirely-willing camp follower after the initial sweeps. All these clues, combined with the fact that she had "ceded" her daughter to a prominent family, paint a picture consistent with her being indigenous.

Marta Acosta learned from neighbors that Carmen had been seen wandering the streets in Viedma after the Cabrera family had moved to Buenos Aires without notice, abandoning the girl. The police placed Carmen in the care of the Salesian sisters. Acosta had a neighbor write a simple letter to the judge requesting that the court return her daughter "at their earliest convenience." The judge was unconvinced and demanded proof of her maternity, which she could not provide. Testimony from prominent neighbors similarly failed to convince the authorities, forcing Acosta to write a second letter. The sharply written missive was probably authored by a lawyer instead of a neighbor. In the second letter Marta Acosta demanded (rather than requested) that her "abducted" (rather than "ceded") daughter be returned to her immediately, citing *patria potestad*, natural law, and the civil code.[64] Judge Abraham Arce refused to release Carmen, placing the minor in the care of the Salesian nuns "to receive an education" until a more permanent solution was found.

Judge Abraham Arce's decision in this case was not an isolated event. He believed that the government needed to move decisively and robustly to shore up the state's legitimacy on the frontier by eliminating two related issues: indigenous slavery and child abandonment. One of the first federal judges in the region, Arce articulated an ambitious social program to systematically institutionalize the children of indigenous families, with the Salesian missions at its very core. In 1890, he ordered all the justices of the peace in the Río Negro Territory to "round up" and send to Viedma any "unsupervised" children they found in their districts. He felt that it was his implicit mandate to "protect the scattered youth" of the region, particularly those who were "orphans, abandoned, under bad examples, or denied an education."[65] Although it was framed as an effort to "protect" young people, the enumeration of likely targets was underscored by cultural constructs of what appropriate role models looked and acted like. We can assume that people perceived to be criminals, itinerant, or who otherwise appeared indigenous would have their parental rights undermined by Judge Arce's plan. Additionally, the focus on children who were denied an education, as outlined above, targeted not only indigenous children but most people in rural areas, where state schools would not appear consistently until decades later.

Judge Arce's plan to mobilize the meager resources of the frontier state to "alleviate" the plight of indigenous children requires us to consider the consequences of his plan independently of its intent. The process by which "Europeans have settled, where their descendants have become and remained politically dominant over indigenous people, and where a heterogenous society has developed in class, ethnic and racial terms" is called *settler colonialism*.[66] This "distinctive kind of imperialism" can be best understood as a series of institutions that facilitate the dispossession of indigenous people while erasing the evidence of that process.[67] As one of the leading articulators of this way of understanding this process, Patrick Wolfe, asserts, "settler colonialism is inherently eliminatory" since indigenous people in settler colonies were not necessary or desired, and their continued existence threatened settlers' claims on the land.[68] In this framework, we can understand Judge Arce's plan as part of a set of "policies of exclusion and segregation . . . central to the development and administration of settler colonies."

Even if we take Arce's formulation at face value (that he intended to improve the lives of indigenous children by protecting them from their unfit parents), such a program constituted a settler-colonial practice. As Margaret Jacobs contends, compulsory education of indigenous children in white schools was "another crucial way to eliminate indigenous people, both in a cultural and biological sense."[69] Although there is much debate between scholars as to whether the Argentine colonization of Patagonia fits the settler-colonial model or a more extractive colonial model, indigenous child removal as envisioned by Arce was a common tool of settler societies, as Margaret Jacobs shows for Australia and the western United States.

Judge Arce's 1890 order to the justices of the peace to "round up" indigenous children was issued in response to the social displacement resulting from indigenous children growing up alone. Arce argued that there were at least three ways in which indigenous children were being failed by their parents. First, during the cruelest periods of the military occupation of northern Patagonia in the early 1880s, some indigenous families grew fearful of having their children sent to the camps and had attempted to hide them. Accounts of children left behind in abandoned tolderías, stashed in makeshift caves, or hidden under piles of hides as troops moved into an area to avoid having them kidnapped, relate the depth of parents' fear and desperation to avoid the "death camps."[70] In many cases children emerged from their hiding places as orphans since their parents perished or were taken away themselves. These kinds of desperate tactics exacerbated the displacement of the military annexation and reinforced the authorities' prejudice that indigenous parents could not be relied on to properly care for their children. Additionally, in his appeal to the Supreme Court, Arce alluded to the common practice, during the military campaign, of commanders "gifting" orphans (and other children) to supporters and followers. He intimated that the practice continued unabated after the end of the military occupation, and that its eradication required "energetic action." The case of Marta Acosta's abducted daughter fits this pattern of abuse by military leaders: a young girl presented to a military commander as a domestic servant ended up in the streets without much explanation.

Finally, Judge Arce believed that his plan would prevent the development of future criminals, by removing them from "dangerous" situations, while also dismantling what he understood to be a flourishing trade in slaves. His concern for the trade in sex slaves seems noteworthy, if nothing else because it might reflect a cultural misreading of indigenous nuptial rituals, as Flora's example in the following section suggests. Arce's plan was the result of racialized misconceptions about indigenous parentings in a context of displacement following the military invasion, and the lack of funding for state-supported social services. Effectively, Arce mobilized the police and the justices of the peace to serve as a link between the withdrawing military force and the "civilizing" embrace of schools.

The Supreme Court found the idea of summarily detaining, transporting, and housing minors not only legally untenable but also economically unappealing, and ordered Arce to desist. In trying to convince his superiors of the economic feasibility of his plan, Arce highlighted the possibility of using the two "comfortable and well-managed" Salesian schools as an institutional repository for the children, saving the government considerable sums. He explained that "here in Viedma we have a [pair] of comfortable and well-managed schools [one for boys and one for girls] run by the Sisters of Charity . . . where the most prestigious families send their children, and they open their doors to the orphans and any minor that requests it, who are fed and taught without charge, and without any contributions from the government . . . they are always willing to accept any *incapaz* (uneducated child) seeking an education."[71] Having found a way to defray the cost of boarding and educating indigenous children, Arce only needed financial support to transport the minors from the hinterlands to the schools, but the government balked at even that small contribution. Arce's plan failed to gain significant traction with his superiors and was ultimately abandoned, but he continued to "refer" abandoned children picked up in the streets of Viedma—like Carmen—to the Salesian order in an ad hoc manner.

Arce developed a seemingly counterintuitive rationale for his proposed program. He argued that the government's legitimacy would suffer in the eyes of the "indigenous classes" without the ability to preemptively step in to remove "at-risk" indigenous children from precarious situations. After all, he claimed, indigenous parents already feared the representatives of the state "just as much" as they had feared the cavalry.[72] In Arce's thinking, the state needed to remove indigenous children from their homes, preventing them from being "ceded" to powerful families, to make indigenous people fear the state *less*. In other words, according to the top civilian authority in the Río Negro Territory, not removing indigenous children from their families was a hurdle to the full incorporation of indigenous people into the nation.

Judge Arce, and other state officials in Patagonia, continued to upend parental rights to ensure that indigenous people could exercise "self-supporting citizenship," as the dismissal of Marta Acosta's claim on her daughter exemplifies. As his counterparts in the United States would argue later that decade, "the true object of [coerced indigenous education] is to accomplish the release of the individual Indian from the slavery of tribal life, and to establish him in the self-supporting freedom of citizenship and a home in the life of the nation."[73] Abrogating the civil rights of indigenous parents was understood as a logical extension of the "struggle between races, in which the indigenous one has been damned to disappear in the name of civilization itself" as Julio Argentino Roca had articulated in his proposal for the military campaign against the indigenous people of northern Patagonia.

These practices form part of what scholars label the "systematic disarticulation of indigenous society" by the Argentine state. By grouping a series of seemingly unrelated government policies on the frontier, like fencing of fields, criminalizing rustling, and child removal, these scholars try to explain how settler colonialism operated in northern Patagonia. These processes were usually driven by individual settlers and police officers, but they could count on the complicity of the territorial authorities, who would turn a blind eye or even encourage abuse and dispossession. Maria Argeri, a historian of state policy against indigenous people in northern Patagonia, finds as much when looking at cases of patria potestad. She finds that when the police decided to remove minors from female-led indigenous households (commonly widows, since they had weaker parental rights claims than married women) to place them in family homes or convents, the prosecutors and judges rarely questioned their judgments. Police, prosecutors, and judges shared the assumption that "immoral women could not have parental rights."[74]

These cases remain hard to isolate in the court documents. When Argeri looked specifically for cases involving indigenous children, she found only six cases between 1880 and 1910 that mentioned indigenous minors being removed from their homes. A survey of the index of court cases in the archives returns eighteen cases in which individuals challenged someone else's patria potestad claims. Twelve of those came in the first twenty-five years of Argentine rule when the indigenous population in the region was a larger proportion of the total, while the remaining six were pursued in the following quarter century after more settlers had arrived. This seems to confirm Argeri's claim that the Argentine state disproportionately challenged the parental rights of indigenous peoples. Oral tradition and travelers' accounts, however, suggest that the number of cases that show up in court documents do not capture the full extent of the practice.

Carmen Acosta's journey through the bureaucracy of the frontier state, however, was not over with her arrival at the colegio. Three years later, in 1892, one of the Salesian Sisters wrote to the judge, asking him to keep Carmen from leaving their care. The nun, aware that the court was considering a "permanent placement" for the teen in a family home, wanted to request continued custody of the girl. The placement of orphans and other vulnerable minors in the homes of prominent families served the dual purpose of cheaply monitoring the minors and purportedly teaching them skills, usually related to domestic chores, in a "positive" family atmosphere. In this case the nuns wanted to keep the "orphaned teen Carmen Costas" permanently in the colegio and requested so in forceful terms.

The nuns argued that the practice of placing the girls in family homes after they had spent some time in the colegio had two negative effects: it prevented the teens from continuing to receive an education and learning "a variety of small domestic tasks," while also depriving the colegio from collecting "some money" from those skills. Without "some kind of reward" for having educated the girl, the nuns argued, they could not feasibly continue "educating and training *hijos del pueblo* [the poor children of the community]."[75] As with many colonial-era colegios, the nuns in Viedma depended on charity and the labor of the orphans to continue to operate as auxiliaries of the state without receiving public funds to serve as jails. The judge agreed with the nuns' argument, placing Carmen under the tutelage of the nuns until she got married or turned eighteen.

The colegio in Viedma, as well as other religious institutions, played a key role in the functioning of Argentina's early colonial arrangement in northern Patagonia. Without the resources to better assimilate the scattered indigenous groups, or to prevent the abuse of minors by unscrupulous adults, state representatives, spearheaded by people like Judge Arce, experimented with different arrangements that would help shore up the state's legitimacy. Over time, these temporary arrangements became more permanent, as lack of resources made children's labor a particularly affordable solution for the state and the colegio. As Hannah Greenwald and others show, the unpaid labor of indigenous children fueled the urban economies of the larger Patagonian towns. In fact, Arce's fear of "indigenous slavery," for example, fits this broader pattern of conflict over the labor of children. Settlers operated from an understanding—a perception—that the indigenous population in Patagonia lived under an entirely different set of legal codes and traditions, an unwritten "Ley de Indios."

Persistence:
The "Ley de Indios" and Indigenousness as Reasonable Doubt

In the decades after the military conquest of Patagonia, people inside the administration and in the population spoke of a parallel legal system challenging Argentina's hegemony in Patagonia: a so-called Ley de Indios. A collection of practices and cultural norms rather than a codified set of laws, this legal framework was understood to operate alongside the official legal regime, uncontested and tolerated by state officials. It should not be surprising that indigenous people would continue to follow practices and norms after Argentina attempted to impose its own legal and moral code.

Australian historian Lisa Ford labels the process by which the sovereignty of indigenous people was undermined by settler jurisprudence "settler sovereignty." It operated somewhat similarly to how customary law operated alongside colonial law in India under British rule—different regions preserved traditional legal practices regulating marriage, trade, family life, while also observing British colonial laws—but in settler-colonial societies "the legal obliteration of indigenous customary law became the litmus test of settler statehood."[76] In other words, the legitimization of Argentine rule in northern Patagonia required that indigenous people's submission to Argentine law was "guarded not just by governors and courts, but by farmers and local constables."[77] Ford identifies the control of indigenous violence in Australia and the American South as the driving engine behind settler sovereignty. But in northern Patagonia the military occupation largely settled that issue by resorting to overwhelming violence. Instead, the conflicts over Argentine law and the "Ley de Indios" played out in bedrooms and homes, shifting the focus to how settler expectations blistered indigenous domestic rituals and practices.

The Ley de Indios was an unwritten set of practices, a lex non scripta (an unwritten, common, law), that structured not only how indigenous people related to one another but also how settlers and state authorities related to people they perceived to be indigenous. Recall how Nahuelcheo played on frontier tropes of "mock kidnappings" to buttress his complaint against his wife and her lover. The perception of this enduring indigenous legal culture prompted state officials to reinterpret criminal investigations in positivist ways. Judges, police officers, prosecutors, and settlers more broadly found that sometimes they could highlight someone's indigenousness—the cultural traits that marked them as enduringly noncivilized—to affect how the cases played out. Finding traces of these unwritten customary laws requires reading the court cases "against the grain," and a little bit of luck, since indigenousness was not always apparent when deciding to read a case.

Consider how indigenous customs and practices were reframed by crafty settlers to their own advantage by using coded language in one particularly sad example. In the early days of 1892, one of the residents of the hamlet of Aguada de los Loros complained to the local authorities that his indigenous neighbor, Martín Suárez, "had purchased an Indian girl" as a slave.[78] The justice of the peace of nearby Cubanea, Manuel Rial, referred the complaint to his supervisor in Viedma, the judge, citing the gravity of the case. The file that Judge Abraham Arce received from Rial contained a reference to the anonymous complaint against Suárez as well as testimonies from two "prominent landowners" corroborating the complaint. Judge Arce, in the throes of deploying his scheme to institutionalize "orphaned" indigenous children, proved a receptive audience for the salacious allegations of indigenous slavery.

According to the coordinated testimonies by landowners Santiago Moreno and José Quiñelas, the girl's stepfather, don Juan Sefiche, had arranged the exchange. Suárez had agreed to pay "eight healthy animals" for the "eleven-, or twelve- at most, year-old girl" Flora, who had consented to the exchange. Judge Arce responded zealously, commissioning a special prosecutor who quickly apprehended Suárez and Sefiche while they found themselves in Viedma on business. The police declined to register a last name for Flora, who simply appeared in the records as an "approximately twelve- or fifteen-year-old indígena" from the País de las Manzanas without a profession, but a self-described "wool spinner." Flora, her four-year-old sister, and their mother, María, were placed under the tutelage of the Colegio de las Hermanas de Caridad until the case was settled. Women, particularly indigenous women, were often deprived of their freedom during investigations, even when they were the victims—the ways in which this practice could be used by the women as a tool against male authority is the subject of the next chapter.

The depositions by Sefiche and Suárez confirmed the exchange, but framed it in cultural terms. Martín Suárez, an unmarried forty-year-old sheep herder from Chile, denied intending to turn the girl into a slave, indicating that he simply lived with her as husband and wife. He confirmed that Flora had been "ceded [by her parents] to be [his] wife and as a reward [he] gave them two horses and two mares." Besides articulating the perceived sale as a dowry of sorts, he further explained the degree of commitment that the couple had since they "lived a married life . . . following the Ley de Indios."[79] For the most part, Juan Sefiche (a fifty-five-year-old sheep herder born in Argentina) confirmed that account, claiming that he and his wife "ceded" Flora to Suárez to become his wife, and that for the previous four months they had been "living a married life." Flora's mother, María, confirmed the marital transaction as an explicitly indigenous act: she claimed that her husband and she had "ceded" Flora as a wife to Martín Suárez, who "gifted us some animals as reward, according to the custom among Indios."[80] The prosecutor decided to proceed with the charges against Suárez for corrupting a minor, and against Sefiche for "enabling prostitution." From the prosecutor's perspective, the case was fairly straightforward: all the parties had confessed to an illegal transaction involving cattle in exchange for "ceding" a young girl to another.

Flora's own testimony revealed the circumstances that had made Suárez's marriage proposal impossible to refuse. She explained that she "was forced to accept Suárez's proposal, because a gringo from Aguada de los Loros called Antonio Pilla took advantage that I was alone in a clearing, . . . grabbed me, and forcefully raped me, about ten months earlier."[81] Flora's mother, María, confirmed that her daughter had been "forced by the circumstances" of that rape to accept Suárez's marriage proposal. The family had reported the rape to the local authorities but had been "offered no justice." Corroborating her allegations of a cover-up, the judge did not find any record of their complaint or of any investigation into the allegations against Antonio Pilla, who was not brought into questioning for this case either. Justices of the peace and police often handled complaints informally to keep local conflicts corseted, and it bears reasoning that they did the same here, either ignoring it altogether or reprimanding Pilla without leaving a paper trail. The accusation against Pilla does help explain why the "gringos" in Aguada de los Loros were so keenly concerned with criminalizing the marriage practices of their indigenous neighbors as retaliation for reporting Flora's rape.

State officials did more than simply ignore the settlers' efforts to muddy the investigations. In some cases, they advocated for a heightened awareness of the frontier's multicultural reality. For example, while Flora was in the care of the nuns in the colegio, the state assigned her a public defender (*defensor de menores*) by the name of David Logan to look after her legal interests. The public defender reviewed the information in the case and took the unusual step of writing the judge a scathing critique of how the state had handled her case. Logan challenged the way the state had interpreted the language of the accused literally, rather than considering them in their cultural context, seeing that they spoke in terms of reciprocity. Logan went on to explain that "all of them are indígenas: as such they do not speak, let alone understand, Spanish very well, so it would not be strange that Suárez spoke poorly of the girl being 'delivered to him,' or that he 'offered a reward' for her."[82]

Deepening his ethnographic report, Logan echoed the persistence of a "Ley de Indios" that included the practice of exchanging gifts for a wedding:

> Very few people are unaware of the habits of these poor beings. It is known that *the Indian is haughty and proud* of the fact that he does not purchase the woman he takes as wife, since it is his custom—or one could say *a law unto his race*—that upon being presented with a future partner, he has the duty to gift in exchange, to the parents and family members, clothing and animals which prove or showcase his wealth.[83]

Logan's articulation of indigenous culture was a product of the prejudices of his period, but it represents a prescient analysis that bears closer attention.

I think David Logan's interpretation offers three key insights into how indigeneity entered a legal process that tried hard to pretend it did not exist. First, it highlights the degree to which individuals handling a criminal case used an array of cultural markers to frame a defense for a suspect. For example, difficulty speaking Spanish served as a marker not of poverty but of *otherness*, in this case indigenousness. Second, it offers a corroboration of the coexistence of the customary "law unto their own race" that operated alongside the Argentine civil and penal codes. Logan even suggests that these "habits" were known to most people in Viedma. Third, that it was possible to use the perception of indigenousness to buttress (rather than undermine) their innocence. This might seem counterintuitive given the rhetoric at the time of "civilizing" and "destroying" indigenous culture, but Logan's blend of positivist and colonial-era legal ideas of how the law ought to apply differently for indigenous people was not unique in the nineteenth century.

As the historian Gil Joseph puts it, while "liberalism carried the day politically" in Latin America during the nineteenth century, "conservative modes of thought endured." In terms of indigenous legal exceptionalism, we can trace them to the Inquisition's exclusion of neophytes, which safeguarded indigenous people in the Americas from its jurisdiction. Other practices stemmed from a framework from the period of Spanish colonial rule. The so-called República de Indios, created parallel legal systems that siloed complaints against indigenous defendants through a special tribunal, distinct from the tribunals used by Spanish subjects. Since northern Patagonia was outside Spain's colonial order, the persistence of these "conservative modes of thought" requires some more explanation.

When Logan argued that "the Indian is haughty and proud" he was borrowing ideas from "positivist criminology," popularized by the Italian Cesare Lombroso in the late nineteenth century, which "posited that biology played a determinant role" in people's propensity toward criminality. Lombroso and his followers conceived of some people as "born criminals" who had atavistic deficiencies: he thought that women, indigenous, and people of African descent, in particular, fell under this category.[84] Logan seems to have borrowed Lombrosian ideas of indigenous people as "born criminals" and flipped them on their head to suggest that biological determinism meant that the state could not hold indigenous people "morally responsible" for their actions.

State agents could use a person's *perceived* indigenousness to excuse, or contextualize, criminal accusations against them. This involved racist assumptions about the mental capacity and "moral tendency" of indigenous people, but they proved surprisingly successful in reframing criminal investigations. For example, when Margarita Anelaf de Cayul was questioned following the disappearance of her three-year-old niece Leonarda, her indigeneity became central to the police investigation.[85] Struggling to explain how the child could have wandered off by herself between the Laguna Grande and her *choza* (hut) in the heart of the central plateau early in the winter of 1907, a very pregnant Margarita Anelaf offered several implausible explanations. She feared that Leonarda had probably perished due to the cold or might have been eaten by a *puma* (mountain lion). After some further questioning, she suggested that perhaps "some malicious person hiding in the hills" might have kidnapped her, echoing the fears of an earlier generation of indigenous parents that "abandoned" their children to protect them from being abducted by the invading Argentine army.[86]

Ultimately, the investigation was inconclusive. The hard, frozen ground and the girl's light footsteps made a sustained tracking almost impossible, even for an experienced transhumant like Higinio Cayul, Margarita Anelaf de Cayul's husband, who did manage to trace the child's footsteps up a rocky, scraggly hill about a mile and a half away, only to lose the trail unexpectedly. The police investigator keyed in on the couple's indigeneity in his report, highlighting that the missing girl "spoke the indigenous language easily, but only a little of the national language."[87] In an unusual step, the investigator explained to his supervisors that he had not arrested his only suspect, Anelaf de Cayul, because she was indigenous.[88] He explained that "her carelessness was a result of her pregnancy and the ignorance that is ingrained in the indigenous folk, which led her to carelessness in the guise of kindness."[89] The investigator's perception of the "ingrained ignorance" of the indigenous suspect justified and excused the potentially criminal actions of an individual.

Margarita Anelaf herself might have encouraged this interpretation. She emphasized that her niece spoke "the indigenous language" better than Spanish and self-identified as an *indígena* in her deposition. She also alluded to the ongoing fear of "malicious stranger" lurking in the hills. Much like David Logan, the unnamed investigator in Leonarda's case introduced his own positivist legal understanding into a judicial process, not to criminalize and punish indigenous behavior, but to exempt it. As Charles Walker argues when looking at attitudes toward indigenous people in late colonial Peru, "prosecutors and the defense shared an understanding of Indians as inferior, irrational beings," a sentiment that echoed a century later in the courtrooms of northern Patagonia.[90]

The prevailing understanding of the judicial system in Patagonia as primarily a tool to disarticulate, disband, and destroy indigenous culture leaves little room for people like David Logan. In the disarticulation narrative that we introduced earlier, the entire judicial apparatus worked to "civilize" indigenous subjects by criminalizing their cultural practices. Insofar as Argentine settlers were able to establish "settler sovereignty" in northern Patagonia, they did so while other settlers worked to advocate for a legal sensibility to indigenous people within settler society. Logan—as well as the unknown persons who helped Nahuelcheo and María Acosta with their complaints—used the perception that indigenous subjects followed "a law unto [their own] race" as a legal tool in framing their cases. Cases like Flora's are surprising and suggest an unexpected degree of flexibility by regional authorities, particularly when we consider the zealousness with which Judge Arce attempted to institutionalize indigenous children and the use of the courts to delegitimize other indigenous cultural practices like rustling.

Part of the endurance of a sociopolitical arrangement like the one that developed in northern Patagonia was the spaces it provided for an array of actors to inject themselves and their sensibilities into the process that legitimized the state's presence on the frontier. It would not be unreasonable to consider that people like Logan made the state's efforts to establish hegemony more successful by insisting on its flexibility. Put differently, the state's strength and resilience in the frontier stemmed from its flexibility and its impossibility to forcefully dictate the terms of assimilation. This precedent, practiced during the early years of occupation against a mostly indigenous population, became in subsequent decades the way in which frontier justice was administered.

Whether the Ley de Indios existed in practice or it was a mere positivist construct, representatives of the state on the frontier acted as if it existed. Unexpectedly, considering the relentlessness with which other indigenous behavior was prosecuted, they continued to see the surviving indigenous cultural practices as attenuating circumstances for potential crimes. This Ley would continue to exist in the background, away from the gaze of state agents, and occasionally intersecting with criminal investigations by the state in the first decades of the twentieth century, suggesting at best a partial disarticulation of indigenous practices. For example, during an investigation into the disappearance of Rolando Sandalio's wife from their home, the police learned that Sandalio had kidnapped her when she was fifteen, and her family had declined to press charges, conceding that he had taken her "rightfully."[91] This echoed the indigenous practice of raiding for captives, which had been outlawed after the military annexation, but appeared to continue as an acceptable practice in some social settings, not unlike how Juana Legipán was "kidnapped" from her home.

In an interesting footnote to Flora's and Suárez's case, once the judge determined that the teen had not been sold, and that the couple "wished to marry" he ordered her to remain in the colegio until her Catholic education was completed. The night before their marriage the nuns reported her missing to the judge, and they suspected she had been kidnapped. After an extended search by the Viedma police, Flora was arrested just as Suárez and she were signing their marriage certificate in the office of the justice of the peace.

The old practices continued even as new ones were observed.

Conclusion

Until fairly recently, most studies of indigenous peoples in Patagonia aimed mainly to prove that they survived Argentina's military annexation. From demographic studies of original census forms and oblique government communications to careful examinations of travel narratives and local histories, scholars established the survival of indigenous people in Patagonia that the triumphal narratives of the 1890s and beyond had tried to erase. The disjointed nature of the government action in Patagonia during the military campaign and immediately after left a large number of indigenous people dispersed across the region, with the expectation that they would slowly incorporate into the nation. This chapter has argued that the structure of the state in northern Patagonia (the centralization of power in the judicial branch, the absence of local government, and the reliance on nonstate institutions of social control) proved critical to the partial assimilation of indigenous people to broader Patagonian society. It has also pushed back on the notion that the judicial system in Patagonia was geared *exclusively* toward breaking down ("disarticulating") indigenous cultural norms, criminalizing their economic activities, and disbanding their families. Although these actions took place—as the example of Judge Arce's ambitious scheme—they were part of a broader judicial attitude toward indigenous subjects that did allow them to practice citizenship in piecemeal fashion.

The courts offered indigenous people in Patagonia an array of tools with which to interact with the state to achieve their goals. Together with their allies and advocates, indigenous people were keen to mobilize "indigenousness" to both compel the state to act, or to block its actions. Nahuelcheo, for example, emphasized his own "civilized" behavior in his attempt to spur the state into action, while subtly painting his rival's behavior as "indigenous" and worthy of police attention. The existence, or the perception of the existence, of a quasi-clandestine Ley de Indios was used by indigenous people and their advocates to inject positivist judicial principles into the proceedings, resulting in the legal incompetence of suspects and victims. On the other hand, the perception of a wide-ranging cultural network of indigenous practices (like the sale of teenage brides) justified the creation of a system of abduction, detention, and indenture to prominent families or religious institutions. Ultimately, the centralization of state power in the judiciary, in particular prosecutors and judges in Viedma and not in local governments, meant that the concerted efforts by communities and individuals to try to scapegoat indigenous people by alluding to their "otherness" had limited success. In the eyes of the state officials, indigenous people were more than "warriors turned into criminals." In idiosyncratic ways, they helped shape Patagonia's own variety of citizenship and established the parameters of exclusion, belonging, and access to justice.

Shorthanded, the state began to lean more heavily on nonstate actors to help it administer the national territories; these relationships prioritized economic convenience over establishing legitimacy. Religious orders, military bases, and private families became ad hoc solutions to house, educate, and punish poor (mostly indigenous) transient people. Government policy toward the conquered indigenous people lacked any consistency other than cruelty, oscillating from incorporation to exclusion, and leading to the *perception* that indigenous people—or at least indigenous culture—had disappeared. Throughout the period, however, state representatives, settlers, and indigenous subjects used indigeneity as a powerful legal tool to either incriminate or exculpate suspects, tapping into a deep reservoir of shared cultural misreadings. Allusions to people's indigenousness made their way into official documents, ultimately changing the way those individuals were treated. The changes in the documents were subtle—more a shift of *tone* and attitude on the part of the witnesses, lawyers, prosecutors, or investigators rather than a marked transformation of the legal process itself. These subtle manipulations of the judicial process were not unique to cases involving indigenous people. In a pattern that later chapters will confirm, the power of federal appointees in the territorial capitals proved instrumental to defusing local prejudices and attempting to prevent brutal frontier justice, even when the investigations themselves were disruptive to local communities. The judicial system in northern Patagonia—which balanced local authorities sensitive to communal pressure with regional ones impervious to them—offered some safeguards to indigenous subjects. This relative equanimity should not be overstated; after all, these were the same regional authorities that had attempted to institutionalize all indigenous children a decade earlier.

The frontier state that had emerged to discipline and "safeguard" indigenous subjects changed very little once its task turned to governing cosmopolitan settlers. Ill-prepared to govern a multiethnic, fragmented frontier society, the state concentrated its efforts in three main ways: buttressing a regime of private ownership by persecuting crimes against property, like cattle; tamping down violence by investigating assaults, murders, and robberies; and by mediating conflicts between residents. That all the examples in this chapter centered on investigations emanating from family conflicts and disputes over marriage and childrearing is not accidental. As subsequent chapters continue to explore, the regulation of family life, in particular the centrality of issues of gender and the state's ambivalent relationship toward patriarchy, was a central concern of administering the frontier. Order—a recognizable, predictable, and controllable social organization—was of paramount importance for statesmen in Buenos Aires and the regional capitals of Neuquén and Viedma, and they sought to build that order "outward" from the family, as the next chapter demonstrates.

"Public and Notorious"

Reputation, Family Life, and Domestic Violence in Small Patagonian Towns

> I am not sure how, or to what extent, the police can be expected to force a married woman to move back with her husband against her will.
> —Officer Díaz's unprompted opinion on state intervention in family affairs, in 1921.[1]

L ate in the fall of 1924, the boarders in María Anzini de Moriconi's house in Neuquén were woken up by her husband, Ángel Moriconi, standing in the patio and brandishing a gun menacingly. He was threatening to kill his estranged wife and their daughter if they did not abandon the house immediately. María Anzini de Moriconi, a forty-year-old Italian immigrant to Neuquén, mother to a "numerous family of children," left her bed with difficulty, and confronted her husband, forcing him to holster his weapon and leave the premises. He would return weeks later wielding a knife, and causing a scene in the dining room, once again frightening the boarders. Anzini de Moriconi was already pursuing a separation from her "violent, absent, and tyrannical" husband, arguing that his inability to "provide food" for the family gave her reason to dissolve the marriage.

While the courts decided that issue, Moriconi's threatening outbursts led his wife to write an impassioned letter to the judge asking for a restraining order to protect her life and livelihood by preventing her husband from entering the couple's property. In the letter she alleged that her husband's "excesses" had caused a miscarriage that not only put her life in "immediate danger," but also "denied the family of the mother's labor" and risked leaving her children without "sustenance and without their protector." She also demanded the immediate return to the family home of three of her daughters who Marconi had sent away, because she was growing worried of the "harm, and moral prejudice on the innocent minors" of being treated like "criminals."[2] María Anzini de Moriconi's pleas to the authorities in Neuquén illuminate how patriarchy operated on the frontier—the laws that underpinned it, the social constraints placed upon it, and the ways in which family members sought to escape its more rigid aspects.

This chapter proposes two interrelated arguments about the role of the frontier state in family dynamics. First, it argues that both settlers and the representatives of the state attempted to use the meager resources of the frontier state in creative ways to protect vulnerable women and children, with limited success. For example, Anzini de Moriconi's boarders not only interceded when her husband began threatening her, but a couple of them "threatened to beat" him up, and several others voluntarily suggested to the police that Moriconi's actions might stem from "somewhat altered mental capacities." The local police—both as state representatives trying to shape the state's response to these cases and the main resource that other actors tried to mobilize—reacted swiftly and creatively. They ordered Moriconi's detention and psychiatric evaluation immediately upon receiving the complaint. They managed to temporarily block his efforts to evict her and demonstrated the state's capacity to exercise discretionary coercion even before a case was adjudicated.

Each one of these steps required the deployment, and renegotiation, of various individuals' reputations: Anzini de Moriconi's reputation as a wife, mother, and businesswoman, Moriconi's reputation as a father, husband, and neighbor, and the boarders' reputations as trustworthy mediators. An individual's reputation in a community dictated how likely they were to receive help from the police—how quickly the police responded, how severely they reacted, and how many informal avenues (like a "psychiatric evaluation" to extend Moriconi's detention) they were willing to use. The importance of reputation on the frontier to accessing justice is the second argument that this chapter advances. To put it boldly, reputation was the main constraint on an individual's ability to exercise citizenship.

At the same time, reputation served as both the impetus for, and limit to, the desire by state representatives to become entangled in a family's private affairs. As the discussion of David Logan in chapter 2 suggests, the representatives of the state on the frontier (not only police officers, chiefs of police, prosecutors, and judges, but also public defenders, juvenile defenders, and social workers) infused their understanding of the law with their own morality and prejudices, making the state's role as a guarantor of domestic order piecemeal and contingent. Settlers' effective power at the communal level depended on how successfully they mobilized sympathy in their communities, which was closely related to their reputation. In other words, successful settlers gained political power in small towns by heading orderly families, avoiding scandals, and assisting in the lodging of vulnerable members of the community. Public scandals arising from domestic disputes eroded the basis of that power.

In short, this chapter considers the ways in which struggles at the heart of families, usually considered a "private" realm, were resolved by "public" avenues, even when the legal system could not offer any redress. In a frontier space like Patagonia, as historian Lisandro Gallucci puts it, "the private sphere, in which everyday life unfolded for most people, was never completely separated from the public one."[3] And, I would add, family life was a crucial nexus for this overlap. The ability to navigate the imperfect split between public reputation and domestic order allowed family members to draw the state into their family affairs. By emphasizing how the reputation of individuals and families affected the kind of justice they could expect to receive, this chapter continues to sketch out the ways in which settlers understood and exercised citizenship in northern Patagonia.

Changing Perspectives:
Why do Scholars Care About Family Conflicts?

Why did Moriconi not fear publicly threatening his wife and daughter with violence? The answer is complex and ultimately unknowable for us, but Moriconi was certainly operating from a position of immunity because of the patriarchal arrangements in place at the time. To better understand the context in which Moriconi seemed to operate, this section defines the concept of "patriarchy" and how it changed during the nineteenth century, outlines the connections between processes of state formation, family life, and changing notions of "honor," and introduces the ways in which patriarchy functioned differently on the frontier.

Broadly speaking, patriarchy is a set of practices, beliefs, and regulations that organize social life under hierarchical gendered roles. As Adrienne Rich defines it, patriarchy is "a familial-social, ideological, political system in which men—by force, direct pressure, or through ritual, tradition, law and language, customs, etiquette, education, and the division of labor, determine what part women shall or shall not play; and in which the female is everywhere subsumed under the male."[4] Conversely, historian Merry Wiesner-Hanks defines it as "a social system in which men have more power and access to resources than women, and some men are dominant over other men."[5] Critics have noted that these definitions build on sharp binaries (male dominance/female subordination) that "homogenize men and women as rigidly defined social groups, excludes other identities and forms of oppression and entails the risk of essentializing power relations or overestimating women's victimhood and lack of agency."[6]

To hedge against those risks, scholars have reframed patriarchy in three important ways. First, by considering other forms of social control and oppression like class and race (what theorist Kimberlé Crenshaw terms "intersectionality") since these relations of domination operate "not as unitary, mutually exclusive entities, but rather as reciprocally constructing phenomena."[7] Second, by highlighting the ways in which patriarchal control was not absolute; in fact it "produces multiple demands that are in tension with each other," and creates spaces for agentic norms to take hold.[8] Third, by historicizing patriarchy to show how it has changed through time and place. We understand patriarchy as historically contingent; it changes with the times, adapts to new realities, responding to shifting pressures and incentives. As Susan Amussen posits, patriarchy's "perseverance [was] made possible by its shape-shifting adaptations."[9]

In Latin America, it adapted to changing times adroitly. For example, during the colonial period (1492–c. 1810), patriarchs in Spanish America, with the expectation of preserving family honor, were expected to discipline those in their households (spouse, offspring, servants, apprentices) while providing security and sustenance to them. Enlightenment ideas of freedom and self-determination and the socioeconomic dislocation of the independence wars changed public and private roles for men and women; with men swept up in military mobilization, women carried larger roles in their communities.[10] The nineteenth century saw a rapid change in how people understood the role of fathers as patriarchs throughout Latin America, and these changing attitudes shaped how settlers and state agents sought to deploy, protect, and challenge patriarchy in northern Patagonia. By the middle of the nineteenth century, liberal reformers sought to shore up and stabilize family life by strengthening the power of fathers in the civil codes (for example, by changing how inheritances were distributed), weakening the rights of children born out of wedlock, and by creating state institutions to act in patriarchal ways (military academies, orphanages, public health initiatives). Scholars refer to this as the "new patriarchy" of the late nineteenth century.

This "new patriarchy" saw the state assume some of the roles that husbands had previously held, making ideas and policies surrounding family "essential" to state building. Central to those roles was the management of "honor" as a form of social currency that expanded or contracted an individual's power in society. Latin American governments in the nineteenth century "sought to check private authority" of men in various forms, distributing honor more directly. As Lara Putnam, Sarah C. Chambers, and Sueann Caulfield explain it, "those who were not able to display the markings of honor—for men, economic independence and patriarchal authority; for women, sexual propriety and a dependent position in a patriarchal family—found it exceedingly difficult to defend their rights before the police and the courts."[11] This expansion of government power, the take-over by state officials of patriarchal duties, deferred to "honorable men" in their absolute authority of their households, including their wives, children, servants, or other dependents. The nineteenth century, in short, saw a reduction in the patriarchal authority of poor, "dishonorable," and marginal men. As Juandrea Bates argues in a recent study of immigrant youth in Buenos Aires, "family policy gave meaning to citizenship, molded legal processes, shaped popular politics, and engendered class inequality."[12] This process was particularly poignant on the frontier.

Family was at the center of state formation in the nineteenth century, and how families acquired, preserved, and redeployed "honor" was central to how citizenship was exercised on the frontier. As Ana María Alonso discovers in Chihuahua, "honor was central to the construction of subjectivity." She argues that honor was a key ideology organizing "relationships of domination, the distribution of social prestige and status" that helped legitimize "the deployment of violence on the frontier."[13] In the context of the Argentine state expanding to Patagonia this meant that for people like Ángel Moriconi, maintaining his honor by loudly disciplining his estranged wife was a central way to preserve his own status as a "civilized settler" in command of his household. In small northern Patagonian towns, family struggles could quickly become public spectacles, affecting how family members were treated by the police and the courts, which played a central role in mediating strife and adjudicating conflicts.

Scholars of Latin America have highlighted other processes that changed the parameters of patriarchal authority during the nineteenth century: urbanization, the secularization of society, and the expansion of the reach of the state, both in terms of its sophistication and the colonization of formerly independent indigenous territories. As small communities transformed into less personal cities, notions of honor, community, and reputation began to change dramatically: they became more institutionalized and less informal.[14] In Argentina, rapidly growing cities not only drew rural migrants searching for economic opportunity, but also became home to large numbers of immigrants from Europe, further eroding "traditional" ways of assessing honor. As liberal states moved aggressively to curtail the power of the church—perceived as an impediment to modernization—they begun reserving for themselves the right to regulate marriages and to register births and deaths. The transition was not seamless.

In places where the Catholic Church had a long-standing presence, or where indigenous traditions had become socially codified into mestizo society, historians have highlighted the resilience of those older ways of organizing society.[15] When change did happen it often played out as part of the broader shift from ecclesiastical authority to a secular one, with state institutions taking over the role of guarantors of family order and patriarchy.[16] Courts, in particular, served as "a nexus for gender disputes within the family" as well as a space where broader political developments intersected with private lives—while family disputes had previously been strictly "private" affairs, they crept into public forums, and were increasingly responsive to forces outside of the family.[17] The records left behind by the courts (investigations, testimonies, summaries, rulings) have helped scholars trace how updated civil codes and constitutions affected gender roles within the family and in society as a whole.[18] The transition from colonial to republican rule presented everyday challenges to Latin Americans as they adjusted to new laws, practices, and even institutions governing family dynamics.[19]

One could interpret Moriconi's brash display of violence as a performance by a diminished patriarch to attempt to re-establish control over his family by threatening to evict them. If it was indeed a semipublic performance, how was it understood by the "audience" (his family, the boarders, and ultimately the state representatives)? In other words, did northern Patagonians understand patriarchy differently than their counterparts elsewhere in the country? One striking difference is the absence of a strong church presence in the area. As a space that had existed mostly outside Spanish colonial rule, northern Patagonia did not have strong church institutions before the military annexation. In other contexts, the struggles between the church and the state in the late nineteenth century provided women like Anzini de Moriconi with "alternate patriarchs" in the clergy. For example, in Arequipa (Peru), María Ignacia Baldivia, turned to the vicar to complain of her husband's (otherwise legal) beatings.[20] Settlers in northern Patagonia had few authority figures outside of the government to mediate the excesses of their husbands, and Moriconi's semipublic performance benefited from that vacuum.

A second distinction is chronological. In other places, the changes brought by the "new patriarchy" of the nineteenth century happened gradually and took generations to internalize. In northern Patagonia, where state institutions arrived suddenly and fully formed, responses to state policies were more spasmodic and urgent. For example, as Argentine jurists began trying to modernize the civil code to weaken paternal prerogatives in the family in the 1920s as a response to shifting attitudes about women's rights, government officials in northern Patagonia were still trying to establish their own legitimacy.[21] This collapse of two process that elsewhere were separated by almost a century were happening in northern Patagonia concurrently, showcasing how changing attitudes met unchanging laws—or how different actors at the most basic level of the government injected their own perspectives into legal proceedings.

One example helps illustrate this point. One of the people who witnessed Moriconi's outbursts was Marcelino Huemul, a twenty-six-year-old immigrant from Chile who worked at Neuquén's public jail. Although Huemul initially attempted to disarm the unhinged patriarch, he quickly relented, claiming that "it was after all Moriconi's house, and his wife was the sole victim of his assault." In fact, Huemul found it "more prudent to shut up and leave the house" which he never visited again. Huemul seemed to intuit that Moriconi was exercising his prerogatives as a patriarch, or that he was willing to use extraordinary violence to exercise what he though was his patriarchal prerogative, but how typical was that understanding? It is hard to tell; even though studies of gendered conflicts in Argentina during this period exist, they rarely venture into the interior, let alone the frontier.

A final striking difference is the frontier setting itself. Judges and lawyers acted differently on the frontier than they did in Buenos Aires. For example, in a study of how patriarchy was contested through the courts, historian Donna Guy mentions in passing a case from the National Territory of La Pampa, when the *defensor de menores* (juvenile public defender) acted in a completely opposite way from his peers in Buenos Aires, upholding the father's rights over an infant despite the mother's complaint, suggesting the existence of a *distinct* legal culture in northern Patagonia.[22] As noted for the American West, family life was "the most conservative area of frontier life . . . its behaviors, its rituals, and the attitudes associated with it," and government officials might have taken their cues from the population on these issues.[23]

I think their behavior reflected not only the scarcity of the state's presence on the frontier but also the different social realities stemming from the violence of the military annexation. These have already been discussed in chapter 2, but they included high rates of "orphanage," placement of children as wards/servants, the preponderance of informal marriages and unwed mothers, which underscored the perception by judicial authorities that families were fragile in the frontier. It seems clear that while nationally courts had moved to thinking of families in structural terms (prioritizing legal and biological relations), the realities of life in northern Patagonia forced the court to continue to think of families in functional terms (prioritizing the roles that undergird relations).[24] The importance of local authorities attuned to the needs and demands of the community, including "interests of households," echoed similar strategies to gain and maintain legitimacy in plebeian Buenos Aires a century earlier, as Mark Szuchman finds.[25]

Consider the example of fourteen-year-old José de la Rosa Carrasco, who ran away from his guardians' home to find Bautista Carrasco, who he thought was his biological father.[26] De la Rosa's mother, María Molina, had died when the boy was just two years old, and he had been raised by Nicanor Ramírez and his wife in an isolated hamlet near Chos Malal, in northern Neuquén Territory. Based on what we know about how courts handled these kinds of cases in Buenos Aires, the child's inability to provide documentation related to his birth should have stymied his quest to find his biological father. Particularly given the family's background: Maria Molina had been born in Chile, and José de la Rosa was described as "indigenous" by the man who raised him. As Juandrea Bates puts it, "making citizens legible though the creation of government-issued identification was part of an extensive process of nation building" that judges took to heart. The "inflexibility" of judges in cases when plaintiffs could not produce adequately "Argentine" documents proved "particularly problematic for immigrant families."[27] Similarly, judges in Buenos Aires would balk at legally empowering "married women whose husbands had abandoned them," nor "poor men who could not produce baptismal certificates," making them legally impotent.[28] But young José de la Rosa Carrasco's example points to a different practice in northern Patagonia.

Faced with an issue of parentage without documents, the authorities in Patagonia attempted to shore up the functional bonds of family as expressed by the community. When the boy introduced himself to Bautista Carrasco, the court bypassed the lack of birth certificates or baptismal records to establish his parental rights, resorting instead to popular opinion. Since "the majority of the

FIGURE 11. "Isleños de Choele Choel. El Padre Juan Acero, en un rancho de vie-
jos pobladores. Río Negro, 1910" (AGN-DDF, Caja 2948, inventario #144941). A
few things to note: the multigenerational family, the precarious dwelling in
the background, and the (somewhat staged) warm reception to the visiting
priest. Rural isolation made it harder for women to mobilize allies against
abusive husbands.

neighborhood" where the kid grew up considered Bautista Carrasco the father, and because María Molina had lived "in concubinage" with him before the kid's birth "she considered him the boy's father." In other words, society ascribed paternity on the basis of social bonds more than biological heritage, and in these cases "society was represented by witnesses and neighbors."[29] The prosecutor and the judge found the evidence from the community adequate enough: though they could not legally certify Carrasco as the father, they instead named him as de la Rosa's guardian "indefinitely." The informal solution shored up a family, preserved the boy's reputation, and maintained the legitimacy of the frontier state—an example of the arrangements central to how frontier justice was administered in northern Patagonia.

Similarly, when Hermógenes Garabito wanted to allow her fifteen-year-old daughter to marry her intimate partner, she could not produce a birth certificate, and the court used the testimony from three neighbors to establish parentage. One of the neighbors, don Juan Ochoa, stated that he knew Garabito's daughter "since she was five, and that he believes, and knows her to be, the girl's natural mother because she is always with her." Another one, Ángel Colombo, ascertained Garabito's parentage because "he saw the girl breastfeeding and she always lived with her."[30] The remoteness of northern Patagonia convinced settlers, lawyers, and state agents that special dispensations were required in the frontier to shore up patriarchal rights of adults over children, even if their actions and desires went against the ways the laws were interpreted at the national level. This process—the pursuit of informal solutions through formal channels—was a continuation of the ways in which some state agents had interacted with the displaced indigenous population, resolving conflict in ways that were both lawful *and* consistent with community expectations.

Perhaps what made northern Patagonians act differently in issues of family dynamics, in issues of intimacy, violence, trust, and desire, was not "the frontier" but the strength of interpersonal relationships and the weakness of the institutions. Huemul, a state employee intimately involved with the administration of justice and the maintenance of order, initially reacted to Moriconi's semipublic assault on his wife by trying to stop it, but when faced with an escalation, he not only relented but retreated as well. As Susan Socolow finds for the southern Buenos Aires frontier, rural men "lived in a world over which they had little control . . . [and] armed with knives, they turned their frustrations at their economic and social roles on the nearest available victim," which usually meant their wives and children but could easily be a nosey neighbor. Huemul seemed to understand this, citing his own understanding of patriarchal privileges to justify his inaction: "it was Moriconi's house" and "his wife" was the only victim. He also recalled Moriconi's reputation in town as an "impulsive, despotic, ruthless, highly untrustworthy" individual when explaining his passivity that evening. Huemul was not a reactive product of "the frontier" shaped by living in a "less cultured," "remote," "desolate field" at the margin of Argentina. He was, rather, a rational actor, adjusting his expectations of whether a conflict was a public or a private affair while assessing his own safety.

Patriarchy is still a useful way of understanding interpersonal dynamics in northern Patagonia, as long as the concept does not flatten the varieties of experiences and responses to patriarchal authority. Changes in law and society placed conflicts over families (and family conflicts) at the heart of processes of state formation in nineteenth century Latin America, making the family a key area of contestation over citizenship and rights. Although patriarchy seemed to operate differently on the frontier, we can understand those differences as concrete responses to the realities of violent times, precarious conditions, and "functional" exigencies.

Family Violence and Negotiating the Power of Patriarchs

During the investigation into María Anzini de Mariconi's complaint against her husband, the police attempted to ascertain the exact violence used by Mariconi against his family. Anzini de Mariconi alleged that his "excesses" had caused a miscarriage, but when asked directly whether he had "ever hit or struck her or her young children *brutally*" she equivocated, answering that "he had never hit her children or her, even though he did not lack the will to." One key battleground over patriarchal rights was parental and spousal abuse—what was the line between "correcting" and "abusing" a spouse? Was that line similar for children? During the colonial period in Latin America, as well as in early modern Europe, enslaved people, women, and children (broadly speaking, the dependents in a patriarchal household) contested the right of males to mete out physical punishment. As Jorge Uribe-Urán finds for late colonial Mexico, law and custom "did not provide a clear definition" of what counted as "cruel and atrocious" violence, or what permitted violence looked like since it had to be "discreet," "moderate," and "reasonable."[31] In a detailed survey of women's experiences on the Buenos Aires frontier, historian Susan Socolow concludes that rural women, in particular poor women, lived lives marked by men's violent behavior—and often they were the victims of "family, friends, acquaintances, or neighbors."[32]

Despite efforts to "modernize" family life by reserving the right to violence exclusively to the state, civil law in Argentina at the beginning of the twentieth century was still geared to protecting the power of the father within the household.[33] When a patriarch's abuses became "intolerable" the victims could run away from the family home in an effort to avoid further violence, but also to bring the state's attention to their plight. The police treated these *fugas del hogar* (home abandonments) by wives and minors as serious criminal offenses: they took depositions, conducted extensive searches, produced lengthy handwritten reports, and made sure they were forced back home or faced institutionalization.

Although wives and underage children were both under the legal control of the patriarch, their responses to domestic violence were different for a variety of reasons. Wives could usually call upon friends or relatives to try to intercede on their behalf, even hiding them or helping them flee. Underage children usually did not have these kinds of networks. Children also risked institutionalization in the *depósito de menores* if their attempt to bring their abusive parents to heel failed. Children also carried the burden of their parents' reputation as well as their own, the combination of which affected how effective their pleas to the state turned out. Both groups' attempts to bring state attention to their suffering succeeded to the degree that they were able to mobilize popular sentiment to their cases. In other words, local social networks, and the reputation of those involved, influenced the state agents' resolve to seek out creative, semilegal ways to protect wives and children from abuse without openly challenging the law.

Wives

When a battered, runaway wife successfully mobilized local allies to intercede on her behalf, she dramatically increased her chances of remaining outside of her husband's orbit, as the case of Remigia Álvarez (a twenty-three-year-old housekeeper) illustrates.[34] Her husband, Sandalio Rolando, a thirty-two-year-old laborer, grew frustrated by her refusal to return to the family home, deciding on 29 July 1923, to denounce her to the San Antonio Oeste police. As a husband, Rolando had the legal right to force his wife to live with him. The Argentine Congress amended the original 1869 civil code through piecemeal legislation throughout the second half of the nineteenth century, incrementally but unevenly, bringing it closer to the modern civil codes flourishing in Europe.[35] One of the biggest changes came in 1889, when the Argentine Congress passed a set of modifications to civil marriage, through Law 2393, spelling out the rights and responsibilities of spouses.[36] Art. 53 of that law established that

> the wife is forced to live with her husband wherever he establishes residency . . . if she fails this obligation, the husband may request the necessary judicial measures to force her to comply . . . the courts, knowing the particulars of the case, can exempt a wife from this obligation when complying with it could result in *danger to her life.*[37]

The law explicitly mentioned the role of the judiciary in keeping households together and, introducing an area for individual variance, allowed an exception based solely on the discretion of the state agents involved in the case.[38] The vagueness of this provision gave settlers and state representatives a degree of leeway in their interpretation of the law, specifically with regards to the protection of abused wives.

The provision was also vague about the role of the courts and of law enforcement in retrieving runaway spouses. Consider the fairly typical example of Tránsito Álvarez (though he has the same last name as the previous family, there is no relation). In 1909 he spent a few nights in the Viedma jail for having "corrected" his wife's "lewdness."[39] Upon his release, he discovered that his wife had abandoned their home and had gone across the river to Carmen de Patagones. Álvarez requested in a letter to the judge that he use "all the public force" available to bring her back, invoking his rights as a husband. Because Álvarez was illiterate, his father-in-law, don Mateo Barone authored and signed the letter—a tacit alliance between husband and father—that signaled to the police that Álvarez's wife (who was not named in the case files) had no other options. Without any neighbors willing to approach the police to make a case for her independence from Álvarez (or with the police unable to find any), the case was swiftly resolved with her arrest and forced relocation back to the family home. In his complaint, Álvarez himself volunteered that he had just left jail following a domestic violence incident, suggesting that the judges had wide latitude to interpret what counted as a "danger to her life."

Remigia Álvarez, in her own contest against her husband Sandalio Rolando, used two interrelated strategies to affect the investigation. First, she commandeered the deposition using it as a platform to expose her husband's abuses, and, second, she was able to have neighbors contribute to the investigation with incriminating evidence against her husband. During her testimony, Remigia Álvarez took the chance to answer the police's open-ended queries with as much detail as possible. She explained how, when she was just fifteen years old, she had been kidnapped from her mother's home in General Conesa, dragged to Viedma, and forced to marry her kidnapper, Sandalio Rolando. Within a month, he had begun to violently punish her and cut off any communication with her brothers and mother.[40] She went on to explain how he "continually beat me, and one time, in the town of Nahuel Niyeo, because of a fit of unwarranted jealousy, Sandalio forced me to strip naked and had me stand in the corner of a room for about an hour, while he beat me hundreds of times, causing me to fall ill."

The beatings had only gotten worse since then, and she worried that he would "one day kill her." Tired of her husband's abuse, and fearing for her safety, she had simply walked off on the evening of 21 May, while Sandalio was outside chopping wood. She headed east, intended to brave the cold winter night, and walk all the way to her sister's house on the plateau, about thirty kilometers ("six leagues") away. She never made it that far, and the police found her hiding in the home of a male neighbor, creating the appearance that she had been unfaithful. Since the law allowed husbands the right to "discipline" their spouse, simply proving abuse was not enough. She had to establish that the abuse was both "excessive" and "unwarranted."

The investigation itself provided a platform for the community to publicly determine whether the abuse was "warranted" by voicing their concerns about him, and highlighting her good standing in the community. Armed with a long list of witnesses furnished by Álvarez herself, the police confirmed in no uncertain terms Sandalio's violent tendencies. Zoilo Manuel Olivares (a twenty-eight-year-old clerk) insisted that Sandalio was known "by all the neighbors" to abuse her continually. Rudencio Sosa (a sixty-year-old day laborer, who rented the couple the room in which they lived) claimed that, though he never witnessed the abuse firsthand, he often saw Remigia whimpering and crying. He dismissed the notion that she might have had extramarital affairs (which could make Sandalio's violence "warranted" under the law) since he never saw her talking to other people and she mostly stayed in her room by herself.

The most damning testimony came from César Severino, an Italian-born bricklayer who had lived in the country since age sixteen and knew the couple well. In the five years that he had known them, he stated that Sandalio Rolando had "always abused" his wife, who often received "beatings and abuses . . . continually being punished and mistreated in every way possible." He went on to explain that "there is a widespread indignation in this town towards Rolando, because the brutal way he treats his wife is public and notorious." Severino claimed to have witnessed the violence several times, even having to intervene at times "to prevent him from continuing to *mess her up* (*estropear*)." Severino's testimony also highlighted Sandalio's other negative traits: he had "very little affection for work" and he had a "sketchy" past. After two days of questioning, the police concluded that Sandalio Rolando's neighbors held a "general negative opinion" of him, and some even alleged that he was involved in "illegal activities."

Remigia Álvarez requested not to be returned to the marital home while the police investigated her *fuga* "since she feared for her well-being, and after eight years . . . of abuse, she did not feel that she could continue to live with her husband." Having already relocated to the home of a friend, whose husband (Everindo Herrera) was a police officer, the investigator honored her request not to return to her home. The stalemate—she did not have to go back to her abusive husband, but he would not face legal repercussions for abusing her—exemplified the limits of how justice was administered on the frontier. The informal arrangement by the police and the prosecutor curtailed Sandalio Rolando's patriarchal prerogative to discipline his household, without altering the broader legal or social structures. By placing Remigia Álvarez in the custody of Herrera and his family, the police effectively recognized her independence and provided some degree of safety. Arrangements like this one, which stuck to the letter of the law but conformed to social pressures, underscored how the weakness of the frontier state allowed individual state agents to devise flexible solutions to local disputes.

The police, the prosecutors, and even the judge not only adapted to the limits placed on them by the law and scarcity; sometimes they could creatively reinterpret the law itself in such a way that it would align with their sensibilities. Consider how the police handled Jesús Manuel Rebolledo's complaint against his wife. Rebolledo claimed to have returned home on the evening of 3 June 1921 to an unexpected scene: his wife, Benita Barrios de Rebolledo, had abandoned their home taking all of her clothes with her and leaving their three children sleeping in their beds.[41] Since she was seen taking the train heading to Bahía Blanca in the company of a minor (Quintina Esquiza) and a guide, Albino Reggano, he assumed she was trying to reach Buenos Aires, where her close friend Estella Goñi worked as a seamstress.

Rebolledo filed a police report requesting they find and return her to their marital home, insisting that she had not run away with a lover, but she was probably following the encouragement of her mother, who did not like him. The police ordered her immediate capture, as Rebolledo had requested, and by the next afternoon they received a notification that the three fugitives had been detained in Bahía Blanca. Unable to find a place for them in the local jail, the Bahía Blanca police lodged them in an unguarded room in a local hotel. By the time the investigator, Officer Díaz, arrived the next morning to escort them back, only Albino Reggano remained. The women had escaped and were headed toward Villa Mitre, in Buenos Aires.

Frustrated by the wild goose chase, and introducing an uncommon degree of candor when forwarding his incomplete investigation to the judge, Officer Díaz angrily questioned the purpose of the investigation itself. Unprompted, he explained that "in this town, *it is well known* that Rebolledo's wife is the victim of abuses from her husband and on one or two prior occasions she had run away from home, only to be persuaded to return by friendly conciliators." Making matters worse, Díaz remarked, "it is also well known that he is now *publicly threatening her*, assuring anyone who will listen, that as soon as he finds her, he will murder her in broad daylight." Most of the time, investigators simply forwarded their findings to the judge without much editorializing, but Díaz seemed keen on establishing beyond a doubt that Rebolledo's violence qualified for the exemptions in Art. 53: he was a "danger to her life." Officer Díaz added a bold questioning of the role of the police in these kinds of disputes, asking "I am not sure how, or to what extent, the police can be *expected* to force a married woman to move back with her husband against her will." In a one-page note attached to an incomplete investigation, Díaz communicated in no uncertain terms a shift in attitudes that was broader than his own sensibilities.

The prosecutor answered Díaz's rhetorical questions earnestly and dryly. He wrote back to the officer indicating that "in accordance with the provisions of the civil code, this office believes that you *can* force Barrios to live with her husband in their home." Noting that the appropriate procedure would entail an additional step: the police would have to "notify Benita Barrios de Rebolledo to present herself to the courthouse to offer a statement as to why she left the marital home . . . [and] only then can you decide whether to force Barrios to live with her husband." This answer appears callous and obtuse: how could Díaz be expected to notify Benita Barrios of the summons if she was a fugitive?

It strikes me, however, that the prosecutor's obstinate interpretation of the law intentionally stalled the investigation. The federal judge, Ramón Garriga, expanded this clever workaround in his own recommendation when he returned the file to General Roca with clear instructions: "notify the [husband] that he needs to provide a (current) home address of the runaway for the investigation to proceed." In the judge's interpretation of the law, the police had to compel a runaway wife to court, but they did not need to locate her, which they had traditionally assumed as their task in most of the previous cases. By narrowly reinterpreting the role of the police, the judicial representatives of the state exerted influence within the state, changing the ways in which it operated in regard to patriarchal rights. This was not dissimilar to how the police in San Antonio Oeste resolved Remigia Álvarez's refusal to return to an abusive husband, or how the police in Anzini de Moriconi's case used a psychiatric evaluation to "cool off" her violent husband. This combination of adherence to the letter of the law while adapting the spirit of the law to fulfill the will of the informal networks in the local communities was a hallmark of how justice was deployed on the frontier.

The police and the courts in Río Negro Territory refused to intervene in "runaway wife" cases after 1925—ahead of the passage in 1926 of Ley 11,357 expanding civil rights for women at the national level.[42] But since the new law did not change the expectations that wives live with their husbands, the changes seem unrelated, and suggest that Garriga's workaround became part of a general praxis after Barrios's case. Patriarchs still tried to get the police to retrieve runaway wives, but they were met with a less accommodating state. For example, when Crescencia Galeano abandoned the family home "without any reason" in 1925, and moved into a local hotel before leaving the town altogether, her husband Baltazar Piñero asked the General Conesa police to detain her and bring her back.[43] The Conesa police requested their peers in Viedma and Carmen de Patagones to capture Galeano. Instead, they received a reply from Viedma reminding them that "you ought to notify Baltazar Piñero . . . that this being *a private affair*, he needs to pursue a civil action" instead of involving the police. The cases in Neuquén followed a far less delineated timeframe (there were also fewer of them). However, by 1930, the Neuquén court was routinely refusing to consider cases of runaway wives as "criminal matters" even in extreme cases. For example, when Benedicto

Carrasco's wife abandoned the home that summer, he filed a police complaint not only to compel her to return but also to send her to jail. Carrasco's appeal to the court framed his wife as criminally negligent claiming that she had left behind two children, one of which had died without maternal care. Despite his efforts the court declined to get involved.[44]

The state agents in Patagonia did not have the power to alter laws: individually they lived under the same political restrictions as other Patagonians, and even as representatives of the state, they had little legislative input. Despite their disenfranchisement and the constraints of their official positions, judges, police officers, and prosecutors found ways to make the state accountable to the settlers by creatively reimagining the way they carried investigations, and how they resolved them, or failed to do so. Throughout the pivotal 1920s, the police and the courts in northern Patagonia increasingly found ways to decline helping husbands keep their households together. This change in attitudes aligns with broader shifts in the rights of women at a national level, in particular the 1926 overhaul of the civil code that reaffirmed parental rights for single mothers, as well as the right of women to choose their profession and keep their earnings.[45] By interpreting Art. 53 as narrowly as possible, the representatives of the state effectively removed themselves from the business of returning abused wives to their abusers. These strategies were not limited to runaway wives.

Children, Teens, Minors

Family law in Argentina during the first decades of the twentieth century gave parents considerable latitude in how they handled their underage children. In cases of runaway teens, state agents also devised creative ways to limit the power of patriarchs. For example, in early 1921, a month after Eloisa Sinski had run away from her parents' home in San Antonio Oeste to live with her boyfriend, Alfonso Salas, her father finally got around to initiating a police complaint to get her back.[46] She had left her parents' home because she had grown tired of the *malos tratos* (abuses) from her father José Sinski, claiming that "whenever he was drunk, he wanted to kill the rest of us." The police eventually forced Sinski back to her abusive father. But the details of the case suggest a set of extralegal measures deployed by the police and the community in an attempt to ensure her safety. The night she ran away she was picked up by the police and spent the night in the police headquarters, then a month with her boyfriend, and ultimately, she was placed in the care of

Tomás Clipton Goldney, a prominent neighbor. When Clipton Goldney suddenly informed the police that he had changed his mind and could no longer house the teen, she was placed under the explicit guardianship of her mother, Catalina Lillo de Sinski, who agreed to take her back and shelter her from abuse.

The police had already managed to stall José Sinski's pursuit of his daughter even before he filed the complaint. The police informed José Sinski (a forty-eight-year-old Polish mechanic) that they would not receive his complaint about Eloisa's disappearance until he paid a fine for "abusing his wife." According to Sinski's own account, he had "punched his wife twice with his fists, believing that she was responsible for their daughter's disappearance," when he found out that the teen had run away. I was unable to find any other records of a system of fines against abusive spouses, so it remains unclear if this was a measure particular to this police detachment, or a widespread policy that simply did not make it to the archives explicitly.

Although Sinski singled out the police as the source of the fine, it might have stemmed from the local justice of the peace, since their jurisdiction included issuing small fines for disturbances of the peace. Alternatively, the fine might have been an attempt by the police to shake him down for money, knowing that, as an impoverished immigrant with a bad reputation, he would not complain about it too loudly. A final possibility was that the police demanded a fine that they knew Sinski could not afford to stall him in his pursuit of his daughter, who had spent the first night away from home sleeping at police headquarters. This last interpretation is consistent with other informal efforts by the police to resolve conflicts in ways that did not disrupt their communities. It also does not preclude corruption as a contributing explanation: a win-win arrangement that informally punished an abuser and helped support the functioning of the frontier state in the hinterlands.

In trying to determine to what degree the police response to Sinski's abscondence was atypical, it bears placing it in the context of the changes taking place at the national level at the time. As the historian Donna Guy finds, as the Argentine state sought to curb child delinquency in the early twentieth century, it eroded patriarchal rights over minors.[47] With the passing of a watershed 1919 law that allowed the state to remove children convicted of a crime from their parental home, the state assumed a more central role in bringing up Argentine youth when their parents had failed to do so. Sinski's case fits that pattern, as the frontier state intervened quite aggressively to remedy her home situation. Of course, two major differences emerge between the broad national trends and Sinski's case: she had not been accused, let alone convicted of, any crimes, and she initiated the process of supplanting the parents as patriarchs *herself* by abandoning the family home. Her fuga invited the state to make her family dynamics a matter of public interest. Running away from home brought public attention to their situation, forcing the community, and ultimately the state, to monitor the way her parents ran their household more closely.

When minors abandoned the home, triggering investigations over their fugas, they often resorted to language of abuse to underscore the untenable conditions they lived in, and to maximize chances of getting the state's attention. Admittedly, we probably cannot answer decisively how much children, minors, and teens understood the subtleties of the law—that is, how can we know that the testimonies by children, often ones raised in precarity and isolation on frontier towns, represented an intentional strategy to manipulate the adults around them? Scholars have noted in other contexts how legal documents, such as the ones discussed here, were seldomly the expression of singular individual's perspective—they were written interpretations of oral testimonies that could have been shaped by advocates, allies, or even be the reflection of communal experiences. This is what historian Natalie Zemon Davis calls documents of "mixed authorship": polyvocal documents that reflect joint responses to legal needs.[48] It is striking, however, how often minors resorted to the language of "abuse" to bring adult attention to their private lives, how successful that strategy was, and how many different ways they found to talk about abuse, be it physical, moral, or even economic.

Understanding that maintaining a good reputation in town was fundamental for later access to justice, some minors emphasized the multiple ways in which their parents could harm them. Although claims of children growing up in immoral environments were often overblown, their exposure to "greed, godlessness, and frequent profanity" on the frontier was a recurring worry of reformers.[49] The perception that they lived in "damaging moral environments" had real consequences for teens. The example of Delia Barrientos, in particular, showcases just how well teens understood their vulnerability to their parents' bad reputation, and how they could use that vulnerability as leverage when attempting to seek protection from the state. Delia ran away from home on 8 October 1914, and her father, Gregorio Barrientos, immediately accused her boyfriend of kidnapping her.[50] Gregorio Barrientos demanded, as many other fathers faced with a runaway daughter did, that the police compel the boyfriend—Juan Leiva, whose longtime courtship the family did not approve of—to marry her. Otherwise, he wanted her placed in the care of the state, rather than returning her to the family home.

These kinds of cases of elopement make the bulk of chapter 4, where they are explained and analyzed in more detail, but suffice to say that Delia Barrientos's handling of her father's objection to her intimate partner was unusual. The teen told police that she had "grown tired of being forced to work in the *boliche* (general store/saloon) that her mother managed . . . without allowing her to talk to anyone and having to endure the impertinences and indecent swearing which the drunken patrons constantly directed at her." Explaining that her family life only exposed her to "poor examples," she requested that the police find a more suitable place for her to live, and she was ultimately placed under the care of a respectable neighbor, Dorila Quintana. Delia Barrientos's decision to frame her *fuga* as a logical response to being exposed to an abusive moral environment where "impertinent" drunks harassed her mirror her parents' concern with the dangers of her "talking to other people." In fact, both parties in this case shared a concern about Delia Barrientos's reputation in town and how that could limit her rights in their community.

Delia Barrientos's concern with how her parents' reputation could affect her own was not unfounded, as Roberto and Flora Rivero found out when they were kicked out of their mother's house by her drunken partner in 1933.[51] In the remote town of Zapala, where the Patagonian plateau turns into Andean valleys, a neighbor (Irene Jara, a twenty-two-year-old washerwoman) alerted the police that she had seen a group of strange men lurking outside Fidel Cuevas's room. Concerned that Cuevas was running a clandestine brothel, the police raided the apartment before sunrise, capturing Cuevas and four teenagers. Far from being child prostitutes, the teens were two sets of siblings: Fernando and Magnolia Quesada, who lived there permanently, and Roberto and Flora Rivero, who had arrived that night invited by a Quesada sibling. Jara justified her concern to the police because she had identified one of the two recently arrived teenagers as the "daughter of the so-called Chilena Juana, a woman of ill-reputation." Juana Rivas's standing in Zapala caused her children to be treated as if they themselves were "lowlifes." Jara went on to explain that "despite her young age [Flora] leads a suspicious life, always bouncing from home to home, and away from her parents, who are also lowlifes."

Jara's negative assessment of the teens based on their mother's associations seems to corroborate Delia Barrientos's concern about working in her mother's boliche.

Roberto and Flora were temporarily homeless and forced to move frequently to escape a bad home situation, adding their own rootlessness to the family's bad reputation that they carried. Juana Rivas intimated in an off-the-cuff remark to the police that she was considering asking the state to take care of the teens but, for unexplained reasons, had "not gotten around to it." Ultimately, the Rivas teens had fewer options available to them to escape abuse. Similarly, after a short stay in the neighbor's care, Delia Barrientos struck a deal with her father to return to the family home, underscoring the limits of teen mobility. Donna Guy argues that in Buenos Aires "the technical project behind the incarceration of poor young girls on the street was to create a rite of passage that removed them from the streets, and, through the powers of public officials, returned them to private, domestic society with new identities that acknowledged their inferior social status." In northern Patagonia this ritual was truncated by the impoverished frontier state, which relied almost exclusively on neighbors to house and "redeem" them.[52]

Being placed in an institutional framework allowed a degree of leeway for teens that found both their parents and any prospective guardians too stifling. For example, in Viedma, during the early months of the winter of 1930, Juana Godoy left the house of her "temporary guardian," the Spanish tailor Jesús Avalle Fernández, a widower who had been entrusted with the care of Godoy by the girl's mother, Felipa Sandeyu Godoy.[53] Juana Godoy explained that she left "out of fear of being punished by my mother . . . who wants to keep me from even looking at people who pass in front of the house, let alone talk to anyone," adding that "she keeps me locked in, not allowing me to leave, not even on Sundays." She adamantly refused to return to her guardian or her mother, claiming that "rather than to go back to that kind of life, she preferred to be in police custody." The police obliged and she was sent to the *depósito de mujeres y menores*, where she stayed for several months until she was placed in the home of a court-appointed guardian instead. One interpretation of this saga suggests a fairly bleak legal process in which a teen who had not committed any crime found herself detained for months and subsequently sent to work as a domestic servant in an elite home. But this outcome

FIGURE 12. (*opposite*) "'El Gurí, montado en su pingo, se siente capaz de todo,' Patagonia, Chubut, octubre, 1936" (AR-AGN-AGAS01-Ddf-rg-1676-161057). Rural life could be challenging for young people in northern Patagonia.

seemed to have been Juana Godoy's gambit, as she hoped to trade her mother's relentless control over her for the state's "ritualized" reclamation of her.

The depósito was particularly important for children in rural areas, with scarce alternate guardians. A case from the region around Maquinchao in 1933, illustrates this dynamic as a ten-year-old orphan, Segundo Parra, was found walking along the train tracks, malnourished and badly dressed.[54] Parra told the police that both his uncle Rómulo González, an illiterate thirty-eight years old *puestero* (ranch hand), and aunt had "punished him almost daily without any reason" during the seven months that he lived with them. He was forced to run away because he could not stand the "impossible life, deprived of appropriate food and clothing." The child's testimony equated both the physical punishment that he received and the absence of material comforts, which were underscored by the deplorable state he was in when a railroad worker found him.

Unwilling to be sent back to the plateau, Parra asked the police to locate his grandmother, Hilaria González, who he believed still resided in General Roca. Despite the police's repeated attempts, they failed to do so. Rómulo González denied hitting Segundo, except as a rare disciplinary step, and explained that the minor had already tried running away twice. Characterizing Segundo as "incorrigible" he refused to take the boy back. Instead, he requested that the police place him in the depósito to "reform and educate" him. To underscore his own innocence González provided a list of character witnesses who assessed his parenting in a positive light.

If the parent or guardian had not abused the child, they had to mobilize an array of witnesses to contextualize the child's apparent neglect—for example, was Parra's lack of nutrition the result of poverty or neglect? An initial medical exam of the child did not find any evidence of systematic abuse, but did note his slight frame. A second, comprehensive evaluation of the minor in Viedma found evidence that Parra had some developmental issues: the examiner estimated that due to parental alcoholism the child had a "diminished mental capacity," which a teacher corroborated after further examinations. The teacher concluded that Segundo Parra had an "insufficient intellectual development," which could be remedied "in a favorable environment."

One of his neighbors categorically denied that González or his wife ever "brutally punished" the minor and characterized them as "decent people" who treated Segundo as "a son . . . with much affection and care." González's supervisor, Geraldo Juan O'Neill, the foreman of the Companía Sud Argentina de Tierras

Maquinchao, explained that since the family lived in a fairly isolated rural area without schools for about twenty miles, Segundo was often unsupervised and not receiving an education. In his estimation, the boy "was not fond of life in the countryside and due to that he was not happy living with González." Ultimately, O'Neill believed that to "avoid acquiring bad habits" the child would be better off with constant supervision. The judge agreed with the doctor, the teacher, and community members deposed, and despite the lack of evidence that Segundo Parra had suffered abuse from his uncle, the state assumed legal guardianship, placing him in the depósito permanently.

The creation in the 1920s and 1930s of depósitos de menores in major urban centers across Argentina to house and educate homeless, or troubled, youths represented a shift by the government in how it thought of patriarchal rights. As Julie Hardwick explained for early modern Lyon's Hotel-Dieu, these kinds of institutions were more than "disciplinary sites that enclosed people"; they were also places that provided "care, education, and work placement" for children.[55] On the surface, Segundo's dramatic disappearance into the plateau paid off for him, as he wanted to leave the countryside. But he might have gotten more than he bargained for: instead of returning to his grandmother in General Roca, he ended up institutionalized at a state-run facility in Viedma. By running away the child brought the state into his family life, highlighting his dissatisfaction with his condition and forcing his uncle to publicly defend the way he ran his household. This constant negotiation of public and private spheres—of how private relationships were perceived publicly—held the key to how these cases were resolved.

Teenagers had complex and varied reasons to leave the family home, but they often articulated these reasons to state officials in terms of abuse: physical, emotional, or moral. By invoking *malos tratos*, runaways equated the moral and psychological abuse of bad parenting (which the law did not recognize as abuse) to the physical abuse that the law did protect them against. A corrupting moral environment (like the drunken hecklers at a boliche, or the bad reputation of "La Chilena Juana") was presented to law enforcement as the equivalent of beatings— and the police, judges, and prosecutors were left to figure out how to resolve these conflicts in a socially acceptable way while working within the confines of the law. Their status as minors placed them at a disadvantaged position compared with runaway wives. Children were usually placed with people they had never known before, as the state felt compelled to place them in the care of prominent neighbors, and later in the depósito, while wives were allowed to remain in the homes of friends. However, both groups needed to mobilize broad coalitions to support their challenges to patriarchal rights, and success often came in subtle, extralegal arrangements that required continued support from that broader coalition.

The state presence in northern Patagonia was ubiquitous but ineffective, which meant that conflicts were often resolved informally. This was different from most Latin American contexts in the early twentieth century, and it was unusual even in other frontier settings. For example, Ana María Alonso finds that in a small Chihuahua village "abused . . . wives paradoxically challenged the extent of their husbands' power while affirming their own submission and reproducing hegemonic constructions of femininity" by using the courts to try to curtail abuses.[56] In northern Patagonia, the deciding factor in how family conflicts were adjudicated was social standing that grew out of an individual's reputation, allowing dependents to avoid reinforcing the power of their abusers by participating in the rituals of the state.

Fathers, daughters, wives, and suitors who could show that they had broad communal support for their actions from their immediate community often managed to receive legal, or extralegal, redress for their grievances. Although courts rarely resolved the cases in a decisive manner, the judicial process itself—from the initial complaint, through the investigation, the detention of suspects or victims, and eventually the legal arguments—served as a socially recognized resolution to the conflicts, showing how important the subjects' social standing was to the quality of justice they could expect to have.

Reputation and Innocence

An important part of Anzini de Moriconi's letter to the judge imploring him to restrain her husband was her plea for the return of her daughters. Two of them had been "deposited" in the homes of prominent neighbors, and a third one had been sent "to a town in the province of Buenos Aires . . . not knowing if she's alive or dead." She feared that they were "handed over to strangers as if they were CRIMINALS . . . which results in moral harm and prejudice" toward them. Her concerns were not unfounded. In a 1905 muckraking exposé on white slavery in Tandil (in the province of Buenos Aires), the journalist Atilio Airton spoke on behalf of orphaned rural girls "who found life in foster homes . . . unbearable . . . [and where] mistreatment and overwork forced them into prostitution as a means of escaping their misery."[57] By Anzini de Moriconi's logic, placing her otherwise respectable daughters in "foster homes" was a waystation to prostitution, or at the very least a permanent taint on their reputations. As Roberto and Flora Rivero discovered when the police assumed any place that would house them was bound to be an illegal brothel because of their mother's character, northern Patagonian society—young, rootless, dependent on police and judges for most government functions—was not easy to navigate without a good reputation.

Someone's reputation in the community could result in police operations becoming extremely contorted. Usually, police mobilized only after a complaint—that is, they usually did not initiate, but responded to settlers' demands for, investigations. However, in March 1913, Lina Biorki (a thirty-two-year-old Russian immigrant) had to contend with unwanted police attention on her, and her legal brothel, after an officer heard about a scuffle late at night.[58] The police dragged Biorki in to testify, peppering her with questions not only about the events the previous night, but also trying to establish her relationship to several men seen in her establishment, from the alleged aggressor Rodolfo Marín to her business partner, Gregorio Kreitman. The police had to exercise caution when following these kind of opaque leads, lest they take their zeal too far, as Comisario Luis Guiñazú, in the hamlet of Rucachoray, found out. After receiving an offhand comment that José Luis Cifuentes had covered up his young daughter's infanticide, he launched a heavy-handed and ultimately illegal investigation.[59] Acting as if "the law had placed [him] as a guardian of all of humankind" Guiñazú hounded, deceived, and entrapped the entire Cifuentes family to prove the allegations against them, since even police in nearby "Quillén could confirm the family's bad reputation" in the area. Despite extracting damning confessions from every member of the Cifuentes family, Guiñazú's investigation was thrown out and he was suspended indefinitely without pay because of his overzealousness. It is hard to overstate how unusual this level of police attention to a private matter that did not result in a formal, or even informal, complaint was; as the rest of the cases in this section attest, the police in northern Patagonia mobilized in direct response to the public's desire for it to do so.

Consider, for comparison, the reaction by Officer José Santos Quesada in 1930, when he witnessed Benedicto Carrasco abusing his wife, Adelina del Carmen Campos, in their home.[60] Even though Carrasco was known in town to have starved his wife and children, was notorious for *malos tratos* and *mala vida*, was a "known drunkard" who had repeatedly chased his wife with a knife into the streets on several occasions, the officer limited himself to "chastising" Carrasco privately. Adelina del Carmen Campos recalled in her deposition that the officer "told her to see the judge, or just leave the house" since he feared for her safety. Even when police officers witnessed a potential crime, and intervened informally in the case, they did not usually launch an investigation without a complaint. For men, at least, reputation came into play after a complaint was lodged—during the investigation. The attention placed on Biorki and her domestic disturbances—that is, the erosion of her privacy—seemed to be related to her occupation as brothel owner, which affected her reputation in town.

Similarly, when twenty-three-year-old Carmen Amador was accused of infanticide in the spring of 1932, her reputation in town as an "arrogant drifter" who "detested young children" closed off any doubt of her culpability.[61] Her fellow servant, María Luisa Pérez, confirmed the accusations made by their employer, Carlos Chibitat, that Amador had been unsuccessfully hiding a pregnancy with "a girdle and an overcoat." The police rummaged through the servants' room looking for evidence of a clandestine birth and noted blood-soaked bedsheets in the bed the servants shared, large pools of dried blood on the floor next to the bed, and traces of something bloody being dragged around the room. Pérez was adamant that she had not helped Amador with the birth, had no knowledge of the birth taking place in the same bed as she was sleeping, and had not heard any screaming from either the mother or the newborn, removing herself from any potential complicity in the death of the infant.

This was a common strategy by witnesses in cases of infanticide: no one the police interviewed ever noticed or saw anything. Amador explained that she gave birth unassisted, squatting on the bed, and then the floor, but that the baby was stillborn, which might have explained why Pérez did not hear any baby screams. Fearing "that her employer would find out and chastise her," Amador wrapped the tiny body in a sheet and dropped it in a nearby field where it was found two days later. The medical examiner could not determine whether the baby died of exposure or if it had been born dead, but he was adamant that there were no signs of any violence against the newborn: no suffocation marks, no broken nose, cuts, contusions, or other typical signs of infanticide. Given the lack of hard evidence against her, the judge's ultimate decision to convict her to three and a half years in prison, an unforgiving maximum sentence allowed by the law, seems particularly harsh.

What accounts for the judge's decision? It is not easy to determine how judges thought of these cases because they were exceedingly rare. Out of over 64,000 cases in the Río Negro archive, only 23 were related to investigations of infanticides; it was not a crime that was usually prosecuted, and when it was, it was the result of "murky [birth] circumstances by single mothers" or when there was "a clear indication of what was perceived as abuse or intentional violence."[62] Although we do not have good figures for northern Patagonia, Richard Slatta calculates that in southern Buenos Aires, itself a recent frontier space, "stillbirths and infant deaths (up to six months of age) accounted for 31 percent of all provincial deaths." Because of diseases like diarrhea, enteritis, and respiratory ailments infant deaths (children under one) in Buenos Aires province remained around 10 percent between 1914 and 1920.

In northern Patagonia, where malnourishment and exposure to extreme weather were more severe than in the comparatively more affluent Buenos Aires, we can expect at least similarly high mortality rates. Slatta finds that mortality of children under six, more broadly, continued to account for "52 percent of all provincial deaths from 1892 to 1902, and 43 percent" the following decade.[63] In northern Patagonia, the death of infants, toddlers, and children was not an uncommon reality either. Without direct evidence of the mother (or someone else) ending the life of the newborn, the state would weigh circumstantial evidence—such as Carmen Amador's efforts to hide the pregnancy from her employer and her roommate, her failure to secure assistance during her delivery, or failing to notify the authorities of the birth, and her bad reputation in town—to attempt to resolve the case.

Hiding a pregnancy and attempting to give birth in secret suggested that the mother did not intend to keep the baby, but that was not sufficient proof that she contributed to the death. Consider that when Ramona Contreras gave birth in an outhouse, leaving the fetus in the latrine, she only received a light eighteen-month sentence.[64] By the time her housemate found the baby "in a pile of shit" the next morning, it was already dead, and the investigation likewise struggled to determine whether the baby was born dead or died due to exposure. Unlike Carmen Amador, Contreras had told her mother she was pregnant, and her housemates knew as well. People in the community, even her housemate, vouched for Contreras and went out of their way to paint a positive picture of her for the police.

The apparent lack of care for the body of the baby was also a suggestion of criminal intent, but it was not enough to make a judge pursue the harshest punishment. When Margarita Morón was accused of strangling her newborn baby with a rope and stashing the body under a bush in the plateau to "hide her dishonor" the judge issued a seemingly lenient two-year sentence.[65] Morón not only attempted to hide the body—the dramatic description by the investigator of the way "the chest was somewhat eaten, supposedly due to a dog" before it was found certainly negatively predisposed the police to the teen—but the rope around the baby's neck made it hard to argue that the baby had been stillborn, which she attempted to do. Morón's mother, her employer, and the local police vouched that "she had not seemed capable" of such a crime, reflecting the favorable opinion of her in the community and underscoring the idea that she came from a "good family." Community assessments of someone's reputation were central to moderating the power of the state to enforce the law and punish.

Although the circumstances around Carmen Amador's lonely, apparently quiet, and ultimately tragic delivery did not differ greatly from other young unmarried women accused of infanticide in northern Patagonia, the severity of the sentence—almost double what other women got—suggests that something about Amador made her an unsympathetic defendant. Unlike Contreras and Morón, Amador did not have a network of people willing to vouch for her good reputation. She had never known her mother and had lived most of her life bouncing around from house to house working as a servant. She told the police that she was weary of "finding herself alone in the world, without family, or shelter, having suffered enormously in all the houses she's worked in," stressing the precarity of her everyday life. The police in Viedma were well aware of Amador's background: six months earlier she had spent some days under police care "preventively" since she was believed to be a suicide risk after being fired for "punishing and mistreating" her employer's young children. Because the community already believed that Amador was the kind of person who would harm children, the prosecutor and the judge keyed on those clues, sprinkled throughout the testimonies, to mete out an exemplary punishment.

The consequences of a bad reputation went beyond enhanced police attention and harsher legal punishments. Consider how Leonor "La Ñata" Rodríguez's life unraveled while the police investigated allegations that she corrupted a pair of teenage boys in 1933.[66] Rosario Cárdenas told the police that she had confronted her fourteen-year-old son Rudencio Laurin when she found "pus stains in his underwear," assuming it was from gonorrhea. Rudencio told his mother that a couple of weeks earlier he had been forced to have sex against his will by "La

Ñata" Rodríguez, a twenty-one-year-old laundress who catcalled him from her doorway, "dragged him" to her bed, and forced herself on him.

She contested his account, framing their intimate encounter as consensual and arising from their friendship. Pedro Troncoso, who had rented Rodríguez a room in his house, told the police that he had "kicked her out of the house" following the allegations against her. This sudden eviction must have been particularly hard on Rodríguez because she relied on the Troncoso family to feed her and her two little children as she was often between employments. Others in the community continued to paint an unflattering portrait of Rodríguez, conditioning how the police, the prosecutor, and the judge saw her. Troncoso's adult daughter Delmira "La China" added that the family thought lowly of Rodríguez "because she is always with different men" including another teenage boy, Antonio Nahuelqueo, who confirmed to the police that he had repeatedly had sex with Rodríguez after being seduced by her.

The officer charged with investigating the rape of the teenage boys failed to turn up anyone with firsthand knowledge of the event, but the neighbors "informed [him] that the aforementioned woman is regarded poorly because she doesn't work, is always bouncing from shack to shack, and never misses a party." Other witnesses confirmed the "very bad reputation she had in town," painting her as someone "comfortable with changing men with the seasons" and who "never works because she is only interested in men." The police arrested her in late October 1933 and kept her in jail until April of the following year, when her case was dismissed. During those six months she was not only deprived of her liberty, but her children were placed under the care of the state, and since Pedro Troncoso evicted her, she was homeless. The state could not prove that a crime had been committed, but the scandalous allegation against her, and the consensus in the community that she was a "lowlife" resulted in her life being upended. She even had to beg the judge for a train ticket back home given that she was now destitute.

Whatever we may think about a grown woman aggressively seducing teenage boys and possibly spreading venereal diseases, the process to which she was subjected as the police investigated those allegations reveals some important features of justice on the frontier that are quite different from other areas. Courtrooms, throughout the nineteenth century, played an important role in getting people from disparate "social groups to work out . . . struggles for political control and cultural influence" in frontiers, especially when those conflicts involved family and social order.[67] In other Latin American cases, the contests *inside* the courtrooms decided those struggles, which was often not the case with struggles involving Patagonian families, as most cases found informal resolution before they reached the beleaguered federal judge. This frontier justice—driven by informal standing in the community but reliant on formal institutions like the police and the courts—was also the daily manifestation of citizenship in northern Patagonia.

Put differently, for impoverished and vulnerable individuals in particular, the quality of justice they could receive from the frontier state depended on a series of factors, but chiefly their reputation. Because so much of the state's operation was in the hands of underpaid, undertrained local officials enmeshed in their small communities, their power was both informal and unchecked. Ambiguous crimes like infanticide could have widely divergent outcomes—from going unreported to strict maximum sentences—depending on the reputation of the accused. Hints of improper morals or questionable work ethics fueled investigations that were thin on evidence, with devastating consequences.

Even when cases were dismissed by prosecutors and judges, the process of investigating and detaining someone could derail their lives, taking away far more than their liberty, based on little more than hearsay. No wonder Anzini de Moriconi tried so adamantly to override her estranged husband's decision to place their daughters in "foster homes" to save money. She was desperate to preserve their reputations, and safeguard their access to justice in a society that easily undermined it.

Conclusion

To what degree was patriarchy upheld by the state in northern Patagonia? In other words, did northern Patagonian state representatives make patriarchs more or less powerful than their counterparts elsewhere in the country? Or, to place that question in the framework of this chapter, how likely was Moriconi to get away with his outbursts in Neuquén? The intersection of family life and an expanding state presence in a frontier space shows the way in which the boundary of the public and the private was negotiated, one family at a time. While the family unit remained an important cornerstone of order in northern Patagonia, the erosion of patriarchal power and the increased role of the state in seemingly "private affairs" was a contingent, fraught process that at times expanded and at other times contracted the reach of the state, and its legitimacy, in the region. Men, women, and children attempted to use the representatives of the state to their own advantage by mobilizing their local networks to try to leverage the good will of state agents.

On balance, even if Argentine lawmakers—like their counterparts elsewhere in Latin America at the time—treated the home as a separate sphere and "allowed the prolongation of colonial-era rights specifically made for heads of households, as well as the continuing treatment of the family as a sphere in which a separate set of rights operated," the state representatives on the frontier did not always follow their lead.[68] Patagonia's institutional remoteness, more than the century separating its introduction to liberal jurisprudence to that of the rest of the hemisphere or the absence of alternative sources of institutional legitimacy, accounts for the less formal "rationalization of patriarchy" taking place there in the early decades of the twentieth century. In the cases in this chapter, we see how neighbors, police officers, and community members used the available government institutions to play out their power struggles. Put differently, by cloaking their interpersonal power struggles in legal disputes the settlers of northern Patagonia built the state on the frontier by legitimizing how certain power struggles were institutionalized.

This process of creating and maintaining reputations, of using local authorities to mediate and resolve disputes in informal ways, and of contesting the results of these arrangements with a cadre of outside bureaucrats concerned with long-term stability rather than immediate social order worked to strengthen the settlers' trust in the state. Stonewalling Rebolledo's efforts to get his abused wife back by sticking narrowly to the letter of the law, levying suspicious fines against Sinsky for abusing his wife, investigating Biorki's brothel under spurious circumstances, the dispassionate dispossession of "La Ñata" Rodríguez, the unwanted attention on the whereabouts of the Rivero siblings, were the kind of irregularities that made outsiders accuse the frontier government of corruption and ineffectiveness.

Those accusations, even if objectively accurate, missed the point of how and why settlers continued to rely on state agents to mediate some of the most important and delicate conflicts in their lives. The informal workings of the frontier state did not erode the settlers' trust in the government; they strengthened it by providing a responsive, highly localized local agent and a meticulous, deliberately insular regional institutional setup. With laws generally stacked against them, family members wanting to escape patriarchal abuses needed to be able to bring their communities into their domestic frays, essentially making the private realm of the family a public affair. Unable, and often unwilling, to break the law to assist them, state representatives found creative ways to adjudicate family conflicts in the gray areas around the law, turning lethargy into an informal, selective tool to maintain peace in the frontier towns. As the next chapter on teen elopements shows, settlers learned how to use public attention to private dramas for their own political ends.

"Suspicious Virginities"

Jóvenes, Sex, and Marriage Choice in Small Patagonian Towns

> I decided to leave to secure permission [to marry], either from the parents
> or the courts, since I consider myself to have the right to marry whomever I
> want, and not who I am told to.
> —Edubina Guerra

> It is so easy, so common, in the fields of these desolate territories, to find sus-
> picious virginities. . . . Your Honor is wisely aware of how female adolescence
> develops in these remote regions of the country . . . the social criteria have to be
> different from the one applied in other, more cultured, regions of our country.
> —Adolfo Leon D'Archary

Late in the spring of 1922, in the remote hamlet of Piedra del Águila, along the rocky arid northern shore of the Limay River, thirteen-year-old Mercedes Arraigada unexpectedly left Juan Rodríguez's home, where she had worked as a servant for a couple of weeks.[1] According to her mother, María Briselda Arraigada, a thirty-five-year-old housekeeper from Chile, the minor had left to follow Gabino Ramírez, a twenty-six-year-old fieldhand, who "had been courting her for a while" ("hacía tiempo le requiría de amores"). The police in Piedra del Águila launched a search for the couple, quickly finding them at Juan García y García's *estancia*, where Ramírez worked. María Briselda Arraigada requested that the state return her daughter to Rodríguez's home so that she could resume her employment, and she categorically refused to allow them to marry. These kind of fugas—dramatic and well-choreographed home abandonments by girls to meet up with their intimate partners to "live a married life" (*hacer vida marital*)—were a common fixture of frontier life. Most of them sought to compel their parents to accept their romantic partners by consummating their relationship in a public way, involving complaints, police searches, depositions, and ultimately, judges.

Cases of runaway minors found in the archives in Neuquén and Río Negro suggest that private disputes over marriage and teen autonomy became political struggles when they entered the public arena, inviting neighbors, family members, and state agents to curtail the power of patriarchs. In that context of reduced rights and limited autonomy, female minors were able to turn the moralizing expectations placed on them into a political opening—a space to practice citizenship by manipulating how frontier justice was administered. The particular arrangement in northern Patagonia, characterized by a state presence that relied heavily on the population to function and which sought to operate in community-sanctioned ways to limit the erosion of its legitimacy, was at the center of these conflicts over marriage choice, much like it was for the indigenous litigants in chapter 2 and the abused wives in chapter 3.

The *jóvenes* (young women) running away from home to elope with their intimate partners encompassed a wide range of ages, from twelve to twenty. To our contemporary mind the collapsing of young women, teenagers, and girls into a single sexualized identity can be problematic. Legally, they were all considered minors, subjected to parental authority, and bestowed with special legal protections of their "modesty." Socially, they were "doubly marginalized" because of their gender and their legal minority status.[2] In the records, the term *jóvenes* was used as an umbrella term for most unmarried women and girls under twenty-one years of age. In some cases, when the age of the joven was undetermined or being challenged for statutory reasons, witnesses and state agents flippantly dismissed the difference between, say, "a girl of thirteen or fifteen years" or a "joven of fifteen or eighteen years." Since birth certificates were scarce, and community recollections were relied on to determine age, the cohort was unproblematically treated as a whole. This chapter follows the cue from the archive.

Faced with the restrictions of legal minority, Mercedes Arraigada had few avenues to challenge her mother's decision to employ her in the home of a stranger far from her intimate partner. By running away, she forced a simple choice on her mother: to acquiesce to her desire to live with Ramírez, or to involve the police in publicly retrieving her, inviting the judge to override the parental veto in the process. Mercedes Arraigada's *fuga* was a political act insofar as it was one of the only ways for jóvenes to access the state on the frontier, involving it in domestic disputes, and leveraging that involvement to override parental authority. This chapter considers the role played by jóvenes in the legitimization of frontier institutions—but in doing so it offers a critical evaluation of how they understood their own actions and proposes new ways to think about choice, exploitation, and love.

The cases highlighted in this chapter also illustrate the dangers surrounding the sexuality of girls, teenagers, and young women in a frontier setting like northern Patagonia, including prostitution, rape, and transience. These dangers were extensions of the precarity of life on the frontier, but they were augmented given the ways in which young women were particularly marginalized. Finally, these kinds of cases require us to re-examine the concept of "agency"—that is, how can we conceptualize Mercedes Arraigada's choice to run away and elope with her intimate partner, a man twice her age, when she was barely thirteen years old?

Frontier Danger: Prostitution, Rape, and Abuse on the Frontier

Most aspects of a teenager's sexuality on the frontier were characterized by the specter of sexual violence. As discussed in the previous chapters, spousal abuse, kidnapping, displacement, isolation, and other forms of sexual violence were endemic to the region. It is clear that girls and young women grew up surrounded by constant danger of sexual assault, which some men considered a prelude to "getting a wife"—a cruel twist on the elopement ritual, as fathers might feel compelled to marry their forcibly deflowered daughters to their rapists. It bears repeating that in most instances of sexual abuse the perpetrator was someone the girls and women knew, at least in passing. The immediacy of life in small, isolated communities underscored the relative lack of "strangers" in everyday life. When a marriage was not arranged, raped women faced several bleak possibilities: if they lived with guardians rather than parents, they might end up being kicked out of their homes, those with parents who felt unable to protect or "steer" them could end up with state-appointed guardians (some of whom felt entitled to continue to abuse the girls and teens in their charge), and an unknown number of them found themselves without a permanent roof over their heads, joining *mujeres del pueblo*, street prostitutes.

In rural areas, unmarried daughters rarely left the company of an adult, lest they became the target for predators. As the newspaper *La patria* of Olavarría in the Buenos Aires countryside just north of Patagonia observed in 1897, "women could not remain faithful to husbands who absented themselves for long periods to work on various estancias," an indictment on the pervasive sexual violence of the countryside, and the economic precarity that forced men to absence themselves from home for long stretches of time during harvest, shearing, or transhumance season.[3] Enriqueta Gallego, who was brutally raped in her parent's remote ranch in Las Minas, was targeted by her neighbor Pedro Santos Fuentes when he realized she was alone because all the males in the house were in the wintering pastures. Magdalena Vázquez, a thirteen-year-old in the oil fields of Challacó, was kidnapped by her uncle Marcelino Vázquez, who wanted to "claim her" as a wife, when her father was at work and her mother was tending to a relative nearby. Her two younger siblings saw the kidnapping and notified their father when he returned that night. Magdalena Vázquez "desperately" fought off her uncle's attempts to rape her throughout the first night that they spent in a field not far from her own home.[4]

Likewise, when twenty-two-year-old British fieldhand Eduardo Yenkins saw his employer's thirteen-year-old charge, Ema Fuentes, alone by the edge of the river, he seized the opportunity to consummate with a violent assault what had been a months-long unrequited courtship. She recalled that

> around eight in the morning she went to the shores of the river to gather grasses for the pigs, and Yenkins, who must have seen her going alone, intercepted her as she arrived to the river, and immediately embraced her asking her to agree to his wishes, which she refused, leading to a brief struggle, which he won because he was stronger and since at that point it was impossible to resist, and because she liked him a little, she decided to surrender to Yenkins's desire to make her his, having complete carnal access, which resulted in a lot of blood coming out because she had never before had any loving contact or relations with any man.[5]

After that morning, Yenkins assaulted her two more times, before he was caught by a neighbor who informed her guardian, Daniel Castellano, and eventually the police. After an attempted escape, vigorous denials, and a tearful confession, Yenkins agreed to marry Ema Fuentes in exchange for the state dropping the aggravated rape charges against him.

Castellano acted swiftly and vigorously to bring justice to the man that he had hired for the harvest and who had raped his charge—but in the context of northern Patagonia in the late 1920s, the options available for redress were fairly limited. In fact, everyone involved in this case operated under the assumption that the only way to redress the sexual assault was for Yenkins to marry her. This stemmed from a provision in the penal code, Art. 132, by which a court could under "exceptional circumstances" consider a "compromise" if the victim of a rape wanted to marry her assailant—a "more equitable way to harmonize the conflict" as the text of the law explained it. Effectively, María Beatríz Gentile argued that the "judicialization" of nonconsensual sexual activity with minors (that is, the lodging of a criminal complaint with the police to involve the judicial authorities) was often a "bargaining chip" between grownups, a way to force the accused rapist to marry the teen or to acquiesce to some other demand.[6] Yenkins himself did not act like someone who wanted to "harmonize the conflict:" as soon as the community's attention turned to him, Yenkins fled the area and denied ever knowing her beyond a "casual good morning."

Yenkins's ruse failed because of the amount of evidence against him, but without the eyewitness reports to corroborate the teen's account, he certainly could have muddled the investigation enough to exonerate himself. For example, when Eluterio Ferrada found himself accused of having raped María Trinidad Sambueza behind some bushes near the town's slaughterhouse, he denied knowing the accuser at all.[7] After further questions he admitted to knowing her "casually" when she was employed in his sister's house. Unlike Ema Fuentes, who had been raised by her guardians, María Trinidad Sambueza had bounced around from home to home for most of her life: according to the police file, she had run away from the home of her first guardian, Moisés Schraier; and subsequently ran away from another caretaker, Francisco García; she had also spent some nights in the local police station following yet another exit from a different guardian. She also claimed to have lived with her friend Delia Ferrari, and according to Ferrada's testimony, she had worked as a live-in servant in his sister's house. No one vouched for Sambueza's honor or chastity like the neighbors had done for Fuentes. Instead, Eluterio Ferrada's employer, a well-regarded typographer, endorsed his character and offered a plausible alibi by suggesting that he "often" worked late (but stopping short of confirming that he had worked late the night that Sambueza claimed to have been raped by him). Employers and guardians, as alternate patriarchs, played an important role in buttressing the reputation of the young people under their authority.

There was a lot of variance in the kind of role that guardians played in the lives of the children and teens in their care. Guardians and employers (the categories overlapped and were ill-defined, as Hannah Greenwald shows) were selected by the parents, or by the state, because of their standing in the community. Prominent families would enter into these informal arrangements because they could exchange "lodging, food, and an education" for the domestic service of the minors, but there were no guarantees that they would fulfill their roles as expected.[8] For example, when Corina del Carmen Mariboli ran away from home "to lead an immoral life" her parents asked the police to turn her over to the judge, since "they were incapable of disciplining her," which had led her to become a "prostitute."[9] Corina del Carmen Mariboli explained that it had been her parents' extreme poverty that had caused her to "make common life (*vida común*) with some people out of necessity, and in order to be able to secure necessary resources." Stories like Mariboli's served as the backdrop to choices that other jóvenes made with regards to seemingly undesirable marriages.

When the police found her in the home of a neighbor who had employed her as a cook earlier, she was placed under the care of the defensor de menores, who reported to the court that three separate men had requested permission to marry Mariboli, to "avoid sending her to a reformatory." She was eventually given permission by the court to marry a thirty-nine-year-old mechanic in Viedma. It would seem from her file that there was an informal mechanism by which "honorable men" requested custody of troubled minors with the intention to eventually marry them, which was against the stipulations of the civil code (which banned underage marriages to "keepers and guardians"). The court might have ignored those provisions when the minor in question was perceived to be "immoral" or during times when resources in the depósito de mujeres were scarce. Child prostitution appears to have been fairly tolerated in rural areas, especially when the mothers themselves "ceded" their children to prominent families because of their own "immoral lives."[10] The scarcity of the government in northern Patagonia resulted in practices—opaque and quotidian—that exacerbated the precariousness of those with the least resources and without the networks to ameliorate those practices.

Even when girls and young women were placed under the care of particularly prominent people who could raise them and provide some work, they often faced an uncertain fate. When Salustiana Benítez was placed by her father, Cándido Benítez, in the home of Miguel Esteban Walsh, the steward of the Estancia Santa Genoveva, to work as a nanny for his three children she was repeatedly raped by someone at the estancia.[11] The rapes were only reported to the police by her father after she was unceremoniously dropped off by Walsh, who simply told Benítez that "the girl was feeling unwell" and was unwelcome back at the Estancia. Within a few days the girl had a miscarriage, and the attending doctor recommended the police be notified since she was showing signs of having been raped. Seemingly out of deference for Walsh, the local police buried the investigation (which was subsequently reopened by an illegal order from the governor), but the surviving interviews show that when the steward had to either protect a nanny who his children and wife "loved like our own" or a foreman, he did not hesitate in swiftly removing the minor from the estancia.

On the other hand, Martín Antemil, the fieldhand who was denied permission to marry Edubina Guerra because her father thought he "was indigenous," benefited from the intervention of the owner of the estancia where all of them worked. Enrique Choeneder, a prominent *estanciero* in the Andean valleys around San Martín de los Andes, added his unprompted endorsement of Antemil's qualifications as a potential spouse saying that "he is an Indian, but he is a good man." The different patriarchal relationships that guardians and supervisors had over the women and men under their care were critical in safeguarding them against sexual assault, but also in helping them navigate the fallout.

The dangers of sexual assault, rape, and "compromise" marriages were a daily reality for northern Patagonian women, especially young unmarried ones. These dangers came from family members, neighbors, or relative strangers with itinerant lives—people the teens knew and people who knew when they were vulnerable or alone. This context of violence and fear offers a stark backdrop to the choices that other young women made to marry young, and often not well, as soon as they could.

"Private Crimes": Elopement, Patriarchy, and the State

When Mercedes Arraigada left the home of her employer to elope with Ramírez, she was participating in a centuries-old "script"—a series of ritualized actions that she hoped would result in a specific outcome. Her mother had placed her in the care of Juan Rodríguez specifically to prevent the couple from continuing the courtship, so we can assume that Mercedes Arraigada had discussed wanting to marry Ramírez with her mother in the past. She did not have many other options, as the law clearly stipulated that without a judge's special dispensation, minors could not marry if their parents had already refused to grant them permission to do so.

Historian Kathryn Sloan traces the long history of teenage rebellion in matters of romantic partners and marriage, finding that in most cases of runaway daughters, the minors would leave the home after a protracted disagreement with her parents or guardians over their choice of intimate partners.[12] A lot of the cases she finds in southern Mexico had similar outcomes: if the couple managed to elope (to spend a night together while running away), the assumed consummation of the relationship would break the parents' resistance. Effectively, Sloan finds that by running away (or by staging their own kidnappings by their intimate partners) young women participated in a well-worn "script of seduction" that could overturn parental objections, since "parents often consented to a marriage over having their family honor sullied by a sexual scandal."[13]

As historian Susan Socolow found in looking at the southern Buenos Aires frontier in the nineteenth century, "in rural areas kidnapping and rape of unmarried girls were part of the local courtship pattern." After meeting an eligible young woman, "a man would steal her from her home, usually at night or when the girl's male relatives were temporarily absent. After riding some distance from the 'bride's' family, the girl was deflowered and the marriage thereby consummated . . . [and] the couple then set up a household, publicly living as man and wife."[14] In northern Patagonia, as Geraldine Davies Lenoble argues, "kidnappings" were a crucial aspect of Mapuche nuptial rituals, particularly for non-elite families. In Mapuche tradition, the "groom" would remove his "bride" from the home in the middle of the night, take her on horseback to a remote location where they would consummate their union with sexual intercourse, returning to her family after three days for the father of the bride to accept the union.[15] How did this "script" work in practice in the early twentieth-century northern Patagonian frontier?

Consider how Manuel Pérez, a successful Spanish merchant in Viedma, found out rather quickly how limited his options were once his teenage daughter, Camila Pérez, decided to elope with her intimate partner Fermín Agüero (a twenty-two-year-old clerk).[16] Manuel Pérez went to the police the morning after he realized his daughter was missing, asked the police that, "given his personal standing ("por la situación que ocupa"), they handle the investigation completely quietly ("con toda reserva")." Agüero confirmed that they had spent the night together in his rented room, but explained that she had shown up unannounced the day before and had been adamant in her refusal to return to her parents' house. He presented himself to the police as an unsuspecting bystander, a reluctant player in the teen's plan, emphasizing that he had tried to persuade her to seek her parents' approval for their relationship. The police deposed Camila Pérez, who confirmed Agüero's story, adding that she refused to return to her father's house because "life there was impossible," a common trope in these kind of cases, since it attempted to erode parental authority. Camila Pérez reiterated that they intended to marry as soon as possible.

When the police informed Manuel Pérez of his daughter's testimony and of her reluctance to return home quietly, he decided to resolve the issue discreetly and directly. He asked the police to withdraw his complaint "since it was clear to him that this was a private crime ("delito privado")," which effectively ended the state's involvement in their family drama. The representatives of the state on the frontier showed deference to a prominent paternal figure when he asked for privacy, which it would not always do for single women or men without good social standing in their communities. Ironically, somewhat affluent, or upwardly mobile, families were particularly vulnerable to the careful balance between blocking a disadvantageous marriage and their daughter's standing in the community, having to determine how much public reputation to gamble on a private matter.

Even when it did not involve a fuga, women on the frontier tended to marry before the age of twenty. Data on this are not easy to come by, but contextual evidence suggests that this was the case. For one, the gender and age imbalances in northern Patagonia throughout the period created conditions that favored early marriage ages for girls. Consider that as late as 1947 in the Territory of Neuquén, men aged 20 to 24 outnumbered women in the same age group at a 3:1 ratio (10,386 men to 3,494 women). In fact, girls under 14 made up half of the female population in that territory during that census.[17] From the information I was able to glean from the archival sources, it appears that similar demographic realities stretched back to the 1920s and 1930s, though we do not have census data to corroborate that insight. The pattern might have stretched as far as the middle of the nineteenth century, as Susan Socolow finds—almost half of the "Spanish women" that were taken captive on the Buenos Aires frontier under the age of nineteen were either married or widowed.[18]

The laws in place in the late nineteenth century regarding parental consent for marriage were a product of both colonial-era tradition and post-Independence concerns about making families more legitimate and legible to the state. During the late colonial period, the Spanish reformers had strengthened parental consent for marriage with a series of laws known as the "Royal Pragmatics on Marriage."

The "royal pragmatics" allowed parents to object to "unequal marriages" (often understood in racialized terms, but also socioeconomically) of their underage children, partially replacing the Catholic Church as the arbiter of these kind of disputes.[19] Although the independence wars did away with many colonial-era regulations, the "royal pragmatics" were used until the mid-nineteenth century, as parents and their children renegotiated ideas about patriarchy, self-determination, romantic love, and national identity. In Córdoba, for example, the "royal pragmatic" was explicitly left in place after independence because it was an important way for the government to prevent the disruption of social order—particularly the social mobility of women of African descent in a city where over half of the population had some African ancestry at the time.[20]

By midcentury, as Jeffrey Shumway finds in rural Buenos Aires, cases based strictly on racial objections to marriages became less effective, as judges began siding with minors who sought economically stable partners.[21] For example, María Rodríguez successfully argued to the judge overseeing her petition to override her mother's objection, that "the purity of my blood cannot put food on my table . . . I am destitute and lack the means to survive." The judge agreed to allow her to marry Andrés Lorca, who was a free man of African descent, underscoring how judges had begun to see themselves as being "in the business of propagating legitimate unions in the poorer classes."[22] By the end of the nineteenth century, economic stability was more exigent than racial stability—as Manuel Pérez's insistence that his daughter should marry better than a lowly clerk illustrates.

Even after the royal pragmatic was replaced in Argentina by the new civil code implemented in 1870, the law continued privileging fathers in matters of marriage choice. Based on Articles 166 through 171, Manuel Pérez had the power to block his daughter's marriage: minors under the age of eighteen needed parental consent to marry. If the parents were deceased or had surrendered patria potestad (by remarrying, for example), a judge could grant the minors permission. Young couples could also request a *venia*—a special dispensation adapted from a medieval prerogative—to marry if they could not secure both of their parents' consent. Art. 167 limited the judicial venias to "exceptional cases" and only after "a personal interview with the judge" to assess the minor's best interests. Art. 169 outlined how parents (or other legal guardians) could justify their opposition to teen marriages, which included the minor's "psychological immaturity," or the suitor having "communicable diseases," "grave physical deficiencies," displaying "disorderly or immoral conduct," or demonstrating a "lack of livelihood." These provisions in the civil code both strengthened patriarchy by bestowing on fathers and legal guardians the power to control the intimate choices of their offspring, but it also made their patriarchal rights subordinate to the state.

The subordination of parental authority to the state was contingent on the specifics of each case. Location seems to have played an important role in how judges inserted themselves in family conflicts. For example, in Buenos Aires, judges seemed to be hesitant to override parental opposition to marriages, as Juandrea Bates finds for the 1869–1920 period, since judges were "committed to the ideas of minority and family embedded in the Civil Code."[23] Patagonian judges were less hesitant than their counterparts elsewhere, probably because of the high incidence of "orphaned" children following the military occupation, as discussed in chapter 2, and because they, too, saw themselves as being "in the business of propagating legitimate unions" in a space that had historically favored informal arrangements.

Camila Pérez understood that by running away she was activating an "alternate patriarch." The judge had the power to change her father's mind directly or indirectly on the issue, removing her fate from the domestic sphere and making it a public issue. A series of legal and cultural changes in the late nineteenth century eroded traditional family structures: urbanization and industrialization resulted in young women entering the workforce and leaving their rural towns, the rise in consumer culture and relative affluence gave women more financial independence, and the passage of new civil codes narrowed the power of fathers. The weakening of traditional patriarchy resulted in other institutions and actors assuming for themselves the role of "fathers" who both disciplined and protected women.

This "new patriarchy" was insidious and diffused, taking different shapes elsewhere in Latin America. It could take the form of factory managers imposing curfews for their single female employees to protect the "virtue of our girls," which was "superior to the buildings, the machines, the company's shares." One factory in Colombia, for example, urged female workers to "help, surround, and protect" any "workmate in danger" with the "same zeal that men would use in extinguishing a fire."[24] In the large El Teniente copper mine in Chile, miners and mine operators supported a system that turned single female workers into housewives, by policing female sexuality, encouraging "family wage" for men, and promoting nuclear households for all employees.[25] In the Brazilian northeast, Bahian physicians founded a Childhood Protection and Assistance Institute in 1903 to attempt to alleviate what they saw as the major failing of Brazil's poor mothers: the abhorrently high infant mortality rates, which hovered about 30 percent. These modernizing health-care centers, Okezi Otovo shows, offered programs "catered exclusively to married poor women" insisting on traditional, subordinate, and disciplined female roles for new mothers. Physicians and public health officials in Brazil and elsewhere tried to "influence poor families' childrearing practices," effectively introducing their institutions into family life.[26] In Buenos Aires, magazines in the 1910s and 1920s, celebrated the independence of single working women while offering advice on how to "transition smoothly from modern working girl to married woman." One advice columnist at the time chastised one of her readers for pursuing "a man of higher social status" since "he would never abandon his social circle and she would never be accepted in it."[27] Northern Patagonia did not have modern factories, glitzy social magazines, large mines, or public health facilities—but it had judges.

Elopement cases provide a treasure trove of information to better understand how family relationships affected, and in turn were affected by, the frontier state. Argentine law allowed fathers a great deal of power in determining their children's intimate partners, but daughters could upend that power in a few ways. Because patriarchal expectations of "controlling" their household forced fathers to request help from the police to make their families whole when daughters ran away, the young women had a reliable way of making a private matter very public. In other words, by running away minors used patriarchal expectations against their parents, bringing in alternate patriarchs, like judges, to mediate. Calling on judges to help secure marriage partners might not seem like an intrinsically rebellious thing for a teenager to do, but these minors were exercising agency, as rejection of one set of authority figures often means embracing others, as Susan A. Miller argues when studying youth participation in patriotic association.[28] As fathers played a smaller legal and social role in the maintenance of order in their households, other agents rushed to fill in the space. In short, Camila Pérez ran away with the confidence that northern Patagonian judges would likely assume the role of patriarch, overriding parents whose stubborn opposition to an adequate marriage would harm society by forcing the couple (and their offspring) into illegitimacy.

Parents objected to their daughter's choice of intimate partner for an array of idiosyncratic and paternalistic reasons, but mostly because of economic concerns. When Serafín Guillermo found out that his daughter Ángela had "romantic encounters" with Manuel Martínez, he immediately tried to prevent the young couple from seeing each other. Serafín Guillermo considered that Martínez was a bad match "since he did not have any earthly possessions" and was not "inclined toward work" ("no es afecto al trabajo"). Ángela Guillermo responded to her father's refusal by abandoning her eight-year-old sister in town one day while running errands, and spending the night in Martínez's shack on a nearby island, El Manzano. Ángela Guillermo's daring stunt had defeated her father, who continued refusing his consent to the marriage even as he admitted that "given what has happened, I don't believe that I will have influence over my daughter, who might relapse, which I wish to avoid at all costs," asking the court to place her under their care.

Fathers and guardians offered an array of reasons to oppose their daughter's marriage choices. For example, Guillermo Guerra, explained that he opposed his daughter Edubina's marriage because he considered her choice in partner, Martín Antemil "to be indigenous" ("es de origen indígena"). Although it was not a legally valid reason to oppose a marriage in Argentina, Guerra argued that it was a valid reason to oppose a marriage in his native Chile. Others seemed to have understood that their main legal redoubt to object to their underage daughters' marriage choices was to impute the intimate partner's economic status. When Margarita Soto tried to block her daughter's relationship with her suitor, she cited his age and lack of resources (as well as his criminal past) to justify her decision. Manuel Pérez refused to allow his daughter Camila to marry because her suitor was not as wealthy as himself. Paula Antemil was rebuffed in her desires to pursue a relationship with Valentín Paredes because her mother thought that he was not serious about marriage—the middle-aged farmer claimed that he could not marry her "at the moment" since he had too much travel and too many business concerns. María Briselda Arraigada blocked her daughter Mercedes's courtship with Gabino Ramírez because he refused to continue supporting the mother. Teresa del Carmen Garabito and Rodolfo Cercera Arraigada ran away a few weeks from their expected marriage date, even though they had her mother Hermogene Garabito's consent to marry, because the couple feared that her father would suddenly object, given that he was "very uptight" (*muy nervioso*).[29] These examples align with what the civil code laid out in Art. 169 listing the reasons by which parents (or other legal guardians) could justify their opposition to their underage children's marriages, which included "demonstrating a lack of livelihood" ("la falta de medios de subsistencia"). Of course, for teens willing to engage in the frontier's elopement ritual, a parent's refusal was not the end of their quest.

For young women like Mercedes Arraigada, a poor, uneducated domestic servant in a remote and rugged frontier hamlet, access to a judge that could override her mother's refusal to allow her to marry her intimate partner was almost impossible to secure. Most rural hamlets, like Piedra del Águila was, were a good two hundred kilometers (about a hundred and thirty miles) from the nearest judge, an insurmountable obstacle.[30] Her mother, María, had urged her to have intimate relations with Gabino Ramírez and had used the relationship to secure housing for herself. Ramírez recalled taking them in because "he felt sorry for the misery and hunger" that family was experiencing, arranging with his employer to allow the woman, and her three underage daughters, to live in the room he rented. They lived with him for almost an entire year. After María Arraigada refused permission for the couple to marry, Ramírez kicked the woman out of his house for "living a life of dubious morality . . . and living a licentious life." In retaliation, María Arraigada placed her daughter far away in the care of Juan Rodríguez.

Beyond a petty retaliation, her actions suggest an effort to retain control of an economic asset—her daughter's sexuality. As long as Mercedes Arraigada was unmarried, her single mother retained parental rights over her and could attempt to "encourage" her to find a new intimate partner that could provide for her entire family, since Gabino Ramírez had attempted to separate the girl from her. Isolated and feeling used, Mercedes Arraigada had few recourses available to her. Running away from home, and forcing the mother to mobilize the state to find her, was the only way for young women like her to expand their personal autonomy in selecting intimate partners.

Camila Pérez had lived most of her life on the frontier, but her father had not—he had emigrated from Spain as an impoverished young boy who had never met his own father. Immigrants from Europe to Argentina during the great migratory waves of the late nineteenth and early twentieth centuries, like don Manuel Pérez, brought with them cultural practices that often mirrored the ones in their adoptive countries. For example, as Donna Guy finds, "in Europe, rural sexual customs among some peasants included premarital sex and childbearing as a sign of fertility, while in the Argentine countryside abduction of women was a prelude to consensual marriage."[31] Similarly to elsewhere in Latin America at this time "marriage might have been an ideal for elite and poor alike, but consensual unions were likely the norm" in areas of weak state presence.[32] A century earlier, in southern Buenos Aires "the nuclear family was the survival unit of the frontier," which often included "stable concubinage and common-law marriages" that outsiders found "licentious." What to statesmen and outsiders seemed like a haphazard, casual organization was instead an expediency of life in precarity, since "for most men taking a 'wife' meant setting up an independent household, [as] unmarried adult children, regardless of age, continued to live with their parents."[33] For northern Patagonian families, concubinage, rather than formal marriage, was a common way for couples to establish households, despite the state's desire for legally sanctioned unions.

Besides the cultural acceptance of informal family arrangements, Camila Pérez could expect her father to recognize the "script" of elopement she was enacting because it was a familiar courtship practice. This particular "frontier script" combined indigenous traditions like the mock kidnappings, as well as European peasant traditions like premarital sex as a harbinger of fertility. According to historian Richard Slatta, the frontier poor "relied on folk rather than legal and religious rituals of marriage" for most of the nineteenth century. These "folk rituals" that Slatta recounts for early nineteenth-century southern Buenos Aires matched fairly closely the ritual of elopement followed by northern Patagonian couples:

> A man would first indicate his interest in a woman by hiring her to wash his clothing. With the convenient pretext of picking up his laundry, he could visit her at the parental home, drink mate, and socialize with the family. Later he might offer her gifts of sweets, perfume, or trinkets. Parents ostensibly ignored the man's attentions until one day the sweethearts eloped to his house. The "outraged" father rushes to the house and demanded an explanation from the couple. They in turn begged forgiveness and asked his blessing. The farce of seduction and pardon completed, the pair commenced their life together with familial and social sanction.[34]

This "farce of seduction" and pardon was repeated countless times in northern Patagonia over the centuries, with some variance from case to case, and remained a familiar framing device for jóvenes as they asserted their independence in choice of intimate partner.

For example, in the case of Mercedes Oliva, a thirteen-year-old servant who was courted with gifts by Luis Mases, a thirty-one-year-old Spanish merchant, her story followed the familiar pattern. Mases courted Oliva near her home when they met in the streets, gave her presents when he came to visit her guardian, and patiently seduced her.[35] Under duress Mases persuaded Oliva to "prove her love" (*prueba de amor*) by having sex with him in an empty lot next to her guardian's house. After the relationship had been consummated, Mases left her detailed instructions to follow him to a new town after a few weeks—which she did, prompting a police investigation into her "kidnapping." Northern Patagonian jóvenes used the cultural shorthand that their parents would be familiar with to assert their independence and force the parents into a double bind: accept the informal arrangement or surrender their parental rights to the state.

Although elopement could easily result in young women forcing their parents to agree to their choice of intimate partner, the process did carry some risk: like the minors in chapter 3, they could find themselves institutionalized under the care of the state or a prominent family (with all the accompanying effects on reputation, employment, and dislocation) or they could find that their intimate partners were less committed than they had seemed. For example, Camila Pérez's gambit was a safe one—safer than for most Patagonian young women. Her father, who brandished the outdated title of "Don" in legal documents, did not want to make a public spectacle of his daughter's rebellion. As he told police, he considered his daughter's elopement a "private crime" and one that he hoped they would investigate "completely quietly" given his "personal standing." She could expect her father to acquiesce rather than have her detained. Even if Camila Pérez was certain that her father would buckle before allowing her to be placed under the care of the state "like a criminal," her gambit still carried a social risk. The unwanted police attention could have ended up alienating Fermín Agüero, whose resolve to marry might have wavered once the stakes of the elopement became higher, leaving her with a damaged reputation besides a broken heart. There was always the possibility that her father would not accept her back to the family home, which would have placed her in the care of a prominent family or in a state-run institution.

For some, detention was preferable to the tyranny of their parents. Aida del Carmen Cabrera, who ran away with her intimate partner, Alberto Álvarez (an older carpenter employed by the state-owned oil company YPF), after her mother refused to consent to their marriage, happily accepted state custody to get her way.[36] Cabrera's mother, Margarita Soto, who exercised patria potestad over the minor, refused to let the couple marry. She objected because Álvarez, who had spent the previous two years in jail for arson, was poor and much older.[37] Soto had placed the girl as a servant in don Banazar's house, with clear instructions to

FIGURE 13. "Declaraciones en la puerta de casa, 1936" (AGN-Ddf, Inventario 140985). This staged scene of rural courtship is similar to those in northern Patagonia.

"curtail her wanderings beyond what was necessary for her obligations." A few weeks later, don Banazar's wife informed Soto that her daughter had not returned home the previous night, suspecting that she had gone out to the movies with Álvarez. The police quickly found them and detained them, under the assumption that Álvarez had kidnapped and abused the minor.

Cabrera had not been kidnapped; she had asked Álvarez to take her to a hotel rather than return to the Banazar household because she had found it to be "too much work" for "too little pay" ("demasiado trabajo, poca plata"). The couple decided to move into a more permanent room to live a "married life" as concubines until she was old enough to marry without parental consent. After her deposition, Aida Cabrera refused to be discharged to her mother's care since she felt "abandoned" by her mother, asking the state to find a different place for her to live—most likely the depósito de mujeres or a prominent home in Neuquén—since she remained committed to marrying Álvarez. Notified of her daughter's desire not to return home under any circumstances, Soto relented. Given "what had already happened" ("ante los hechos consumados") she reluctantly gave the couple permission to marry. The police escorted the couple (still under arrest) to the justice of the peace in Neuquén, and once they were married the police released them, ending the case.

Ultimately, Camila Pérez's strategy paid off. Her understanding of her family's standing in the community limited her risk: she counted on her father's distaste for public spectacle to work on her behalf. Her family's position in society added a further safety net—her father would most likely accept the "bad match" for her instead of escalating the power struggle by refusing permission and placing her as a domestic servant in the home of another prominent neighbor. Everyone involved in these fuga cases (fathers, daughters, partners, and judges) seemed aware of the tension added to the patriarchal bonds by the minor's decision to run away from home and elope. In a seminal study of sexuality and intimacy in nineteenth-century Lima, historian Christine Hunefeldt poses a provocative question: "whether virginity, elopement, abduction, and even rape could be social bargaining chips, by which a woman could obtain money or a maintenance allowance in the name of honor."[38] The next section grapples with her provocation, considering the possibility that "virginity, elopement, and abduction" were more than *social* bargaining chips; they were *political* tools.

Eloping as Politics:
Virginity, Reputation, and Accessing State Power

Running away from home to elope with an intimate partner was a political act by young Patagonian women. In the process of forcing their parents to seek the help of the state to make their households whole again, northern Patagonian minors took part in the creation of a political culture in the region. Their actions shaped how police thought of parental authority, effectively challenging social expectations of appropriate gender roles for both men and women. Jóvenes manifested change in mores and practices by putting themselves in precarious positions, running away from home to force their parents to activate the state in a way that they could not do directly, being women and minors. For these teenage girls and women, the personal was the political in very concrete ways. Historian Joan Scott suggests that by examining how gendered categories were constructed and maintained we could understand how power was manifested in everyday life.[39] To better understand how teenage girls wielded the political power that they had, this section defines political power, looks at how it was deployed, explores the consequences of its deployment for parents and their daughters, and introduces some of the ways in which parents could attempt to counter it.

How could elopement be a political act? Rebellion against parental authority has been used by scholars as a proxy for how republican ideas of independence, self-determination, and equality permeate everyday life. The decades after independence in Latin America provided fertile ground for these kinds of studies. For example, in one of the landmark works of this type, historian Mark Szuchman finds that "youthful rebellion represented changes in the attitudes and mentalities regarding established patterns of deference to authority."[40]

In this view, the formation of republican-inclined individuals came downstream from political changes themselves—as society became more open, young men and women began to assert themselves, using the language of affection in marriage choice to insist on their individuality. In a study of marriage choice in central Mexico, Daniel Haworth flips the argument on its head: the efforts by teenage daughters to override their parent's objections was "an expression of affective individualism," suggesting that choices made from personal preference emerged from the constraints and possibilities of the traditional communal practices.[41] Politics and law changed because individuals, in this case teenage daughters, exerted pressure on them to change.

These framings build on the familiar private sphere/public sphere dichotomy, not unlike how "reputation" was framed in chapter 3: since men had expanded opportunities to assert their individuality through "voting, journalism, and . . . associations," women had to "turn to the private realm of affective relations—that is, to family, friendships, community, and the like" to assert their individuality.[42] However, as Ana Lidia García Peña reminds us, liberal articulations of families as "both natural and as constituent of the political" underscore the artificiality of the public/private spheres.[43] In the context of the northern Patagonian frontier, the manipulation of practices and institutions to achieve a particular personal goal in a public setting made personal choices into political acts—even if these young women did not think of themselves as political beings, they did not espouse any recognizable political philosophy, or behave in a coordinated fashion to effect change. Lack of self-awareness does not preclude political agency, nor does the lack of a radical agenda.[44]

Northern Patagonian teenagers understood the ways in which playing into the "elopement ritual" could result in concrete and immediate results. Consider how eighteen-year-old María Enriqueta Molleni, who was known as "Milonguita" in her neighborhood, explained why she had eloped with her intimate partner Joaquín Utor Guerrero.[45] She explained to the police during their investigation that "they decided to leave the home so that they could receive parental consent, which would not have happened if they had asked in any other way." That is, if the marriage proposal was kept private, the minors had no leverage—they were legally subjected to their parents—but by running away they made the proposal public, forcing the patriarch into a bind. As Susan Socolow argues for the pampean frontier a century earlier, "a woman did not lose her honor as much by giving her virginity to the man she was to marry as she did by failing to marry that man."[46] Molleni seemed keenly aware that her father would agree with that insight, and buckle when challenged with a public loss of honor.

Ángela Guillermo told the police when she was apprehended after running away with her intimate partner that "the only objective has been to force my parents to allow me to marry my boyfriend."[47] Guillermo repeated the phrase "to force them" several times in her deposition, underscoring the marked intentionality of her action, which her intimate partner Manuel also echoed in his deposition: "to force her parents to marry us."[48] Fathers had to cede some of their authority in two critical ways: first, by asking the police to help find a daughter in order to uphold their broader duties to maintain the household whole, and, second, by requesting the state's help they allowed the state to override their refusal to allow the minors to marry. In other words, a father could maintain the illusion of his absolute power over his offspring even as one disappeared from home, or he could exchange that illusory power for the concrete power of knowing that his daughter was safe.

How aware were young women of these constraints faced by patriarchs? A decade earlier and hundreds of miles west in the Andean hamlet of San Martín de los Andes, Edubina Guerra had used similar language to explain why she had absconded from home with her intimate partner, Martín Antemil.[49] Guerra told the police investigator that she "chose to leave, in order to secure permission either from the parents or the courts to marry" since she considered herself "to have the right to marry" whomever she wanted to and not "who I am told to" ("considerarse con el derecho para ella casarse con quien sea de su gusto y no con quien se le imponga"). Her use of the phrase "to have the right to marry" implies a degree of consciousness in her actions (and though the testimonies were highly mediated by the state agents taking the depositions, the awkward phrase construction indicates that Edubina Guerra probably articulated it, or something similar). She explained that her elopement was driven by a desire "to follow the good path that every honorable woman ought to follow" in marriage. Describing herself as someone aspiring to be an "honorable woman" was certainly a pointed choice. It reframed her elopement as a necessary step on the "good path" that she imagined herself to be on, verbalizing an often-unspoken notion. Edubina Guerra's choice of words, from her talk of "rights" to the reference to "honorable paths" seemed intentional, purposefully reframing what the stakes of her challenge were.

Similarly, when María Sara Pintos realized that her father was withdrawing his support of her marriage with Robinson Contreras, "she let Contreras know, and together they decided to leave in order to see if with that, they could get his consent to marry."[50] As far as we can tell these young women arrived at these decisions independently from one another. They lived far from one another, their cases did not reach regional newspapers, but even if they had, regional newspapers did not make it to remote outposts like Cerro Buitre, where María Sara Pintos lived. They shared an insight into the constraints of patriarchy on their fathers and an understanding of their limited rights under the civil code. This shared insight allowed them to project political power from a position of relative weakness to both their fathers and the state, leveraging them against each other.

Patagonian minors were able to use what scholars term the "legal weapons of the weak" created by the patriarchal provisions in the civil code, but they also had to capitulate to "traditional gender norms that undergird law and society by appearing as passive victims" of the courtship.[51] As Sloan pithily puts it, runaway daughters exchanged their virginity for the opportunity to "reorder power relations in [their] families."[52] The practice was not confined to the nineteenth century. For example, in interwar Brazil, when deflowering complaints skyrocketed as urbanization and industrialization reordered traditional sexual mores, young women and their guardians relied on the state to remedy the loss of virginity, usually under implicit promises of marriage.[53] In other words, for teens in northern Patagonia, the success in running away required a delicate balance between the assertiveness of deciding to pursue an intimate relationship against their parents' wishes and maintaining the veneer of respectability since their virginity was a "form of capital" that could be used but was destroyed in the process.

The ritual of elopement was a very compelling force, even when used to pre-empt implicit objections. When fifteen-year-old Humbertina del Carmen Castillo ran away from her grandmother's house in the remote hamlet of Auquinco with twenty-six-year-old Juan de Dios Muñoz, she explained the elopement in straightforward terms.[54] Since her grandmother doña Natividad Venega "always chastised her" for her courtship with Muñoz, the couple ran away to consummate their relationship and marry "if they could get her father's consent." Although the father claimed not to know about the relationship, and the grandmother merely "suspected it," the script of elopement—the courtship, mock kidnapping, and elopement—remained an appealing way to assert agency. It seems clear that even when not entirely necessary, the ritual of elopement was a way to publicly announce independence and adulthood—as a way to claim legitimacy and honor even without parental objections. Both men and women may have used it as a way to perform idealized gendered roles by making men feel like they acted in a masculine manner and women in a feminine one. Whether it was deployed to force a parent or a suitor to consent to marriage, or used as an affirmation of idealized gender roles, the entire script hinged on the minor's ability to appear as chaste. That is to say, the key for this gambit to work—the leverage that the teens had over their parents—was their *perceived* virginity.

Reputation and female chastity—in the guise of virginity—were deeply intertwined in northern Patagonia and elsewhere in Latin America, and elopement cases often hinged on how they were characterized by the community. In mid-nineteenth-century Lima, Peru, "tarnishing a woman's social image and creating suspicions about her honor and good behavior made men look less guilty" of sexual assault or indiscretion. Indeed, "when judging rape, a woman's previous behavior was taken into consideration—if she showed the slightest signs of 'public' life she would be considered morally unworthy."[55] Social attitudes, stretching back to Latin America's colonial legacy, and later liberal civil codes, were geared to protect "honest and chaste" women, but "judging a woman's virginity presented numerous contradictions and interpretations." As a young Peruvian man argued in attempting to justify reneging on a marriage promise after consummating the relationship, he claimed that after "making love to her [he] found her as sleazy as any public woman," which "proved" to him that she was not a virgin, as she had insisted she was.[56] Historian Katheryn Sloan finds that ultimately "women had to make the case that they were worth defending and protecting by asserting their reputation as a virgin."[57] In effect, "once virginity was lost, a woman was worth less because she also lost her social standing and perhaps even the support of her family," according to Christine Hunefeldt.[58] That social isolation presented a liability in a legal context in which reputation in the community was tightly correlated with access to justice.

In Argentina, reputation not only changed people's perceptions within their community, but chastity had a legal dimension as well. Art. 120 of the criminal code, dealing with rape of an underage girl, established a jail sentence of "between three and six years, when the victim was an honest woman between the ages of twelve and fifteen." For men accused of rape, establishing that the victim was not "an honest woman" was central to their defense, as dishonorable women had fewer legal protections. Virginity was a contested social construct because even though police wanted to treat it as a biologically determined objective fact, the process used by the community and the medical examiners was subjective and drew on varied factors. In each case of elopement, and in each accusation of rape or sexual abuse, the court would order a medical examination of the victim, to determine whether they had had sex and how recently. Some of the medical exams were not conducted by medical professionals but by employees of the court, prominent neighbors, and in some instances by midwives.

It would be hard to overstate how invasive, and uncomfortable, these exams must have been for teenage girls (also women and, in a few cases, boys) since they were done far from their homes, in isolation, and in the context of a criminal proceeding. The medical report usually included absurd levels of specificity, interspersed with moralizing assessments of the minors. For example, when the court wanted to determine whether Juana Tejero, a fifteen-year-old from the village of Los Menucos, had "casual concubinage" with the director of her school, Feliciano Cabrera, as she alleged and he denied, it ordered a medical exam of her genitals. Since no doctor served that area, one was ordered to come against his will from the nearest town. Noticeably unhappy about the request, Dr. José Novoa blamed "the girl's lack of gynecological hygiene" for his inability to determine when the hymen had been damaged. Ultimately, he reported that she had "been deflowered between six and eight days" earlier, but insisted that it was hard for him to categorically determine it since the "bad hygiene" had resulted in "erosions on the inner labia." With an inconclusive medical report, the school director and the teen's father began hurling accusations at each other to try to establish her reputation in town.[59] The contextual details about the young woman's life contributed to the "socially constructed" part of how virginity was determined in northern Patagonia.

Contests over a teenage girl's virginity could lead to contradictory arguments, as people tried to frame the issue in a way that proved advantageous to them. As it was elsewhere in Latin America at the time, "sex and virginity were essential ingredients in the cultural manipulation of marriage" as Christine Hunefeldt finds in Peru. In fact, she argues that "from a woman's point of view, the loss of virginity could become a legal weapon to demand reparation and support, if not marriage."[60] In northern Patagonia, conflicts over the virginity of jóvenes were similarly wrapped up with marriage implications. Consider the fallout from the inconclusive case of Juana Tejero's allegations against the school director, Feliciano Cabrera, in Los Menucos, that he had scandalously deflowered her on school property. Tejero's father and Cabrera fought very publicly for months in court, in the streets, and even in regional newspapers, as the father insisted that Cabrera "seduced her with praise" and "promises of marriage." It was an ironic twist: to preserve his daughter's reputation, he had to argue that she had had sexual relations with Cabrera. For his part, Cabrera maintained that he was being set up by the Tejero family, who wanted to force a marriage on him. He argued that the teen was chaste, had always been chaste, and that these allegations were out of character for her, to continue to raise suspicions that it was a setup.

Elsewhere, Adolfo Leon D'Archary—the rhetorically flamboyant and prolific defense attorney for Marcelino Vázquez, accused of kidnapping and attempting to rape his thirteen-year-old niece—found himself redefining virginity in a way that exculpated his client. He argued simultaneously that the teen was not "successfully" raped because she resisted, but that she was "not an honest woman" because "her insinuating and youthful flesh" had tempted his client into wanting to marry her. The defense was left to argue that "it is so easy, so common, in the fields of these desolate territories, to find suspicious virginities.... Your Honor is wisely aware of how female adolescence develops in these remote regions of the country ... the social criteria have to be different from the one applied in other, more cultured, regions of our country."[61] D'Archary's meaning is not entirely clear but three things in particular that he mentions bare further analysis.

First, he seems to suggest that the "desolation" of northern Patagonia made it hard for men to ascertain women's sexuality, perhaps tying sexual development not with age but with early onset of adult-like duties in the workforce and the home. He might have been referring to how boys and girls were thrust into adulthood earlier than in the cities, through physical labor, exposure to violence, and poverty, and how that pushed them to form independent households at an earlier age. The second phrase that calls out was his advocating for different "social criteria" to judge sexual crimes. Perhaps this was an argument stemming from the relative absence of unmarried women older than twenty, which distorted courtship of jóvenes as other cases in this chapter aptly illustrate. Last, his mention of northern Patagonia's lack of "culture" echoed familiar articulations of the frontier as a source of barbarism, as a place where the landscape and the precarity devolved human behavior to a more primitive state. Regardless of his exact meaning, the attorney was advocating for some sort of frontier exceptionalism. In D'Archary's formulation, virginity was not only a social construct but also one that was specific to each location. For his legal needs it was an objective medical fact when it exonerated his client, and it was a matter of social perception when it absolved him. Reputation was central to the access of justice, as chapter 3 discussed, and the reputation of teenagers was not the exception.

Once it became "public and notorious" that a joven did not lead a chaste life, her standing in the community changed—her political power diminished. For example, consider the case of sixteen-year-old María Domínguez, whose poor reputation in town led the investigator to dismiss the idea that a pregnant young woman could have been kidnapped at all.[62] Domínguez lived in a room with her mother, Inés Fornagueira (who was single, thirty-six years old, and illiterate), in the house of a prominent family in General Roca, where they both worked. María Domínguez had been having "amorous relations" with José Carró (a twenty-four-year-old Spanish-born mechanic) for over a year, after they met in a hotel where the women had worked earlier. On the morning of 17 January 1922, Fornagueira reported her daughter missing to the police, identifying Carró as the likely kidnapper. Challenging the notion that he had kidnapped her, José Carró surrendered himself to the police immediately and explained that he was surprised when his intimate partner showed up at his doorstep. He adamantly insisted that he had not instigated her to run away when she did, but that he had "always intended" for her to live with him, even though the baby she was carrying pre-dated their relationship. When justifying his reason for ending the investigation without further inquiries into Carró and Domínguez's relationship, the investigator wrote in his summary to the prosecutor that "without a doubt, given that it is public and notorious that María Domínguez has had marital relations with lowlifes ("sujetos de baja valía") she did not need any encouragement to go to Carró's house."[63] Maria Domínguez's lack of a father, and her residence in a hotel might have coded her as "public woman" meaning that if she had been kidnapped, the local police clearly believed that burden of proof sat squarely with her.

Similarly, when Paula Antemil left home to live with her intimate partner, Valentín Paredes, in his hotel room, her mother filed the complaint as a kidnapping.[64] To assure the police that he had not kidnapped her, Paredes shifted the focus of the investigation back to the women and their reputation in town. Paredes (a forty-four-year-old farmer from Cinco Chañares) claimed, with some pride, that he had no reason to pressure the teen to run away from home since "he could always come by the house, where [he] had ample freedom and opportunities to abuse of her honesty without needing to remove her from the house, particularly since [he] and Paula's mother, María Rial, used to lead a married life."[65] The police took the bait, asking neighbors to share their assessment of the mother and daughter. One witness recalled seeing Antemil answer the door without pants when she knew it was Valentín who was calling. On a different occasion, the witness added, he went to pick up Valentín from Paula's house and found the couple still in bed together, as her mother sat a few feet away at the kitchen table having breakfast. Not only did Paula Antemil's fuga backfire, because her intimate partner refused to marry her, especially after all the unwanted police attention, but it became further "notorious and public" in the neighborhood that she did not lead a chaste life.

Likewise, when a seventeen-year-old from the remote district of Las Minas, accused a neighbor of violently raping her in a field one afternoon while all the adults were away, the investigation focused on her sexual history.[66] The medical examiners, two "distinguished neighbors" appointed to the task summarized that "it was not the first, or second, time she had intercourse since she is a woman that has had carnal life." The defense attorney doubled down, arguing that "it is public and notorious that the alleged victim, who lives a licentious life, consented to the natural act, as she often does." The judge agreed. Just like it was the case with Paula Antemil and Maria Domínguez (and countless other jóvenes), her reputation not only affected their current cases, but they also limited the kind of justice she could expect to receive moving forward.

Marriage choices, one of the most common aspects of most minors' passage to adulthood, provided legal minors with an avenue to exert control over their lives. As much as contests over marriage choice allowed young women to chip away at the power of the males in their lives, it also resulted in contentious public conflicts over virginity and worthiness. Because the law was geared to protecting victims who could demonstrate "honor," female sexuality remained a contested matter of public interest. For teens, maintaining the perception of chastity was central to their ability to exercise political power on the frontier. That is, their public power to affect how family and state agents reacted to them was tied intimately with the reputation they could maintain in their communities. The backdrop of latent sexual violence and scarcity made it particularly difficult.

Beyond "Agency": Marriage Choice in a Violent Setting

The cases in this chapter, under the broad umbrella of fugas, encompass a wide range of behaviors and ages. The heterogeneity of experiences makes it hard to generalize. In fact, there seem to be at least three ways to conceptualize these fugas. The first frames them as contests between two men, father and intimate partner, over young women. This framework places jóvenes as the passive victims of oppressive structures, as "tokens" being exchanged or transacted. The second conceptualizes them as a way for girls and young women to use the expectations of sexual propriety and passivity placed on them by society to bypass the power of their parents to control their intimate lives. This framework places these jóvenes as agents of their own fate, capable of exerting free will, and wielding political power by manipulating the state to their advantage. Running away from home with a lover, quite plainly, was the only way for many young women and girls to escape from poverty, abuse, and privation in the rural hinterlands. There are some cases, however, in which the particular circumstances surrounding the fuga make it harder to celebrate it as a triumph of agency. This last framework in which jóvenes are neither passive victims nor active agents, invites us to consider the limits and significance of "agency" as category of analysis.

This is not a new question. Critical reappraisals of agency in the last two decades have taken place within gender history, the history of childhood, and the history of slavery. These reappraisals have focused on the context in which people make choices, the paradox of agency as conformity, and the dangers of allowing agency to become a stand-in for speaking of someone's humanity in the face of systems of oppression. Historians of gender have been reassessing the centrality of agency as the be-all and end-all of social history. For example, Androniki Dialeti warned that "overstressing female agency entails the risk of producing an idealized depiction of female communities, networks and relations, diminishing or naturalizing power relations."[67] That is, to emphasize the agency of jóvenes in choosing a marriage partner against their parents' wishes risks ignoring the (limited) choices they could have made that did not ultimately conform to existing gendered roles. Put differently, we should reaffirm that agency does not operate in a vacuum.

Here we can borrow from Karl Marx's observation in *The Eighteenth Brumaire of Louis Bonaparte*. In an oft-quoted passage, Marx noted that people "make their own history, but they do not make it just as they please in circumstances they choose for themselves; rather they make it in present circumstances, given and inherited. Tradition from all the dead generations weighs like a nightmare on the brain of the living."[68] Choices, big and small, have always been made within the context of what the people making them thought was possible, what their peers expected, and what they understood to be the consequences. In the northern Patagonian context, girls, teens, and young women made choices about their intimate partners to start a household in precarious conditions, under the specter of sexual violence, and in an environment of demographic gender imbalances.

In some instances, agency is indistinguishable from conformity. This is particularly relevant when people's choices do not entail revolutionary change of the systems of oppression, but rather focus on accommodation and survival. Historians of gender who overemphasize agency in contexts of hegemonic control, according to Dialeti, have resulted in a "paradoxical identification of agency with conformity."[69] Historians of childhood have also grappled with this question in recent years. Scholars like Susan Miller have urged us to think about the ways in which "children willingly conform to adult agendas, not necessarily because youth acquiesce to power, but because their interests often align with those promoted by adults." Miller encourages us to think of childhood agency as a "continuum from opposition to assent."[70]

In a zeal to "liberate" children from the condescension of history, scholars of childhood sometimes fall into the "agency ideal" trap, as defined by Mona Gleason. She warns that the "imperative to focus upon youthful autonomy and resistance as the main interpretative goal" results in the exclusion of other aspects of children's agentic behavior.[71] That is, understanding the role jóvenes played in the legitimization of frontier institutions entails a critical appraisal of how they understood their own actions and the practical processes through which those actions provided new ways to think about choice, exploitation, and love. In other words, it encourages us to not only tell stories *through* the lives of jóvenes but also *about* jóvenes—even if they are stories that conform to broader expectations, like married life as the only path out of poverty for young women on the frontier.

Scholars have also warned against reducing people's lived experiences to the choices they made and failed to make. It has been easy for scholars to fall back on what Lynn Thomas criticized as "agency as the argument," or to "unthinkingly deploy" agency, turning the concept from a tool or starting point to a concluding argument.[72] Historians of slavery have similarly grappled with how to assess the agency of enslaved people. As Walter Johnson put it, historians ought to "imagine a history of slavery which sees the lives of enslaved people as powerfully conditioned by, though not reducible to, their slavery."[73] Johnson observed that the emphasis on agency becomes a shorthand for classic liberal notions of autonomy, independence, and the supreme value of choice as the defining characteristics of humanity. That is, the quest to find agency in enslaved people becomes an empathetic device to reaffirm our shared humanity with them, one which also "reduced historically and culturally situated acts of resistance to manifestations of a larger, abstract human capacity" for agency.

Indeed, we could reframe Johnson in the context of teenagers in northern Patagonia and consider their lives "powerfully conditioned" by patriarchy without them being reduced to mechanically acting the role prescribed for them. This echoes Joan Scott's argument that understanding the processes and structures of social power, like patriarchy, still allows for "a concept of human agency as an attempt to construct an identity, a life, a set of relationships, a society with certain limits and with language . . . that sets boundaries and contains the possibilities for negation, resistance, and reinterpretation, the play of metaphoric invention and imagination."[74] We can reconstruct the circumstances that framed a particular fuga—the incentives, pressures, and rewards for that given choice—but we can only speculate about the meaning of that choice—how it made her feel, what value she extracted from it, and the significance of overcoming the objections of her parents.

To make this less abstract, consider what happened to Mercedes Oliva, "a child of just thirteen or fourteen" who was seduced, pressured into clandestine sexual intercourse, and removed from her guardian's home by Luis Mases, a traveling salesman in his thirties. Mercedes Oliva's neighbors and the police framed her odyssey in terms of "male domination and female objectification": she was a victim of contest within patriarchy, with an older male "stealing" her from her guardian.[75] Mercedes Oliva herself attempted to present her story in a way that highlighted her own agency: she saw herself as an active individual making an intentional set of choices to start an independent household with a successful merchant. She acted as someone making the best choice possible when the opportunity presented.

It is hard to overlook, however, the inherent power difference in their relationship. He was older, literate, wealthier, able to purchase gifts for her, and promise a financially secure future. He had traveled across the Atlantic from his native Spain, and throughout Argentina before arriving to northern Patagonia. On the other hand, she was barely a teenager—a "child" in the police complaint—who was left at a young age in the care of a stranger, Tomás Cueto. Cueto, a successful Spanish merchant himself, claimed to love her like a daughter, but she was willing to leave his care in the middle of the night with just a terse note. She had never left the town she had been born in, owned nothing except a bundle of clothes, and had recently had a violent and traumatic sexual encounter, as described by the medical examiner.

The police rallied to her defense, punishing Mases for his transgression by keeping him in jail for a month, without charging him with any crimes, or elevating his case to the judge—an example of the kind of informal arrangements that chapter 5 explores. One of the neighbors testified that Mases offered to give him Mercedes Oliva "as a servant," which echoed the treatment of indigenous children discussed in chapter 2. Mases denied everything—he claimed to only have seen the girl when he delivered sodas for her guardian's business. In an irate letter, he threatened the judge that he would withdraw his investment in a soda factory because the police had allowed the minor's allegations to "gravely threaten to alter the harmony of social relations." A prosecutor who picked up the case two years after the complaint was filed wondered rhetorically if the state should continue to pursue the case given that "the victim had requested permission to marry *another*, which the judge granted."

Was Mercedes Oliva a victim of patriarchal institutions and expectations that compelled women to remain in a state of legal minority through guardianships, and later marriage? Or was she a savvy operator, slow playing a courtship with a promising entrepreneur, securing for herself a comfortable life outside of the destitution of her youth with a well-timed sexual intercourse? A satisfactory answer remains unknowable. It is certainly true that social expectations and the violence of her youth stacked the deck toward early marriage—even after the events with Mases, she married before she was fifteen. It is also true that in a world of bad options Oliva took initiative, welcoming the merchant's advances, denying him sexual intercourse until she was certain that his promises would be kept, and securing a train ticket out of town.

It is also true that her prospective husband might have wanted to marry her in order to place her somewhere as a servant to supplement his own income, and that after the events with Mases she faced mounting pressure to marry *anyone*, lest her standing in town continue to deteriorate. Romantic relationships between girls and much older men were common in northern Patagonia, where about half of the female population was under the age of fourteen. As Camilla Townsend argued when reconstructing the choices available to indigenous women during the Spanish conquest of the sixteenth century, "they survived the most trying of circumstances with as much dignity as they could muster . . . they are never seen in all their complexity, as the real people they once were."[76] Relationships with much older men represented one of the only avenues out of poverty for jóvenes that found themselves thricely marginalized: by their gender, their minority, and their ruralness.[77]

Did Mercedes Oliva have agency? Certainly. But what does that tell us about gender relations on the frontier and the choices available to her? Not much at all, and it further risks only valorizing contributions to history of young people like her when they acted recognizably as adults. Ultimately, when faced with inconclusive and contradictory fragments of information, historians, as Lynn Thomas urges us, have to "attend to the multiple motivations that undergird meaningful action, motivations that exceed rational calculation and articulated intentions to include collective fantasies, psychical desires and struggles just to get by."[78] To echo what Mona Gleason articulates for a different frontier setting: only when historians engage with the complexity of little lives and move toward a "nuanced engagement with agency and age as relational, contextual and constitutive of unequal relations of power" will we fully understand their role as architects of historical change.[79] Those unequal relations of power between jóvenes and their intimate partners, and the choices they elicited from the less powerful individuals, remain at the heart of our understanding of why and how things change. That might be a tall task, but a necessary one if we hope to understand not only their world but also how it continues to affect people today.

Conclusions

If, as Marx suggested, "the tradition of all the dead generations weighs like a nightmare on the brain of the living," we have not realized that we are still asleep. Argentina finally repealed Art. 132 of the criminal code—the one concerning *avenimiento*, the provision which allowed for rapists to avoid further criminal punishment if they married their victims—in 2012. The law was repealed following the brutal murder of Carla Figueroa, in the northern Patagonian town of General Pico, the previous year.[80]

Nineteen-year-old Carla Figueroa was stabbed to death eleven times by her brand-new husband, Marcelo Tomaselli. Tomaselli had raped Figueroa at knifepoint the previous year, and was serving a lengthy prison sentence, when Figueroa, under duress, agreed to marry him, enabling the legal "conciliation." Within a week of his release, he murdered Figueroa in their shared home in northern Patagonia, in front of their two-year old child.[81] It would not be hard to imagine a future historical account highlighting Figueroa's agency in deciding to marry her assailant to take ownership of her life. But that she had a choice is the least interesting thing about her story—or the stories of all the other young women in this chapter.

Throughout Latin America, and especially in Argentina, civil and criminal codes have been revised to promote and protect gender equality. At the same time, the country has seen an increase in feminicides, domestic violence, and state complicity in promoting impunity measures for the perpetrators. The capacity for women to exercise agency, to act politically in matters big and small, runs into a relentless patriarchy that refuses to recede.

Indeed, the past is never dead, and it is not even past.

"The Most Respectable Neighbors"

Vecinos and Local Politics

The territories don't need anything more than good justice and heavy policing.
—Manuel Láinez, senator from Buenos Aires, arguing in 1907 against a
spending bill for Patagonian infrastructure.[1]

I invite all of those who were born here or adopted it as a home to show
their affection for this homeland. . . . I invite everyone, manual laborers and
thinkers, humble homesteaders and wealthy ranchers, professionals, teachers,
students, established *vecinos*, travelers and tourists, state-employees, civilians
and military, so that together they celebrate [the anniversary of the Argentine
flag being raised in Nahuel Huapi for the first time] . . . since remembering
glorious events is not about politics . . . nor it affirms political agendas.
—Primo Capraro, speech delivered in 1932 to commemorate the 1881
raising of the Argentine flag by General Conrado Villegas on the shores of
the Nahuel Huapi Lake.[2]

I n 1924, in the Andean agricultural town of San Carlos de Bariloche, a group of
successful immigrant merchants lodged a complaint against the local police.
They claimed that the Comisario Guillermo Schultz had ordered an officer
and a convict to unceremoniously drag the body of a recently deceased teenager,
Laura Haneck, through the streets of the town as a vendetta against the teen's
father.[3] The complaint was spearheaded by Evaristo Gallardo, a Chilean merchant
who a few years later would be part of the first elected municipal government in
Bariloche. The complaint was backed by several other foreign-born settlers (mostly
Spaniards and Chileans, but also Italians and Germans) including breeders, peons,
and merchants. When confronted with the accusation during an investigation into

the complaint, Comisario Schultz framed the incident more mundanely: following an order from a judge, he sent his only officer to exhume the body, but lacking any tools or transports, he asked a convict to help out. According to Schultz, the two men were forced to improvise because neither the state nor the community had properly provisioned the police force with wheelbarrows, carts, or even horses.

The testimonies by the settlers labeled the incident as an "inhumane act in this *pueblo culto*" ("civilized town" but also "civilized people"). The almost thirty settlers interviewed by the investigator used very similar phrases to express their outrage, suggesting a complex level of coordination among the neighbors. To them, the police's behavior was aggravated because it disrespected one of the town's founding fathers, Herman Haneck—he had arrived to the region as the teenage cook for the border commission and had received land as a reward for his services. The idea that immigrants and their families were some of the "original settlers" of the northern Patagonia might sound ridiculous to the indigenous people of the region, but it carried considerable weight in the minds of fellow settlers. In a young town like Bariloche, the creation of a "pantheon" of town elders, people whose lives became enshrined and whose experiences of the frontier were a self-validating mythology, was a decisively political act that elevated some members of the community while erasing others. Hence, the desecration of that particular corpse, they insisted, went against "the culture of the *pueblo*."[4] The perception that the police had not respected one of the "original" families was a political undermining of the town's self-construction as a pueblo culto.

In fact, this chapter argues, settlers came together under the identity of vecinos (neighbors) to challenge how the police operated in their communities, to attempt to mobilize police for their own economic and political goals, and to articulate an informal political vision that built on the state project but diverged from it in important ways. The relationship was central to the working of the state, and it was fragile. Consider how Comisario Schulz explained that the officer had no choice but to "drag" the casket through town because the community had failed to lend the police a wheelbarrow or a wagon to carry the casket from the cemetery. In other words, we should understand the community's unwillingness to provide needed supplies to the police as an indication of a much deeper schism in the town. The Argentine government delegated the responsibility for supporting and maintaining the police to the vecinos, who seized on that opportunity to either co-opt the police as their own personal tool or to challenge how the police behaved. The circumstances of semicolonial rule in northern Patagonia (appointed rather than elected authorities, scant resources to support local state functions, and an emphasis on economic development at the expense of political structures) helped turn the financial success of some settlers into effective political power.

The patronage of police and judges by vecinos was certainly self-serving, but it was also essential in buttressing a fledging colonial order in northern Patagonia by creating a class of people in small towns that had a vested interest in the success of the state's project in northern Patagonia. In other words, the decentralization of the maintenance of order in a frontier setting resulted in abuses and petty power struggles, but also in a lived-in practice of citizenship (assessing municipal priorities, mobilizing communal actions, supporting, supplying, and regulating state representatives), which helped turn settlers into citizens.

Drawing from a wide variety of criminal court cases, from complaints and grievances to thefts and malfeasance, this chapter reconstructs the ways vecinos related to the state agents around them, the tools available to them to control those agents, and the effects of this power on the growing state presence in Patagonia at a time of dramatic change. The vecino identity was consciously cosmopolitan: it turned a heterogenous mix of immigrants and settlers into a cohesive political unit. It was the dominant political discourse through the 1910s and 1920s in northern Patagonia, before being challenged by nationalist groups in the 1930s. A concerted effort by nationalist groups in the second half of the 1920s resulted in challenges to the power of the vecinos in the region, ushering the end of this ad hoc political identity.

Vecinos in Northern Patagonia

Vecino politics emerged out of a specific historical context. The cases in this chapter focus on mostly foreign-born settlers living in small towns and villages, between the late 1910s and the mid-1930s. Why limit to those specific groups? There are three reasons for this particular scope. First, small towns and their rural hinterlands have been *especially* understudied in Patagonia, and in frontiers more broadly. In northern Patagonia, where more than 80 percent of settlers lived outside the main cities by the early twentieth century, this means that we still do not really understand how the vast majority of Patagonians experienced political life in this period.[5] The sort of informal arrangements that underpinned political life in northern Patagonia were more salient in small towns because of the absence of any of the formal political institutions available to settlers in the capital cities (elected municipal councils, personal access to governors and judges, partisan press, for example), as discussed in chapter 1. In other words, small towns are more representative of northern Patagonia *and* offer a clearer picture of the interpersonal, informal dimensions of local politics.

Second, immigrants were particularly effective in mobilizing as vecinos in northern Patagonia. The politically charged identity of the vecino was built on the same kinship networks that had brought immigrants to the frontier in the first two decades of the twentieth century and turned their economic success into social and political capital.[6] As Lisandro Gallucci argues, the "image of the *'vecino de arraigo'* [established vecinos] became one of the strongest bulwarks of local political imaginings, while its opposite, the lack of established roots, became one of the most effective ways to undermine the legitimacy of rivals."[7] Although Gallucci observes the phenomenon exclusively in electoral contests, a close analysis of criminal complaints in small northern Patagonian towns without formal political rights suggests it applies there as well. The category of *vecino* was capaciously inclusive for male residents of a town. The documents include a broad spectrum of vecinos, including successful merchants, day laborers, transatlantic immigrants, people from Chile, and indigenous peons. In practice, however, not all vecinos had the same power in the coalition, and not all of them embraced it as fervently.

The first generations that had risked their meager fortunes and their lives to try their luck in the state-sponsored colonization of northern Patagonia had sought to build the scaffolding of civil society in the frontier. Recall that many of the Bariloche vecinos deposed during the investigation into Laura Haneck's exhumation considered her father, Herman Haneck, a noteworthy *compadre* and were appalled that the body was exhumed without family and friends being present. They argued that Haneck did not deserve this affront since he was one of the "original settlers" of the area and had long worked to establish the "culture of the pueblo." Brígida Baeza notes that even as late as the 1970s, Patagonian elites would use the category of "original settler" as a way to differentiate themselves from "outsiders" who had arrived to the region more recently—and these internal differences were materialized in segregated neighborhoods, political access, and economic influence.[8] As discussed in the previous chapters, immigrant elites gained political power in small towns by heading orderly families, avoiding scandals, assisting in the lodging of vulnerable members of the community, and supporting social and cultural institutions. Their reputation held the key to their political power at the municipal level.

Third, the informal arrangements that turned settlers into patrons of the state lasted for only two decades, roughly between 1910 and 1930. These arrangements blossomed in a period of rapid demographic change and lagging state reaction to those changes. Northern Patagonia's population ballooned from almost 25,000 in 1895 to over 71,000 in 1914, plateauing until the late 1920s. New colonization efforts arising from the 1908 Ley de Fomento, which sought to encourage the surveying and sale of public land in the arid central plateau, stimulated the colonization of those areas, which were harder to police effectively given their remoteness, even after the area was serviced by a state-owned railroad. The number of police officers per capita in the region actually declined during the period, going from about 8 police officers per thousand residents in 1914 to about 5 per thousand in 1934. The broad trend of population growth obfuscates the steady increase of Argentine-born settlers as a share of the population. For example, by 1931 in the Territory of Neuquén, Argentine-born settlers outnumbered foreign-born settlers three to one. The continued replacement of immigrants by Argentine-born settlers marginalized the old vecino elite.

Additionally, by the mid-1930s, a series of institutional developments by the nationalist elite in control of the Argentine government during the so-called "Infamous Decade" (a period between 1930 and 1943 characterized by electoral fraud, economic policy advantageous to large landowners, and concession in international relations) greatly increased the state's autonomy in northern Patagonia. For example, when the Nahuel Huapi National Park was established in 1934, it displaced rural dwellers from their suddenly protected forests and rivers, and transformed the agricultural town of Bariloche. Similarly, in the early 1930s, state-run oil towns grew around the oilfields outside Neuquén in Cutral-Có and Plaza Huincul. The nationalist governments of the "Infamous Decade" also presided over massive expansions of roads and bridges that allowed for increased transportation of people and goods, lessening the reliance on local benefactors as well as the construction of police buildings and customs offices, which professionalized the police and increased its independence from vecino patronage.

Our understanding of the ways in which northern Patagonian vecinos aligned politically, and the ways in which they related to the state and its agents, borrows from three broad scholarly trends. First, though they ultimately formed a heterogenous group of professionals, laborers, landowners, artisans, and speculators, vecinos' political outlook was derived from their most prominent members: merchants. Merchants took a leading role coalescing other settlers into self-conscious and politically engaged vecinos. Critics have characterized their political activities as a reflection of their economic standing: "a population that sought to secure their material condition and who leaned on discourses of progress and civilization that allowed them to demand from the state the necessary order."[9]

Their economic success, and the social ramifications of that success, meant that they not only had the means to sponsor and support the state on the frontier, but also could easily mobilize employees, associates, and co-nationals to their political goals. As their peers in other frontier contexts, merchants in northern Patagonia were "more conformist than revolutionary, more backward looking than progressive [and] often defended the status quo," especially when they had a prominent role in that existing order.[10] Recall how Evaristo Gallardo and the vecinos of Bariloche framed their conflict with the police as a defense of the town's "culture" rather than as an issue of governance, financial support, or illegality. In northern Patagonia, the centrality of merchants in civil society infused local politics with their "backward-looking" defense of the status quo—often articulated in abstract liberal, or nationalist terms.

Second, the vecinos of northern Patagonia share some traits with a type of municipal-level citizenship that was typical of the national and popular period in the middle of the twentieth century. That municipal elite emerged from an active, participatory local political life centered in neighborhood associations and a political culture that superseded institutional limits. They organized in the absence of a functional state presence on the edges of booming cities, remaining autonomous through interwar years, until the consolidation of Peronism in the mid-1940s.[11] The key to this novel political culture was the rapid urban growth that cities—in particular Buenos Aires—experienced in the first decades of the twentieth century, as the interaction between skilled workers, shopkeepers, small merchants, tradesmen, and their families resulted in the proliferation of a "dense network of associations" such as community libraries, municipal councils, and an array of political associations. In these accounts a "neighborhood elite" emerged naturally as a response to the shortcomings of the government: a middle class forged in the shared experience of an urban frontier.[12]

This approach builds on a longer tradition of urban popular involvement in high politics that reached as far back as the early independence period.[13]

FIGURE 14. "Gendarmeria Nacional, destacamento de frontera, Chubut 1941" (AGN-Ddf, Inventario #29813). Infrastructure like border crossings proliferated after the 1930s, short-circuiting trans-Andean trade and eroding the power of vecinos.

Urban "plebeians" throughout the nineteenth and twentieth centuries defied the exclusionary politics prescribed by the elites to mobilize, sometimes violently, for political ends or in support of their preferred leaders.[14] Studies of municipal-level political engagement in Buenos Aires, for example, in the 1870s and 1880s have revealed an active political life centered on demonstrations, mobilizations, and "get out the vote" campaigns that prefigure the growth of political involvement and demands for reform in the 1890–1910 period.[15] When scholars of northern Patagonia emphasize the ways in which vecinos coalesced in multiclass alliances to support the functioning of the state, they frame vecino-led politics as a supplement to the state, as an independent constraint on the power of established elites, and as an yet-untapped constituency for emerging political coalitions.[16]

Borrowing from the vast literature on colonial Latin America, a third historiographic tradition conceives of vecinos as elite urban dwellers rather than a counterbalance to them. During the colonial period in Latin America the term referred to elite urban dwellers (people having *calidad*, or honor and status) who thought of themselves as neighborhood leaders, the auxiliaries of state magistrates when they attempted to reform colonial cities.[17] In this context, a vecino was a largely exclusionary identity, reserved for those at the highest rung of the social hierarchy, the distinguished few that sat at the top of the urban, colonial social pyramid.

Building on these findings, historians of postcolonial Mexico continued to find vecinos at the heart of local politics. These vecinos were crucial in maintaining order in their communities during a period of increased violence and constant civil war, and offered a sense of stability during a period in which a series of incompetent national administrations threatened to erode the government's legitimacy.[18] The vibrancy and autonomy of local elites in Mexico carried through the nineteenth century and into the Mexican Revolution (1910–1940), shaping the decentralized and experimental way events unfolded.[19] When scholars of northern Patagonia emphasize the ways in which vecinos assumed informal leadership of their communities, imposing "order" by encouraging crackdowns on cattle rustling or banditry, or by persecuting police that acted independently, they frame vecinos and their politics as a continuation of the ways in which elites deployed, consolidated, and replicated their own power.[20]

While vecinos emerged from an expressively exclusionary political system designed to exclude direct political participation from plebian masses, they rarely mobilized in support of individual political leaders, as part of political machines. Despite the economic profile of their leadership, vecinos preferred to frame their grievances in cultural and social terms, or as issues of good governance. They sought to accommodate to, rather than modify, the ways their communities were run, cutting a conservative, rather than reactionary, political outlook. Their goals and methods were locally based: each community mobilized in defense of their particular grievances and used strategies that worked for their local context. In short, vecinos benefited from the semicolonial arrangement in place on the frontier, and they sought to preserve their prominence in the system rather than overhaul it.

The Arrangement: *Vecinos* as Patrons of the State

For most settlers in northern Patagonia, the police represented their main interactions with state authorities—and in those encounters the state presented an anemic profile. Budget constraints meant that the police could not afford to cover their own lodging, transportation, or equipment, and often relied on prominent neighbors to rent buildings, horses, and pastures.[21] The relationship between vecinos and the police was a complicated one. It was built on the material precarity of the frontier state, but it extended into a much wider set of social relationships.

At the core of this social tapestry of violence, coercion, dependence, and magnanimity was the patronage of the local elite toward the police. From providing buildings (offices, warehouses, barns) for the police to operate from, to offering credit, vecinos kept the police force in operation. In exchange, they expected the police to maintain order, foster an environment conducive to commerce, protect their personal well-being, and assist them in enforcing contracts or collecting debts. The effects of that patronage radiated outward in often-unexpected ways, involving police officers who were both tools of the vecinos and constraints on their power, extending to marginalized rural people whose own precariousness was preyed upon by vecinos and the police. Part corruption, part clientelism, the symbiotic relationship between police and prominent neighbors structured everyday life in northern Patagonia.

Consider the arrangement in the small hamlet of Chipauquil, in the central plateau, a rugged thirty miles from Valcheta, the county seat. A prominent vecino, Ricardo Bruce (an Argentine merchant and landowner in his forties) worked closely with the Sub-comisario Servellón Ortellado to facilitate the work of the police in their remote community.[22] When the two men had a falling out in early 1923, the police investigation into the merchant's complaint laid bare three key aspects of how the informal arrangement between vecinos and the police worked in small communities. First, it underscored that the relationship was grounded on the precarity of the frontier; second, the relationship was predicated on an expectation of preferential treatments by prominent vecinos; and last, whenever possible, the police and the vecinos would seek out informal solutions, channeling conflict into extrajudicial avenues. These relationships, much like the conflicts over indigeneity in chapter 2, abusive spouses in chapter 3, and teenage runaways in chapter 4, made up the foundations of how frontier justice was administered.

The material scarcity of the state on the frontier was the foundation of the spatial and social proximity between vecinos and the police. According to Ortellado's own testimony, the police detachment in Chipauquil was headquartered "in Bruce's house." This was not entirely uncommon, as insufficient infrastructure was a constant complaint of travelers, reformers, and critics, who mockingly highlighted the "imposing majesty" of makeshift courthouses in "mud huts."[23] Despite yearly complaints by governors of insufficient infrastructure when requesting additional funds for their budgets, the Argentine state did not prioritize building headquarters for the police in rural frontier districts.

The dramatic lack of basic resources to conduct police work had consequences, since officers, supervisors, and community members lent personal items when the government-issued ones failed or got lost. The case of Pedro Sandoval (a twenty-five-year-old born in Chile) illustrates this precariousness. Sandoval, a police officer in Valcheta, was forced to borrow money from a local merchant in the early months of 1908 to settle an onerous debt owed to his immediate supervisor.[24] Comisario Francisco Perelli had personally loaned Sandoval a revolver to use in pursuit of a fugitive since the department lacked enough weapons for all the agents. Sandoval lost the borrowed revolver during a shootout with the fugitive in a remote rural area. Perelli threatened to garnish Sandoval's wages until the cost of the weapon had been recouped, which he estimated at eighty pesos—four times its actual cost. Sandoval borrowed the money from a local merchant, Carlos Leandroglio (a forty-nine-year-old Italian immigrant), and repaid Perelli. With Leandroglio's support, the officer filed a complaint against the comisario. The court ordered that the garnished wages be restored and proceeded to reprimand Comisario Perelli, who at this point had relocated to a different town.

Leandroglio's extension of credit to the police force was not an isolated event, as a select few merchants in each rural outpost had permission from the state to issue "advances" on police pay. This was an advantageous arrangement for merchants since it allowed them to pay out the advances in goods rather than cash and gave them a material and a relational windfall.[25] By offering advances in kind, they secured a captive customer base for their stores, as individual police officers faced two unpalatable options: waiting for the usually late and incomplete official payment to arrive or accepting the merchants' inflated valuation of their own goods. These arrangements also strengthened the merchant's relationship with the comisarios, who were eager to keep their police stations staffed. In Leandroglio's case, the extension of credit to Sandoval allowed him to further his patronage of the police. Effectively, he had covered up the state's failure to supply police with the necessary equipment, and he had strengthened his relationship with the officer, who was now indebted to the merchant in more ways than one.

The state's dependence on settlers was widely discussed at the time and has continued to interest scholars and critics who try to understand the significance of these arrangements. These relationships have been interpreted in three main ways. Inflamed by complaints of police abuses and merchants' complicity in those abuses, contemporaries understood these arrangements as evidence of the enduring barbarism of the countryside, as relics of a frontier that they considered already civilized.[26] A second interpretation highlighted the resourcefulness of the pioneering spirit of the immigrant settlers, arguing that these informal arrangements showcased the ingenuity of vecinos who supplemented the state. The lived spaces of Patagonian towns embody this interpretation: streets were named after "pioneers," plazas and schools commemorated their resilience, and they lent their last names to the landscape around them.[27]

More recently, scholars have articulated a third interpretation, which understood the role of the vecinos in these relationships as a junior partner to the extralegal order established by state representatives in rural areas to cushion social conflict and resolve disputes away from the courts.[28] Police commanders and justices of the peace deliberately crafted what Gabriel Rafart terms a "network of firm loyalties" to avoid open conflicts by co-opting local elites into their arrangement.[29] This framing suggests that civil society emerged as a restraint on the excesses of the frontier state that it paradoxically also underpinned. But the relationships discussed so far, such as those between Comisario Perelli and Leandgrolio or Sub-comisario Ortellado and Bruce, do not suggest that the settlers were junior partners, or that the police commanders were dictating the terms. These relationships existed as a creative solution to the lack of resources. Complicated networks of loyalties emerged from those creative solutions, but the vecinos were at the heart of those networks.

In fact, their relationship can be better understood as part of a larger complex of networks—in tension with one another but not always in conflict—created by the vecinos themselves, not by the justices and the police. For example, the kind of relationship that Bruce and Ortellado shared defied easy categorization. Bruce not only housed the police, but he also cultivated a close relationship with the sub-comisario: Ortellado could often be found casually sharing a *mate* tea in the merchant's kitchen and talking amicably. In short, the lack of resources drew the police closer to prominent neighbors, and in turn encouraged the police to exert authority in extraofficial ways to ensure their continued support and patronage.

It was more than clientelism or corruption as it showed an investment by all actors involved (police, prominent neighbors, and those caught up in the social networks) in the success of the Argentine state in Patagonia. For the police commanders, these relationships certainly contained elements of corruption, as they found ways to advance their personal goals, but it would be reductive to try to characterize them as such without understanding the institutional framework that re-created practices and processes within which individual agents operated.[30] Perelli, for example, was not solely trying to make a profit by overcharging Sandoval for the lost revolver; he had come up in a system bereft of stability, with rapid turnover of agents, with a lack of resources, and constant pressure from statesmen and settlers to produce results. He was operating within an institutional framework that would punish *him* for providing a revolver to a potentially untrustworthy subaltern. For the vecinos the patronage was self-serving, but it expanded into a political engagement that went beyond a narrow economic concern.

Prominent neighbors like Leandroglio or Bruce certainly seemed to expect that the police they supported would support them back when they needed them. For example, in 1925 the "Merchants of Cinco Saltos" sent a telegram to their judge in defense of a besieged police officer, charged with "abuse of authority" for roughing up a suspect with too much violence.[31] In their letter, the merchants assured the judge that Ibarra was "a staunch warrior against 'thuggish elements'" in their community. He had helped to heal the town with his "correct" behavior in the past, and they "completely trusted" his judgment in this instance. They urged the judge to consider their assessment of the officer's character and his value to their community when deciding the case. Using deferential and candid language they appealed to the judge as trustworthy stakeholders rather than a contentious rabble. With no possibility of input into who made up the police force in their town, the merchants of Cinco Saltos tried to intercede as representatives of the broader community in the decisions of the regional authorities. The arrangement between vecinos and the state representatives did not guarantee a good police force, but it at least ensured a present police force.

This special relationship provided small merchants like Bruce with preferential treatment, like the occasional police escort when dealing with debtors, creditors, and other settlers. For example, Camilo Basualdo, the acting comisario of General

FIGURE 15. "Subcomisario de La Pampa y suboficial, tras atrapar a tres sospechosos, 1921" (AGN-Ddf, Inventario #405641). The impeccable uniforms, matching weapons, and neatly kept appearance of the officers in this picture are probably due to the presence of the camera, judging by contemporary critiques of the police force in northern Patagonia.

Roca, seemingly directed the officers under his command to intercede on behalf of "his friend" Desiderio Tapia, a forty-year-old merchant in town.[32] Tapia had asked Basualdo for help when he found out that a "dangerous anarchist" by the name of Ángel Abad Angulo had returned to town with the intention of retaliating against Tapia, who had testified against him in an earlier case. Claiming to speak for "all the people" (todo el pueblo) who felt that Abad Angulo's presence was "threatening the lives of peaceful vecinos" in town, Basualdo acted decisively. After a confrontation at a bar when the officers provoked Abad Angulo, he was "shackled" and kept isolated in a "dungeon" for two weeks, before being sent to Viedma in a rudimentary stockade, according to his lawyer's complaint. When investigated for these apparent abuses, the officers in General Roca admitted feeling "obligated" to help Tapia since he was a leading merchant and a "friend of the police." Upholding the law and maintaining the patronage of propertied patrons was not always an easy proposition. This was the core tension of the informal arrangements that kept the peace in northern Patagonia for as long as vecino politics lasted.

Police work in small Patagonian towns operated in a dual manner, blending formal and informal deployments of resources and power. For example, during one of their "amicable" sessions in his Chipauquil home, Bruce relayed to Ortellado that someone had been stealing his cattle. According to Ortellado the merchant told him "in passing" that one of his horses had been stolen by a twenty-two-year-old farmhand, José Carrizo. To Bruce's consternation the sub-comisario did not conduct a criminal investigation, opting instead to deal with the complaint informally. Bruce explained that the sub-comisario had first tried to offer him a "replacement horse" from a "friend of the police" and had subsequently organized a private meeting between the two men to resolve the issue. A police agent in Valcheta, Juan Rivas, confirmed that Carrizo had been illegitimately arrested and detained in the Viedma jail, until Ortellado ordered him released after "a deal had been brokered."

The sub-comisario used the police to find, detain, and jail the suspect, but no charges were filed, no complaint initiated, and no investigation recorded. Ortellado explained that he had put forth "informal inquires" to determine whether Carrizo had stolen Bruce's horse, tapping into the community's reputation networks to attempt to resolve the situation. Since Bruce had not filed a proper complaint (he had only "told [Ortellado] about it in passing"), the interactions between the police and any witnesses or informants were not recorded, and the coercive power of the state was wielded informally. The sub-comisario's intervention in the case followed the lead of his patron, Bruce, who signaled his preference for an informal resolution by *not* filing a formal complaint. But, judging from Bruce's complaint, the two men seem to have misunderstood each other's cues.

Bruce's complaint against Ortellado followed a typical pattern in northern Patagonia. When local authorities failed to respond to their informal complaints or acted in an antagonistic way, vecinos moved beyond allegations and petitions, and filed criminal complaints. These complaints usually began with an individual contacting a police officer (or a traveling commander, if the local police were compromised) to formally lodge a complaint, much like Bruce had done when he encountered the visiting comisario in his village (and unlike the *informal* complaints he had filed with Ortellado). The complaint would lead to a formal police investigation to determine whether a crime had occurred and, if necessary, to also gather a list of witnesses who could provide any relevant evidence to solve the case. Countless cases in the archive are just a few pages long, with a complaint that the officer was unable to substantiate—either the details were too vague to follow up on or the person making the complaint recanted and refused to expand on their initial statement. Even when the police failed to establish that a crime had in fact taken place, the process of initiating a complaint, following it up, collecting a list of witnesses, and deposing them disrupted local arrangements by bringing unwanted attention to their actions.

The investigation into Bruce's complaint brought to light several other examples of Ortellado's "informal solutions." Ortellado responded to Bruce's airing of their grievances to the rest of the community with increased police harassment, including the arrest of the merchant's godson, Silberio Moreno. Some vecinos reported similar harassments, which extended to their associates and employees as well, exacerbating tensions between the police and those that imagined themselves as their patrons. Ironically, some vecinos complained that the sub-comisario tended to show too much leniency. For example, a witness complained that following a nonfatal stabbing during a drunken brawl the sub-comisario gave the men a "talking to" instead of booking and detaining them, as the *Código Rural* (rural criminal code) prescribed. These complaints suggest that Ortellado's use of the coercive force of the state as an encouragement to resolve conflicts informally was not an isolated strategy that he employed with Bruce alone. In other words, the dually informal and formal approach to "keep the peace" was not an aberration: it was frontier justice.

These dual arrangements could implicate far-flung actors throughout the region, shaping how state power was experienced. For example, during the investigation into Ortellado's dealings, one of his subordinates, Juan Rivas, an officer from Valcheta, complained that he had purchased a horse from the sub-comisario, which had not been conveyed. Rivas offered proof of payment in the form of a "purchase credit transfer" at a local trading house (Casa Chatier y Cía.). Ortellado had failed to convey the horse because the animal had been removed from its winter pasture by its rightful owner, Valentín Ayelef (an indigenous peon from the rural hinterlands of Valcheta county). Ayelef found himself in an unenviable position following an arrest over a series of small infractions: Ortellado offered to reduce his sentence to "just a few weeks" if the peon "gave him a horse." Ayelef returned to Chipauquil, after spending six months in jail, and reclaimed his horse, complicating Ortellado's sale of the "gifted" animal.

Ortellado took to the streets, berating Ayelef as a "thieving fucking Indian" and a "son of a bitch." The sub-comisario even publicly threatened to kill the indigenous peon unless he turned the horse over.[33] Fearing for his life and following the advice of Bruce and the local butcher, Ayelef left town immediately. The sub-comisario used the dually formal and informal system to dispossess an indigenous peasant for personal gain. But labeling this act simply as corruption misses the larger institutional framework in which his actions made sense. These relationships wove the social fabric of the frontier into tight reciprocal tapestries: if Ortellado received patronage from Bruce, he himself acted as a patron to rural workers, peons, and other marginalized actors who might find the informal arrangements offered by Ortellado preferable to the alternative. Although Ortellado ultimately failed to lessen Ayelef's punishment, the offer was appealing enough (and believable enough) that the peon took it.

Personal relationships worked both ways, and people like Ortellado established relationships with their supervisors in the capital cities. While the police investigated Bruce's complaints in Chipauquil, the sub-comisario's allies in the regional government attempted to intercede on his behalf. The governor and the chief of police sent the court two brief letters in support of Ortellado, highlighting "the great opinion that his supervisors and the public have of him, given the competent and fair way he has performed his duties."[34]

The defense offered Ortellado's "good reputation" as proof that the charges were bogus, even presenting newspaper clippings that highlighted the high opinion that the press had of the sub-comisario. Considering his reputation and record, the judge decided that after six weeks in jail he had already served enough time and should return to his post immediately. Contemporaries often criticized these kinds of arrangements between governors, chiefs of police, and judges that legitimized malfeasance by returning problematic police officers back to service. In the context of vecino politics, however, these informal arrangements were simply part and parcel of how power was deployed on the frontier.

The complicated relationship between vecinos and the public servants that depended on them emerges from the criminal complaints, urging us to consider the ways in which settlers exercised citizenship in imperceptible ways. Consider how Bruce ended his deposition with a seemingly ironic plea: he hoped that

FIGURE 16. "Carros de mulas transportando lanas, Neuquén, c. 1920" (AGN-
Ddf, Inventario #147750). Most rural merchants in Patagonia traded hides
and wool. They would buy them from small producers and resell them to
traders with national connections.

his complaint would help reform the local police to avoid the negativity that
complaints against the police generated in the community. Bruce thought of his
complaint as his way of exercising citizenship in his small community. Although
his original grievance was economic, it was quickly articulated in political terms
as an issue of good governance.

This can seem like a cynical ploy as Bruce complained that the police were
failing to protect his business interests, but his long investment in the community
had made him expect that the police would act in his defense. After all, he justified his grievance by alluding to a greater communal good: trying to eradicate
complaints against the police to preserve the prestige of the police. By going
around the sub-comisario and complaining directly to the authorities outside

town, Bruce attempted to constrain how frontier justice was administered by Ortellado through informal investigation, strong-arming suspects, and peddling stolen goods to his employees.

The cost of exercising citizenship through complaints was potentially high, damaging relationships between vecinos and the police as well as exposing nonconforming settlers to retaliation or harsher treatments, as Ortellado attempted when Bruce first began complaining. One way to defray some of those costs was for individual vecinos to band together to complain as part of a "harmonious people."

A "Harmonious *Pueblo*": *Vecinos* and Social Order in the Frontier

To minimize the risk to their businesses and their well-being, prominent vecinos sometimes sought to build broader coalition in their communities, much like Gallardo and the other settlers in Bariloche had done when they self-identified as a pueblo culto. When vecinos assumed the title of "most respectable neighbors" or "the guardians of the pueblo," they sought to juxtapose their coalition—both respectable and "the people"—from their opponents in town, who were presumably disreputable and illegitimate. They framed their grievances in civic and political terms, even when they had fundamentally material bases. As discussed in chapter 1, their complaints were often directed to the governor, who was seen as an outsider with personalist power who could intervene in local disputes. The governor in turn would forward the complaint to the territory's chief of police for further investigation. These coalitions were effective because they appealed beyond economic classes, transcended ethnic and national identities, and had a certain ad hoc quality to them that lowered the cost of participation.

To illustrate these dynamics, consider the response by Maquinchao's vecinos to the escalating abuse by some police officers in their isolated town in the heart of the plateau.[35] On 20 June 1922, shortly after five in the afternoon, the governor of Río Negro received a telegram from the "most respectable neighbors and industrious businessmen" of the small town of Maquinchao.[36] The "respectable neighbors" complained of daily harassment and abuses at the hands of the local police. The situation had reached a boiling point earlier that morning when the vecinos convened a *magna asamblea* to discuss and work out a unified response to the crisis. During this extraordinary assembly the local merchants made the dramatic decision to close down their businesses to protest the "unusually frequent" abuses. They informed the governor that since their constitutional guarantees as citizens were "virtually suspended" under the current police force, commercial life in the town would stop until he sent an outside investigator and restored peace to their community.

The telegram bore the signatures of dozens of Maquinchao's vecinos, who called themselves a "harmonious people" (*pueblo armonioso*). They had different national affiliations, with the expected presence of immigrants of Spanish and Syrio-Lebanese heritage (the groups which, along with Italians, represented the largest cohort of upwardly mobile immigrants), as well as French, Polish, and even British immigrants with varied lengths of time living in the country. They represented a range of occupations: hairdresser, carpenter, cobbler, trader, and even several illiterate peons. A veritable melting pot of civic virtue that would make the liberal architects of Argentina proud.

The group's decision to combine a civic identity ("respectable neighbors") and an economic one (the "most industrious businessmen") seems pointed. This framing echoed the priorities of the modernizing national elites, as the vecinos explained that their businesses would remain shut "until Your Excellence takes action to restore harmony to this hardworking town, which contributes with its efforts to the greatness of the country." They made the connection between hard work by settlers on the frontier and the national greatness explicit, highlighting the importance of "harmony" to the operation of the town. They identified themselves as "respectable, industrious neighbors," positioning themselves as worthwhile subjects and increasing the likelihood that the governor would intervene on their behalf. The vecinos in Maquinchao leveraged their economic success in the plateau to appeal to the state's desire for economic development in the fledging Patagonian settlements to restore the "harmonious" way that the town had operated before. Like Bruce in his complaint, the vecinos conflated political and economic concerns to mobilize outsiders not to overturn the informal arrangements in place, but to constrain them. They succeeded when the governor took immediate action, deputizing the comisario of San Antonio Oeste Armando Zimmerman the next morning to head an independent investigation.

Although the list of grievances was long, the trigger seemed to have been a series of beatings in early April and mid-June, when several of the merchants' employees were viciously attacked in the streets by members of the police when their supervisor was out of town.[37] That initial complaint precipitated a cascade of accusations being added to the complaint. Some had been lodged independently before: in fact, the archive has several prior complaints by individual merchants that were not pursued when they were lodged but that were added to the file when Zimmerman arrived. Some of the actions of the police had a definite economic goal of either extracting payment from them or harming their businesses. Witnesses reported illegal confiscation of hides and goods, the practice of forcing some merchants to pay a surcharge to transport their goods into town, an armed assault on a logger in the street, and forced nightly closures of legitimate businesses (a selective curfew). These activities directly harmed some residents of Maquinchao but made clear to the entire community the power of the police to protect those within its network of loyalties and harm those outside of it.

Other complaints had little commercial ramifications, but highlighted a sense of social unrest or a lack of order. Vecinos complained of ongoing nighttime dangers, despite the selective curfews, and charged the police with protecting an illegal brothel and organizing a gambling operation during the Independence Day celebrations the previous 25 May. The officers' relationship with the brothel, in particular, led to several colorful accusations. In one case, the police were alleged to have disarmed most visitors to the brothel, except those who had "bribed" the police into being allowed to keep their weapons, leading to a dangerous situation in which only a handful were armed inside the establishment. In another case, a police officer corralled the local schoolteacher and a clerk inside the brothel and proceeded to "rough them up, in a generally jovial manner." The vecinos relayed police abuses that affected every facet of the town's life, from the economic and social, to issues that reflected on the "culture" of the town, and combined them into a single, encompassing complaint. I think we can outline three "factions" in the town: the "ringleaders" who had triggered the complaint and been the recipients of the police abuse; the "respectable neighbors" that had not suffered the affronts but decided that they could not stand idly by; and the "loyalists" who remained allied to the police throughout the conflict.

The group of leaders was immigrant-heavy, and it included a wide swath of the town's merchant elite, from the principal signee Elías Sede (a thirty-four-year-old "Arab" merchant, who had lived in Argentina since he was nineteen) to the carpenter José Vázquez (a thirty-three-year-old Spaniard, who had been living in Argentina for thirteen years), the hairdresser Antonio Sabata (a thirty-year-old Spaniard), the greengrocer Camán Sede (an illiterate fifty-six-year-old "Arab," living in Argentina for only seven years), and Alberto Donato Álamo, the twenty-eight-year-old Argentine manager of the Sociedad Anónima Mercantil.[38] The ringleaders had experienced the brunt of the police's excesses, and once the telegram had gone out, the abuses continued to escalate in a punitive manner similar to what Bruce experienced after his complaint. For example, one of Sede's clerks, Miguel Pérez, recounted being summoned unexpectedly by the justice of the peace, Miguel Ferré, who proceeded to browbeat the clerk, threatening to kick and potentially shoot him for "having signed in support of those fucking Turks" (turcos de mierda). The xenophobic rhetoric by Ferré suggests a reservoir of resentment toward the immigrants' success. The strength of the vertical relationships cultivated by the immigrants, joining employees to merchants and tradesmen, all economically connected, seemed to confound Ferré. According to the testimony, the justice of the peace's outburst escalated as he ranted, threatening first to kick and "on second thought" to shoot the "treacherous" clerk. Ferré seems to have expected residents to band together along ethnic, or national, lines, and their embrace of a more inclusive vecino identity threatened the social order that the justice of the peace had grown used to.

Even though some of the signees to the telegram had not personally suffered any abuses, they explained that they felt it was their duty to join their voices to their neighbors who had been harassed by the police. "As an Argentine citizen, aware of my duties and rights" one of them argued, "police . . . have proceeded mistakenly and with lamentable arbitrariness," which prompted him to sign the petition to ensure that the town did not descend into "tyranny and chaos." Other neighbors reacted strongly to the violence against nonmerchants, particularly since it seemed to be an attempt to intimidate people too powerful to coerce directly. For example, Zacarías Terzaghi (a forty-six-year-old Italian day laborer who had lived in the country for thirty-five years) testified to having witnessed police officers beating up one of Elías Sede's employees (Fredo Lugi, a middle-aged Italian bricklayer) near the train tracks, which the pharmacist (Luis Cazzolino) and a couple of other merchants also witnessed. Terzaghi claimed that when Sede informed him of the telegram being drafted following the general assembly, he agreed to sign it since "all the merchants were doing it." The telegraph operator (Armando Agreenhill, of British descent) claimed to have seen a different beating and signed the complaint "to prevent further abuses to other residents." The Polish cobbler, Teodoro Busdzco, agreed, claiming he signed the complaint after a request by the "merchants who were being abused." The coalition of vecinos taking a stand against the social disruption caused by the police did not seem to care that the abuses had initially been economically motivated—it had grown to be an issue of order and governance that affected the entire town.

The rapid response by the governor and the prompt arrival of the outside investigator allow us to understand the nature of the vecino alliance in a way that other complaints do not. For example, few years later, the neighbors of the Andean hamlet of El Bolsón had a similar set of grievances against some of their local police officers, but their complaint failed to galvanize the population in the same way.[39] Their telegram demanded that the governor "guarantee our lives and livelihoods, which are currently threatened by the lack of real police, since the one we have has been operating outside the law for some time." The local police were accused of an assortment of bizarre actions, including nightly cemetery skulking, theft of an iron fence, and petty harassment. Unlike the swiftness of the Maquinchao investigation, which began less than a week after the complaint was lodged, the El Bolsón one stalled for almost six months.

The chief of police struggled to find an impartial outside investigator, and the one he settled on was delayed by late-fall snow drifts, the remoteness of El Bolsón, and the treacherous canyons and deep valleys that surrounded the town. Dirt paths became impassable due to snow and ice in the winter, while in the spring they disappeared altogether as mudslides and the overgrown temperate rainforest devoured them. Once the investigator arrived in El Bolsón, he failed to find any witnesses willing to ratify the complaint: unable to find any material evidence beyond hearsay and the victims' own accounts, the case was dismissed without detaining any of the accused police officers. Those six months between the original complaint and the arrival of outside authorities to investigate probably accounted for the lack of popular fervor in support of the complaint. Either the police managed to intimidate the would-be "respectable neighbors" into sitting out the conflict, or the delay in getting the investigation started might have calmed tempers down, as vecinos upset with nighttime skulking in the cemetery or the theft of the iron fence either forgot or lost interest. Ultimately, the vecinos in El Bolsón failed to relay to the investigators their grievances in the same way that their Maquinchao counterparts had.

In a sense, the fragility of the vecino coalitions was part of their appeal—they did not always develop into coherent organizations, or political factions, or even "interest groups." They were low-stake commitments that did not necessitate broader political alliances or precluded other ways of being politically organized.

At a certain point, the critical mass of peers joining the complaint made neutral neighbors feel the pressure to add their voices. For example, the French merchant Luciano Berbecke explained that he signed the Maquinchao telegram "to support the businesses, and *to not look bad*." These dissents, timid and quiet, speak to the power of the vecino identity articulated by settlers on the frontier. Because of its inclusivity and lack of overtly political goals (like electing a councilman or mayor), there was a fairly high social cost for those refusing to join their neighbors in attempting to reform the police. The flip side of the openness and unity of the vecino identity was a conformist pressure, and a reification of the town as a bastion of civilization in juxtaposition with the barbarism of the countryside—it was hard to be seen as standing against civilization.

This stark binary between town and country carried more than a cultural messianism, it was a struggle for political power wedded to nascent social identities. For example, in 1927 in the town of Zapala, on the eve of the first-ever election for a municipal council, a series of candidates from the Unión Comercial y Obrera presented a complaint against the local comisario for issuing voting cards to people from outside town (mostly rural workers and small ranchers).[40] Three of the four candidates identified themselves as merchants, and the witnesses they offered for the investigation were either merchants or "trustworthy employees," all representatives of the vecinos of the town. They had filed their complaint to ensure that both members of the community and regional authorities in the capital monitor the police on the eve of the election. Their criminal complaint ultimately collapsed when, after the election had already taken place, one of the signees recanted his support for the continued veil of suspicion on the newly elected council. Máximo Besoky, a forty-two-year-old Russian mechanic, confessed that they had issued the complaint pre-emptively to influence public opinion if the election went against their party. He retracted the claim, and said he fully supported the elected officials, who needed the support of the community instead of sowing distrust. The alliance between "merchants" (*comerciantes*) and "workers" (*obreros*) in that municipal political party and their fear of "rural" elements "interfering" with the election embodies the small-town ethos of the vecino identity, similar to the petite bourgeoisie of early modern German towns.[41] German "home towns" and a fledging Patagonian town might not seem like the most likely paragons of civilization—they were not Vienna, or Buenos Aires—but the residents of those urban enclaves understood them to be. This shared social purpose bound vecinos together even when they had few other goals in common.

This group of "respectable neighbors" were the heart of vecino politics: they joined the fray without being directly affected by the abuses because they understood it to be their "duty and right" to prevent "tyranny and chaos." In other words, they acted as bulwarks of civility in a roughshod environment. Whatever arrangements had worked informally before, the police's recent excesses in Maquinchao had tipped from frontier justice to lawlessness. It would seem that part of the appeal of the vecino corporate identity for townsfolk was that it was an ad hoc arrangement—a sui generis coalition kept together by virtue and shame.

The characterization of the police as violent and out-of-control was not shared by all in Maquinchao. We know the least about the people who remained loyal to the police in this case. Two witnesses in particular came forth in defense of the police: the Australian-born foreman of the Estancia Maquinchao—a massive sheep-raising enterprise that owned a significant amount of land in the county and employed a lot of the rural peons in the area—as well as the owner of the brothel. Their support for the police was tepid at best. In remarkably similar statements, both the foreman and the brothel owner claimed that the officers had generally behaved appropriately and fairly toward them, and declined to add anything else—a conscious strategy to stall an investigation. Without more context into their particular circumstances and relationships, it would be safe to assume that those siding with the police were people who had benefited from the informal arrangement in place in Maquinchao.

Some clues as to the inner workings of this set of relationships and alliances can be gleaned from the fallout of the investigation. The relationship between the police and the vecinos in Maquinchao was in flux, since a couple of years later, in the outskirts of Maquinchao, the police were accused of moonlighting as hired guns for immigrant merchants and landowners.[42] In that case the victim of the police excesses was an illiterate Chilean breeder, Arturo Fuentes, whose cattle were forcibly removed from his land by Officer Libermann at the behest of Mustafa Zain, a local trader to whom Fuentes owed some money. A different crew of police officers established different alliances in town, responding to different patrons and antagonizing a different cast of "outsiders" as frontier justice continued, differently but unabated. As suggested during the discussion in the previous section, police in northern Patagonia had no institutional culture other than adapting to the bare necessities of operating in the scarcity of the frontier.

The investigation into the complaint in Maquinchao reached an anticlimactic end, buried in a desk drawer in Viedma for several years. It resolved the situation in the only way that it could: since the merchants could not produce any material evidence of the abuse and harassment their case had little legal weight. But the show of force, the investigation, and the attention given to how the police operated resulted in the disbanding of the abusive police gang. Two of the officers relocated elsewhere and were frequently recalled to Viedma to ratify, dispute, or supplement parts of the case. The two other officers were considered fugitives of the law and were never captured, which probably meant that they had to lay low and forgo any official police duties wherever they ended up.

By the end of the decade merchants and landowners in Maquinchao had coalesced around a more hierarchical, institutionalized organization—the Liga de Defensa Comercial y Ganadera de Maquinchao (Maquinchao's Commercial and Ranching Defense League). The Liga de Defensa interceded in cases of police abuse, as the sprawling complaints against comisario Ángel Martínez in 1928–1929 exemplify.[43] The group's president, an Argentine merchant by the name of Julián Pérez, sent a formal complaint to the chief of police alleging that the police in the area were confiscating the hides of guanaco fawns (*guanaquitos* or *chulengos*) from local peons. Pérez piggybacked a series of complaints on that original one, claiming that comisario Martínez tried to blackmail Elías Sede to return some of the hides; that he ignored verbal complaints about abuses by one of his deputies, Officer Gregorio Luján; that he illegally detained several people to extort them for a release fee; that he mishandled the kidnapping of a teen by failing to report her abductor to the courts—among other complaints. Unlike the impromptu 1922 complaint, this one was done in a meticulous manner, witnesses were marshaled and detailed beforehand and the evidence against Martínez and Luján painstakingly collected and presented by the Liga de Defensa. Despite the thoroughly documented cases against Martínez and Luján, neither was convicted, as the investigation failed to produce material evidence, and the defense lawyers introduced enough probable doubt to muddle the narrative crafted by the well-organized vecinos.

Luján's example, in particular, illustrates how frontier society had changed and how much remained the same. According to the police records Gregorio Luján had an eventful life: in 1918 he was convicted of murder in Ensenada (Buenos Aires) but received a pardon in 1923, after serving five years of an eight-year sentence. He relocated to the frontier and joined the police force, where he was arrested for battery in 1925, but served no time. At the time of the allegations against him, he was also facing charges for assault and illegal detention elsewhere in the plateau. In 1931, he was accused by Juana María Peña of rape and aggravated assault—but the judge dismissed the charges due to lack of evidence. By 1931, however, his employment was listed as a "former police," and he had spent most of 1930 and 1931 shuttling through different towns in the Río Negro valley and the Andean valleys looking for permanent employment. The police were more professionalized, but the limits of the official dispensation of justice continued to force informal solutions—like de facto exiles.

A few things appear to have remained constant in Maquinchao during the interceding years: prominent merchants cultivated patronage relationships with their workers, immigrants continued to be engaged in broader economic and political endeavors, and the police dispensed frontier justice with frustrating opacity. But other things appear to have changed significantly as the decade progressed: the more professionalized police conducted longer, more thorough investigations, the vecinos were organized primarily along economic roles, and Argentine-born settlers were firmly in control of these multiethnic coalitions, signaling the demise of the immigrant-led vecino identity that had been forged earlier in the decade.

Throughout the 1920s merchants and their allies used collective written petitions to attempt to effect change in their communities. Even though they had limited political rights (Maquinchao, El Bolsón, Chipauquil, and Cinco Saltos, for example, did not have any elected local government of any kind at the time of the complaints), these vecinos thought of themselves as part of a civil society, a counterbalance to the coercive power of the police and remote institutions of the national territories—and acted accordingly. Their political order faced a serious challenge toward the 1930s.

The Nationalists' Conspiracy: Turning "Vecinos" into "Gringos"

A new wave of arrivals to northern Patagonia transformed the region in the second half of the 1920s. Hard data on this transition are hard to come by, since national censuses skip three decades between 1914 and 1947, but anecdotally, these new settlers were more likely to be born in Argentina and boasted connections with established authorities in Buenos Aires, like the national doctors in chapter 6. These newcomers were also better equipped to weather the economic uncertainty of the Great Depression, and they quickly came to resent how the older vecinos marginalized them by continuing to wield outsized influence in their communities. These sentiments of exclusion from the networks of loyalties that made up the vecinos coincided with, and were fueled by, the rise of a nationalist paramilitary force at a national level, the Liga Patriótica, to challenge the inclusiveness of the vecino identity. Appropriating certain features of vecino politics, but adding robust connections to power in Buenos Aires and the regional capitals, these new nationalist coalitions began to remake the frontier in their image.

Scholars have recently begun to seriously look at the influence wielded by nationalist groups in Patagonia. Nationalism in Argentina underwent a xenophobic and antisemitic turn in the first decades of the twentieth century as a response to the growing sense that cosmopolitanism had diluted the national character. As historian Ernesto Bohoslavsky puts it, in the late nineteenth century, nationalist elites "imagined a new Garden of Eden, open to any *cosmopolitan entrepreneur* willing to challenge with their pioneering spirit the hostile geographic and climactic conditions."[44] But, starting in the 1920s and 1930s a new generation of nationalist elites "championed the idea that Patagonia needed to be protected from greedy actors who were infiltrating it stealthily."[45] Whereas nineteenth-century nationalists had conceived of northern Patagonia as the key to unlocking the country's economic potential, they began to see it instead as an area susceptible to foreign meddling, in particular from neighboring Chile.[46] For example, Col. José María Sarobe, a notable conservative thinker of the 1930s and 1940s, argued in his 1932 treatise *La Patagonia y sus problemas* that frontier towns in Patagonia needed to "constantly contemplate" historical monuments to "keep the national sentiment alive."[47] The change in attitudes from cosmopolitanism to nationalism must have been a disorienting reversal for the vecinos who imagined themselves as the harbingers of culture and civilization in northern Patagonia.

Col. Sarobe was not an isolated voice—in their 1927 Congress on issues pertaining to the national territories, the members of the Liga Patriótica put forth a dual plan to Argentinize northern Patagonia: increased education, and the "official colonization with rational, fundamentally Argentine settlers of good disposition, able to build the future they yearn for with hard work, and who feel responsible for the success of the *patria* [homeland]."[48] The Liga was formed in 1919 in Buenos Aires as a reaction to the perceived instability caused by foreigners to Argentine social harmony. The Liga, which under the slogan of *patria y orden* (homeland and order) conceived of itself as the "guardian of the Argentine essence," grew in importance in Patagonia during the mid-1920s. According to Sandra McGee, a historian of the right wing in Argentina, about 15 percent of all Liga brigades operated in Patagonia, a striking percentage since the region only held about 1.5 percent of the national population during the period. In other words, people in Patagonia were ten times more likely to be part of the Liga than people elsewhere in the country.[49]

The Liga's preoccupation with national integrity and political purity made the national territories—sparsely populated by Argentines, along international borders, and stripped of effective political rights—a central concern for the group, culminating in their hosting of the 1927 general congress on national territories. In fact, while other political parties tended to forgo any political organization in northern Patagonia (since the population was disenfranchised), the Liga was an early proponent of mobilizing and formalizing political associations in the national territories—so much so that their central committee had representatives from each of the national territories as well as the provinces and the federal capital.[50] In other words, the Liga made the political organization of the national territories, and discussion of issues related to them, a priority in the 1920s, which began to bear fruit and disrupt the vecino-led municipal arrangements that had emerged organically up to that point.

To illustrate how nationalist groups began to exert influence in northern Patagonia, consider how Bariloche had changed in the decade following the complaint against Comisario Schultz. By 1934 the immigrant merchant elite of the "first settlers" in Bariloche found itself economically ruined and politically marginalized. The town and its old guard of immigrant merchants would finally lose their grip on the area when the national government established a massive national park just outside the town, forcefully injecting itself in local politics, rearranging landownership patterns, and refocusing its economy toward tourism and the service industry. The decline had begun in the late 1920s, when Bariloche and the entire area of the Andean valleys grappled with the consequences of a series

FIGURE 17. (*opposite*) "Monumento a Julio Argentino Roca en el Centro Cívico de San Carlos de Bariloche, el día de su inauguración—Río Negro, 1938" (AGN_DDF/ Caja 3083, Inventario #36600). Patriotic monuments like this iconic one in Bariloche's civic center were the direct result of agitation by the Liga Patriótica.

of tariffs implemented by Chile and Argentina which suffocated the trans-Andean trade that had fueled the regional economy since the military annexation of Patagonia.[51] The economic crisis arising from the "disarticulation" of trans-Andean trade networks, coupled with the collapse of the world economy in the early 1930s, destroyed the agricultural economy of the area. Large multinationals, like the Sociedad Anónima de Importación y Exportación, as well as smaller family firms, found themselves overleveraged and in ruin. The national park established in 1934, which coincided with the arrival of the transcontinental railroad, was the death knell to the vecino politics as it had existed. Their plight was punctuated by the influx of a new generation of settlers to the Andean region who brought heightened anti-immigrant sentiments.

The most emblematic example of the rise and fall of the vecinos-led citizen model in the region was perhaps Primo Modesto Capraro. His businesses, political engagement, and cultural activism helped define the region around Lake Nahuel Huapi during the first three decades of the century. Capraro had become so interwoven with the region that he was eulogized as "the soul of the Nahuel Huapi" lake after his untimely death in 1932.[52] Born in Italy in 1875, he emigrated to Mexico without any money at the end of the century and found his way to the Andean valleys, through Chile, by 1903. He used a small land grant on the northern shore of the lake to stage a logging business that supplied the main cattle company in the region, eventually expanding on to a larger parcel as a lessee where he grew and processed award-winning wheat. Soon after he partnered with the comisario of Bariloche, José Alanís, to start a brick factory. He spent the 1910s traveling throughout the region selling his building materials and applying the building skills for the rugged mountainous area he had acquired during his duty with the Italian army in the Alps. By 1920, he had reinvested his earnings into an integrated construction empire in the Nahuel Huapi region, owning a power plant (*usina*), a lumber mill, a smith, a mechanics shop, as well as several general stores, a hotel, and a dock.

His prominent position afforded him a steady patronage from the state, which contracted him for almost every infrastructural project including the much-delayed transcontinental rail line that would link the Andean valleys with the Atlantic ports. By the time of his death, the state owed him "vast sums" in unpaid labor, material advances, and other unfulfilled contracts.[53] The state patronage had more political than economic windfall. From his position of prestige, he encouraged greater immigration of Italians into the region to work for him, further broadening his base of support. He was appointed to the municipal council on multiple occasions, and earned a minority seat in the first elected council. He was active in the Italian cultural association as well as the German one (his wife and son were German), while serving as the local representative of the Italian consulate and of several international companies. During Primo Capraro's life in northern Patagonia, he epitomized both immigrant archetypes articulated by nationalist elites: the coveted industrious cosmopolitan pioneer and the greedy foreigner infiltrating the frontier.

In Bariloche, the Liga first organized in 1925 and was presided over by the recently arrived medic, Dr. Luis Pastor. It included prominent Argentine-born vecinos, police officers (including Chief Benítez), and a teacher (all of them recent arrivals in town), who distrusted and disliked Capraro and his associates. Convinced that the foreigners in town wielded too much power (having dominated the unelected municipal council for over a decade), Dr. Pastor, on behalf of the Liga, demanded an elected municipal council, in 1926.[54] Governor Quaglia, who was a guest of honor at the 1927 general congress on national territories, balked at that demand and appointed a municipal council headed by Capraro and consisting of five foreigners with established roots in the region. The Liga Patriótica, using an aggressive toolkit that characterized their political engagement, launched a three-pronged attack on the municipal government: the chief of police began arresting and detaining members of the Italian community; Pastor directed the Liga to "paper over" the town with broadsides and cartoons defaming the municipal authorities and Capraro in particular; and through the local correspondent to the national daily *La Prensa*, they amplified the allegations "insidiously."[55]

Building on the kind of tools that had become typical in northern Patagonian towns, the conflict played out publicly and centered on personal attacks as a way to erode the legitimacy of the rival. Incensed by these attacks on his character and by the complicity of the local police, Capraro filed a complaint against Luis Pastor accusing him of slander and libel.[56] His complaint included familiar outrage at police provocations, beating of employees, and illegal fines, but added specific ethnic language. The complaint described the victims as "peaceful foreigners" who were "punished violently" and their tormentors as "minions" egged on by "rough police" (*policia brava*) who sought to "publicly demote the gringo." For a while, each tourist that arrived in Bariloche received an envelope in their room, containing a letter "defaming" Capraro, and warning the newcomers that the old pioneer was "power-hungry" and lacked any scruples.[57] When the conflict escalated into broken windows and "false-flag" pamphlets (allegedly by the Italian community) threatening to "carve [Dr. Pastor's] flesh with an Italian knife," the governor requested the police investigate. Once again, the regional authorities resolved the conflict in informal ways: Chief Benítez was reprimanded and some of his agents transferred to different posts, while the governor sent a personal letter to the Hygiene Department in Buenos Aires requesting the "permanent transfer" of Dr. Pastor out of the town, alleging absenteeism and lack of medical care.

The political turmoil in Bariloche eroded Capraro's political capital with the national and territorial authorities, even as the immigrants continued to defend their version of "el pueblo culto" against the newcomers. In late 1929, the Ministry of the Interior authorized municipal elections in Bariloche for the first time, but irregularities in the confection of the voter registry which excluded foreigners and added Argentine-born residents from rural districts marred the election. Capraro gained a seat on the council, but the candidates backed by the Liga took the other three seats. Although that municipal council was dissolved after the 6 September 1930 coup, Capraro was unable to recuperate his political clout, since the new government was aligned with the Liga, which reconstituted in Bariloche in 1931, counting among its members many of the new state authorities in town.[58]

The collapse of the world economy in the early 1930s decimated Capraro's holdings, taking away the economic underpinning of his power. Through tireless advocation and politicking as more moderate factions took power nationally in early 1932, Capraro was appointed as the top municipal authority in May 1932, but famine, lack of electricity, and mounting debt wore out his diabetic body.[59] Exhausted and broken, he took his own life in October 1932. A well-known hagiography of Bariloche's "pioneer history" eulogized Capraro thus: "like his forefathers, wherever he went, because of his civilizing instincts, he became a conqueror of deserts, a builder of cities, and a tracer of roads."[60]

Although the scope and size of Capraro's enterprises in northern Patagonia made him a highly unusual example, his experience on the frontier was representative. The merchants in Maquinchao, for example, operated single trading houses but aspired to diversify their businesses in the same way that Capraro did: as immigrants accumulated capital in the frontier they tended to invest it in diverse ventures in their communities.[61] While Capraro was connected to national and international institutions (newspapers, embassies, companies) in a way that only a few people in each town were, even smaller merchants like Bruce could count on some degree of support from outside allies in their contests against local authorities. By the end of the 1930s, witnesses walking into the police department would not be entering into the home of a local merchant—no matter how big or small their businesses, their role as patrons of the police had been taken over by a more robust, and chauvinistic, national government.

Conclusion

Like Capraro, early Patagonian merchants (many of European descent, but a significant number of Argentine and Chilean ones as well) worked to parlay economic advantage into social capital and political ambitions, forming the backbone of a broad-based *vecino* identity. The examples in this chapter offer a cross section of the interplay between social networks and patronage networks in northern Patagonian towns, as well as the ways in which they interacted with powerful yet passive regional authorities. The peculiar institutional arrangement in northern Patagonia created the conditions for this neighborhood-centered kind of citizenship, which built upon local, regional, and even national socioeconomic relationships to emerge and flourish.

The first generation of settlers (the "pioneers" of settler mythology) grew adept at using the material scarcity of the state to their advantage, and learned how to use institutional and informal mechanisms to apply pressure on local authorities to maintain "good governance," as defined by themselves. This growing social order needed impoverished state agents to thrive. The police force, in particular, occupied a strategic space in the institutional arrangement in Patagonia—alternately victimizing and protecting the settlers while maintaining a semblance of state presence in the remote towns and hamlets despite a dearth of resources. They were both part of the vecinos' extended networks of loyalties and—as the linchpins of paralegal arrangement designed to restrict access to justice and resolve conflict informally—they were also the vecinos' antagonists.

The resistance to police abuses, and attempts to dislodge informal arrangements and corruption, went from being the purview of independent merchants to collective responses, which minimized the risk incurred and amplified the complaint so that regional authorities had to respond to them. However, just as this vecino-centered system reached a level of self-awareness and self-confidence in the mid-1920s, demographic and institutional changes began to upend the arrangement altogether. The language of a shared *civilized* culture in Bariloche, and the foreign-born settlers' tight fraternity, underscores how self-aware civil societies in small Patagonian towns were becoming by the middle of the 1920s. This collective identity was leveraged against material and moral excesses by the police, using the precarious state presence available to them. These kinds of "mature" political conflicts, which went beyond immediate economic threats and began to articulate a shared culture in the town, came to a sudden halt with the changes in administration and state intervention of the early 1930s. The state that had been distant but willing to accommodate became much more present and intransigent, reshaping the way conflicts were resolved and citizenship practiced in the frontier.

Following the expanded infrastructure of rails and roads new settlers arrived in the plateau and the Andean valleys, bringing a different set of expectations and sensibilities. Mostly Argentine-born, these new settlers resented the power of the tightly knit immigrant communities, and some even boasted competing claims to legitimacy. New federal appointees, and their connections through the Liga Patriótica to those new settlers, provided a counterbalance to the networks that the earlier vecinos had painstakingly crafted. The increase in funding for police (and the reduction in their numbers to prioritize professionalization, discussed in chapter 1) might not have resulted in better police for northern Patagonia, but it certainly made it less reliant on the largesse of local merchants and neighbors. The era of "pioneers" on the frontier was ending, but the community-based system of legitimacy grounded on reputation, cooperation, and reciprocity would prove hard to uproot entirely for the newcomers. To the resilience of that system we now turn.

"A Trusted Doctor"

Legitimacy and Local Power in Medical Practices

Folk medicine, in all its forms, is one of the worst enemies of public health. . . .
Now that we are building the nation . . . *we cannot ignore the public clamor against these professional liars and deceivers*; we cannot be deaf to the educated men and the most renowned scientific associations who demand the complete extirpation of this well-recognized evil.

—José Ramos Mejía, 1906.[1]

Aften jamming a needle into her thumb so deeply that she could not remove it, Tomasa Catalán de Pelletieri, a forty-year-old widow, sent one of her four children to get Dr. Núñez for assistance.[2] Ten hours later, when Núñez finally showed up at her house, he stunned the widow by not greeting her or engaging in small talk, proceeding to "cruelly" remove the needle while cursing "rudely." Ernesto Luis Núñez, a certified "national doctor," had only recently arrived in the village of San Martín de los Andes and was having a difficult time adjusting to the shifting demands of the frontier in 1932. When Tomasa attempted to barter for the service rendered, the doctor refused, going as far as to tell her that he would not see her again until she had money to pay upfront. Worried that the wound was getting infected and unable to afford a consultation with Núñez, she visited the town's older doctor, a German immigrant named Rodolfo Koessler, who happily redressed the wound free of charge.

Citing a provision in the penal code against the illegal practice of medicine, Núñez lodged a formal criminal complaint against Koessler. Núñez claimed that the German doctor's temporary authorization to practice medicine had expired the previous month, and he himself alone had the right to practice medicine in San Martín as the "national doctor" appointed to that town. During the investigation, members of the community offered testimony in support of Koessler and against the new doctor, defending who *they* considered as the town's legitimate doctor. This chapter explores conflicts over the legitimacy of medical practices, highlighting the importance of reputation—the "social good" that an individual contributed—to counterweigh the power of the state-sanctioned actors.

At first glance this case fits with the narrative of vecino decline discussed in chapter 5, as a new generation of Argentine-born settlers replaced immigrants in prominent positions in frontier towns. Most cases against illegal practice of medicine took place in the late 1920s and 1930s, underscoring not only the growing independence and professionalization of the police force but also how the arrival of a new generation of settlers undermined the arrangements that had stabilized municipal life—conflicts were no longer easily contained by informal frontier justice. But the resolution of this case, and others like it, complicate that narrative. The arrival of newcomers was resisted by the population of small- and medium-sized frontier towns, which insisted on their own alternative legitimization of authority.

This chapter argues that even as the frontier arrangement was disappearing, social standing—based on networks of loyalty and reputation in the community— remained a decisive factor in resolving complaints at the local level. Even as the Argentine government attempted to establish a stronger presence and reinforced a top-down legitimacy regime, settlers continued to find ways to practice their citizenship by proposing and supporting an alternative social order. In effect, the reach of the national state continued to be contingent on the local social networks that had contested the deployment of state power for the previous half century.

FIGURE 18. (*opposite*) "El médico César Fausone de la Gobernación de Río Negro examinando al hombre-mujer, 1902" (AGN-Ddf, C2299). Notice the juxtaposition between the medic's urbane appearance and the patient's. Doctors arriving to the frontier had to learn to adapt to the social realities.

Frontier Medicine: Healers, Doctors, and Regulations

The complaint by Núñez against Koessler invites us to discuss three key developments that converged to put the young doctor in conflict with his older predecessor: the culmination of a long-gestating effort to criminalize some medical practices, the government's sudden preference for "national" doctors trained in Buenos Aires, and the experience of a generation of young doctors who took to the countryside in the late 1920s and early 1930s with pastoral zeal but who were ill-prepared for the scarcity of the interior.

The "illegal practice of medicine" was criminalized nationally in 1921 following decades of negotiation and campaigning by doctors to define the boundaries of legitimacy in their profession.[3] The reformed penal code of 1921 (which had been drafted in 1906, but remained stuck in a legislative morass for over a decade) made the lack of medical credentials a serious enough crime to punish with incarceration.[4] Art. 208 had only three provisions, which enumerated the restrictions on practicing medicine and stipulated a penalty that ranged from fifteen days to one year in jail for breaking them. Primarily, it singled out for punishment anyone who "*without a title* or authorization or anyone who *exceeds* their authorization, practices the healing arts, or who *habitually* promoted, prescribed, administered or applied medicine, water, electricity, hypnotism, or any other means to healing diseases, *even without receiving remuneration.*"[5] The other two provisions in the law punished anyone who promised impossible results, as well as any person with a legitimate title who allowed someone else to heal under their name.

The text of the law had both highly specific examples and broad characterizations, which reflected the struggles that had brought the law into being. The specificity of the law responded to the influence of the growing number of university-trained doctors who were coalescing into a medical establishment. As part of the National Hygiene Department, established in 1880, doctors had a growing influence in the state which enabled them to secure their position of privilege, and to exclude alternative practitioners of medicine.[6] The more capacious aspects of the law—broadly proscribing those without authorization, with limited authorization, and those who "habitually" practiced "any other means" of healing—responded to the relative youth of the certification process and the dynamism of the medical practices at the time. Prosecutors and judges had a lot of leeway to interpret this tension in the law in a socially acceptable way: it could be applied broadly and punitively, or in such a specific way as to render it null.

Núñez had hoped that the authorities in San Martín de los Andes would have strictly interpreted the law to punish Koessler for "exceeding" his authority, even if he did not charge for his assistance. The court battles over the "illegal practice of medicine" in Patagonia differ from the conflicts in previous chapters in that local authorities had to contend with a powerful new actor: the National Hygiene Department, which zealously brought complaints made by doctors to the attention of judges, governors, and individual police departments.

In northern Patagonia, the National Hygiene Department began aggressively assigning doctors to particular districts, conferring on them the title of "national doctor" and guaranteeing them a monopoly on health care in their area. This was supposed to encourage city-dwelling doctors to move to the countryside, ensuring that rural patients received "rational treatment" from a reputable source while guaranteeing the doctors an exclusive patient base. When an 1891 law adjudicated the regulation of medicine to provincial authorities, the national territories, like Patagonia, fell under the jurisdiction of the National Hygiene Department, which played a limited role: it would periodically survey the national territories, issue recommendations to lawmakers, and handle epidemics.[7]

Their role grew after the implementation of Art. 208. Doctors within the Hygiene Department developed guidelines limiting the "legitimate practice of medicine" to members of the National College of Medicine, the main guild for medical practitioners. This requirement threatened the legitimacy of medical professionals with international degrees, who had operated freely in the national territories until then. The majority of the cases against the "illegal practice of medicine" in northern Patagonia originated in small towns or in the rural areas immediately surrounding them, which were the places where immigrants had been particularly successful as prominent vecinos.[8] This is strikingly different from the better-studied cases against the illegal practice of medicine in Buenos Aires, where the cases were concentrated in urban marginal areas. This is probably how Núñez ended up as the "legitimate" doctor in San Martín, displacing Koessler.

The newfound self-confidence and power of the medical institutions (the National Hygiene Department and the National College of Medicine) came at a time of acute moral crisis for the medical community in Argentina. The economic crisis of the 1920s and 1930s had exposed and exacerbated the poverty of large swaths of the population in the country's interior, a reality that was foreign to most doctors living in provincial capitals and other urban enclaves. At the same time, national authorities noted glibly that a growing number of doctors seemed increasingly concerned with making a profit rather than providing care to those in need, fearing that the profession had "lost its way."[9] A new cadre of doctors graduating in this period, like Núñez, took these critiques to heart and threw themselves into developing practices in the hinterlands, but many of these new "national doctors" turned out to be ill-prepared for the harsh social, and professional, realities in the more peripheral areas of the country. Even when they did succeed in their fledging frontier practices, there simply were not enough of them.

Consider that by 1940, the entire territory of Río Negro had only 50 doctors (for a population exceeding 128,000—a ratio of 0.39 doctors per 1,000 residents) and Neuquén had a mere fifteen (for a total population exceeding 69,000—a ratio of 0.22 doctors per 1,000 residents). To contextualize those numbers, that same year the entire country had 11,398 doctors (for a population of just over 12 million—a ratio of 0.89 per 1000).[10] Richard Slatta, in a study of a similar frontier space in southern Buenos Aires, estimated that in 1896 a scant 114 doctors served a population of roughly 390,000—a ratio of 0.29 per 1,000, roughly similar to northern Patagonia half a century later).[11] Slatta quoted contemporaries in southern Buenos Aires "alarmed" by the "thousands dying at the hands of illicit medical practitioners" due to the lack of doctors and their "refusal to make house calls" to far-flung corners of the region.

In frontier spaces, doctors occupied a privileged place in local social life and operated in a scarce market, since there never were enough doctors to meet the needs of the population.[12] Doctors occupied a paradoxical position in frontier towns: on the one hand, their robust institutional presence in the national government (through the Hygiene Department) made them powerful outsiders, while, on the other hand, the poverty and remoteness of most northern Patagonian towns meant they had to adapt to local society to succeed. The gulf between their self-regard and their actual standing within their communities often frustrated doctors, who could hardly hide their contempt for the folk healers and the patients who cherished them. To the surprise of many newly arrived doctors, like Núñez, social standing in a community (based on reputation and a sense of belonging to the community) represented an alternative source of legitimacy in the frontier, one that they could not overcome simply with credentials. Núñez's 1932 complaint came in the middle of this process of pilgrimage to the hinterlands, and his zealousness reflected his expectation of exclusivity and privilege for his "sacrifice" to the frontier patients.

Usually, scholars explain the story of the "modernization" of health care in the Argentine interior in linear, teleological terms following a pattern of growing, uniform, popular support for the state-led health initiatives. This approach celebrates important milestones like the criminalization of the illegal practice of medicine, the "pilgrimage" of young doctors to the interior in the 1930s, and the institutionalization of care in the 1940s, as the national government built a flurry of maternity wards, first aid stations, and other medical facilities.[13] The experiences in northern Patagonian towns, as they emerge from the court records, do not fit this general narrative, as the modernization of medicine seemed to follow the rhythms of each particular community.

The cases presented in the following pages highlight the different ways in which Art. 208 was prosecuted in northern Patagonia, which not always aligned with the intention of its framers. Doctors used Art. 208 to root out and combat *curanderos* (healers), to eradicate faith healers, as well as to contest the legality of other, seemingly legitimate, medical professionals. Settlers, on the other hand, exploited the vagueness of the law to thwart these efforts and protect health providers that had served the community. In regard to the adoption of "modern" medical standards embodied in people like Núñez, each community followed a different pace of adoption, one that was dictated less by the priorities of statesmen in Buenos Aires and more by the realities and relationships in each town.

By looking at seemingly low-stakes conflicts like those involving the illegal practice of medicine, we can follow the path laid by Eugene Weber's study of nation building in rural France, where he found that state action was "less welcome" when it "intervened to establish or restore a public order alien to the population."[14] Like in rural France, "most people approached change hesitantly and experienced its effects with great ambivalence." But whereas Weber found his French peasants could not turn back to "irrational" beliefs "once they had drunk from the fountain" of change, northern Patagonian settlers continued to contest the terms of modernization if it did not conform to their expectations and practices rooted in communal belonging.[15] Social standing in a community influenced the likelihood that the police would take the complaint seriously and investigate it, at the same time, local reputation and social networks continued to offer a critical counterweight to the action of the representatives of the state. This delicate balance between society and state, between a community and the authorities outside of it, remained at the core of how frontier justice was administered, even after it was fundamentally transformed in the 1930s.

Defining "Outsiders":
Folk Healers, Medical Need, and Police Investigations

Police investigations into cases of the "illegal practice of medicine" by poor, untrained folk healers tended to have fairly straightforward resolutions, particularly if their practices resulted in harm to the patient or interfered with the work of certified doctors. The prevalence and importance of folk healers in northern Patagonia were well understood by national authorities. For example, an envoy of the Hygiene Department sent to survey the Territories in 1908, recommended a lenient interpretation of the "illegal practice of medicine" for the frontier. In his estimation, simply practicing medicine without certification should not result in prosecution unless the patients had been deceived. He concluded that given the shortage of certified doctors in the territories, medical professionals simply had to coexist and cooperate not only with folk healers, but also with foreign medics without appropriate certification.[16]

At first glance, the persistence of healers in northern Patagonia several decades into the twentieth century seems consistent with notions of the region as an underdeveloped frontier despite the efforts of reform-minded national elites. At the same time, the survival of healers almost five decades after the military incorporation of the region further underscores the limited success of the government in rationalizing and regimenting Patagonian society.[17] The continued reliance by the population on curanderos and the ongoing efforts by certified doctors to coexist with them while managing their reach reflected the reality that medical care on the frontier remained scarce.

Police responded to this reality, as their investigations attempted to determine the urgency of the healer's intervention before sending the case to the prosecutor. First, they tried to ascertain if the violation in question came in response to a critical need—that is, if it was a case of a "good Samaritan" instead of an "illegal doctor." Second, they tried to determine whether the medical intervention was part of a broader behavior—that is, if the suspect regularly wrote prescriptions, attempted to sell remedies, impersonated a certified doctor, or advertised their services publicly. If the accused did not openly confess to a habitual practice, the police tried to find proof of a systematic violation of Art. 208: testimonies from patients alleging a habitual practice, evidence of dispensation of homemade remedies, of charging for their services and remedies, or of impersonating a certified doctor to defraud patients.

Consider how the police handled the allegations against Leopoldo de la Place (called in the file the "Príncipe Indú"), a traveling healer and salesman.[18] He claimed to be a representative of the Centro Religioso Espiritista, a spiritist group in Buenos Aires. De la Place was accused of the illegal practice of medicine by Bernardo Serafín D'Arco, a resident of Viedma, in August 1927. Bernardo's father, Silverio, sought out the healer to treat his oldest son's deteriorating mental health (the son was, confusingly, also named Silverio). The deal that the D'Arcos made with de la Place to treat Silverio the younger with herbal infusions and prayers whenever he had a mental breakdown included a steep fee of six hundred pesos. They also agreed to provide him with room and board in their house in Viedma, and to cover his travel costs to continue to see his other patients in southern Buenos Aires. After six months of having de la Place living in his house, eating his food, and charging his father and brother for treatments and medicines, Bernardo D'Arco feared that they had fallen prey to a skilled quack, and proceeded to get the police involved. The police immediately arrested the tall, dark stranger in a late evening raid more befitting a dangerous criminal than a healer.

The investigation uncovered other patients in Viedma being treated by de la Place, who also remarked on the healer's demands for payment. For example, a neighbor (Lautaro Montalva) with a "mentally deranged" child had requested de la Place's assistance but was dismayed when the healer required a fee to treat the child, in advance no less, since "he could not work for free."[19] Despite the protestations of both Silverios, who insisted that de la Place was a guest in their home and that his cures had been working, the prosecutor was merciless. Arguing that de la Place had impersonated a professional doctor by brandishing dubious accreditation, sold unlicensed medications, and appeared to live solely on the income from his practice, the prosecutor requested three months of jail in addition to a large fine.

Healers accused of illegal practice of medicine highlighted alternative qualifications in an effort to combat the charges against them. Consider the complaint against María Cruz Guzmán (a "robust" Chilean laundress, either forty-three or fifty years old), who was accused in 1930 by Dr. Correra, who administered the hospital for the oil-town of Plaza Huincul. Correra had hastily prepared a splint for a patient who had broken his leg playing soccer, and had ordered him to board a train to Allen for further treatment immediately.[20] Unable to cover the train fare, and feeling an increased pain in his leg, Juan Inestresa stopped by the home of María Guzmán, who had helped his brother with a similar injury in the past. After examining the wound, she determined that the shin bone had come out of place, puncturing the skin. She reset the bone with her hand and "spread a mixture of chicken eggs and flour over the wound" before covering it with bandages previously disinfected with vinegar, using chicken bones to make a new splint.[21] When Correra encountered Inestresa again the next day he was dismayed to find him in agony and his wound draped with a "strange liquid" which, in his estimation, was causing a serious infection.

When questioned by the police, María Guzmán did not dispute the doctor's narrative, but challenged the state's authority to regulate her activities. She defiantly believed that even without "proper certification" she was qualified to perform these cures because her patients never complained and even referred their families and friends to her. During questioning she acknowledged having helped Inestresa's brother, and "many others before as well," never charging for her assistance. The public defender added a crafty counterargument: Dr. Correra "had failed to provide medical care" putting Inestresa at risk of further injury and forcing Guzmán to intervene "humanely" by "giving aid (socorro) to a patient without means." Highlighting Guzmán's "lack of education and extreme poverty," he made a positivist plea for clemency. The judge ordered her to serve the minimum sentence of two months in jail, as well as a small fine of one hundred pesos, showing leniency.

While Guzmán was able to proudly list off patients that she had treated without charge as a way to establish her community bona fides, de la Place was clearly an outsider in Viedma. His dark skin, tall, lanky frame, and "strange ways" marked him as inherently untrustworthy in the eyes of the police, as evidenced by the large raid organized to detain him. His lack of local connections meant that he did not have friends or acquaintances in town that could serve as character witnesses or offer a counternarrative of his intentions and practices. Usually, a healer's social network—as far as they had one—sprang into action to attempt to defend them, much like the networks activated by abused wives in chapter 3, or by prominent vecinos in chapter 5. To deflect police attention, their friends, patients, and patrons tried to use the healer's reputation in the community to reframe or derail the investigation. The case of Filomena Salvo, an illiterate thirty-year-old Chilean homemaker who had lived in Patagonia for half her life, underscores how, even when they fell short of forcing an acquittal, these networks were critical in ameliorating the punishment received.[22]

An "anonymous tip" from a neighbor claimed that Salvo not only practiced medicine without an appropriate license but also charged fees for her services. The police deposed two disgruntled patients who confirmed that she had indeed treated them and received remuneration for her work. Their testimony furnished the police with a long list of other patients and established that Salvo was a "known curandera" in the town of Allen. Like María Guzmán, Filomena Salvo tried to present her reputation as a qualification for healing, claiming that she had treated "many ailing patients without ever hearing any complaints." The long list of witnesses volunteered by Salvo not only supported her qualifications, but they put her practice in a broader context. For example, one of the witnesses explained that the town's physician, Dr. Cámpora, allowed Salvo to treat minor ailments to free him up to attend to more serious cases, suggesting that the healer's work was legitimized by the local authorities. Another witness tried to insist that Salvo was not soliciting patients, explaining how upon hearing through acquaintances of the healer she had doggedly sought her out for weeks. Finally, several of the witnesses insisted that the healer had never asked for money in exchange for her services or her remedies, but that since she was "very poor," she gladly accepted gifts. Despite Dr. Cámpora's conspicuous absence from the testimonies in her defense, the judge was ultimately moved by her defense. He found her guilty, but showed leniency in only sentencing her to time served and no fine. Her support network was somewhat effective, as the judge cited her poverty, as well as the fact that she did not seek out customers or charge for her services as attenuating circumstances.

As these examples showed, successful cases against healers hinged on three key variables which determined if a case resulted in a conviction and ultimately how severe the punishment was. First, the strength of the initial complaint carried outsized weight in the final judgment. Questions like who initiated the complaint, how much detail they added to the complaint, and how readily they could provide a list of corroborating witnesses set the course of the investigation. In the case against Filomena Salvo, only the two initial witnesses (who we can assume were related to the "anonymous complaint") suggested she charged for her services, and they provided the police with a long list of other witnesses to build a case against her. Similarly, in the case against Leopoldo de la Place the initial complaint by D'Arco carried a lot of weight, as the counternarratives by father and brother failed to exonerate him, and in the case against María Guzmán the fact that a certified doctor complained against her almost surely sealed her fate. The relationship between the person initiating the complaint and the local police was paramount in establishing this narrative and spurring police action—a classic feature of how frontier justice rewarded those with good standing in their communities.

The second variable deciding these cases was the disposition of the state agents: police investigators, prosecutors, and judges could either doggedly pursue a case or lazily let it languish. The investigator in the case against Salvo decided to detain her even though he failed to turn up evidence that she received payment, beyond hearsay, and de la Place was also detained based solely on the complaint by D'Arco. Police had to make judgment calls on how to frame some of the details in the case: establishing whether de la Place simply sold herbal teas or illegally peddled homemade remedies was up to the discretion of the investigators and the prosecutor. The "urgency" of the medical intervention in question, as the case against María Guzmán showed, could also be a subjective choice by the representatives of the state. These human moments made the application of the law fairly uneven, even in cases that appeared to have similar details.

The third variable, the social status of the healer, was the only part of the investigation that they could control to some degree. The healer's reputation, broadly defined, had a decisive influence in the prosecution of cases against them. If witnesses could establish their poverty, for example, it could provide an "attenuating circumstance" for the judge to consider a lesser punishment. The healer's ability to summon and mobilize members of the community as witnesses to try to challenge, and change, the initial narrative often proved critical in avoiding a conviction, or at the very least, avoiding a harsh sentence. This variable—let us call it the social constraints on state power—depended in large part on who the witnesses were: prominent vecinos and local doctors had the most influence in investigations, but coordination between the witnesses or legally creative witnesses also had surprising sway.

The vulnerability of the accused in all three cases was remarkable: they lacked strong social connections (though Salvo and Guzmán were not "outsiders" in the same way as de la Place was), did not demonstrate legal shrewdness, or offer clear examples of attenuating circumstances. None had powerful friends who could intercede on their behalf, even if they had a working relationship with prominent people in their towns. None had savvy witnesses who could manipulate the investigation by explicitly referencing the healer's charity work, or by specifically situating their activities outside the particular parameters of the law. The cases in the next section show how healers accused of the illegal practice of medicine could, together with their patients and supporters, craft a narrative during the investigation that maximized the chances of the charges against them being dismissed.

Good Neighbors:
Spiritual Healers, Social Networks, and the State

Some healers, and their followers, found great success in organizing collectively to reframe and redirect police investigations. They succeeded at this by focusing on two related strategies. First, they resisted the police interpellation by refusing to add new information when questioned, by withholding evidence, and by declining to name further witnesses for the police to question. This was not unlike the strategies deployed by community members assisting runaway wives in chapter 3 and by people loyal to the police in chapter 5. The second strategy was to reinforce during the interrogation, in supplemental documents, and through the press, the ways in which their actions did not contravene the provisions in Art. 208.

The successful campaigns to protect healers would repeat four points: there was never an expectation of payment for services, the healers did not solicit patients, they did not attempt to make money by selling home remedies, and, crucially, they described the healers in terms that emphasized their contributions to the community. These efforts to shape the law "from below" echoed the strategies of indigenous people and their allies discussed in chapter 2, and the teenagers discussed in chapter 4. In short, their followers made sure that the police investigation reflected their opinion that the healers were a social good, and that the state should not criminalize their activities and persecute them.

Healers with particularly strong followings operated outside of both folk medicine and the scientific medical tradition. Often, they resorted to prayers, spirits, and positive thinking as avenues to alleviate suffering. These "spiritual healers," or "faith healers" (*mentalistas*) often combined European folk beliefs with indigenous traditions.[23] Their lives and practices were deeply intertwined with the people around them. They presented themselves as neighbors, first and foremost, providing a helping hand when they could, comfort in times of crisis, and hope in times of despair, making their social networks particularly resilient and effective.[24] This relationship, built on trust and the reputation of the healer, should not have represented a threat to physicians, who tended to different flocks. Most established doctors worked in cities or small towns, dealt with acute health crises rather than chronic conditions, and were not always prepared (or willing) to assist people who could not afford their services. Spiritual healers treated people in the countryside (like most curanderos did), with chronic maladies and psychosomatic conditions, and almost always accepted bartering for their services.[25] Cases against spiritual healers could be hard for police to prove, since they tended not to generate the kind of physical evidence that could convince a judge, like the chicken-bone splint made by María Guzmán to stabilize the compound shin fracture.

Besides not having a lot of evidence to use against them, the faith that these healers elicited from their patients could make the police's work particularly difficult. Consider the case against Onofre Morales, a sixty-two-year-old Peruvian farmer, who in 1934 led the police in the upper Río Negro valley on a protracted game of cat-and-mouse for several years.[26] In the almost fifty years he had lived in Argentina, his gift for healing had built him an impressive following among the impoverished rural population of the small hamlets that dotted the rich agricultural valley. When an anonymous complaint resulted in his capture in the village of Chinchinales, the police swiftly compiled a list of patients to question as witnesses. But the witnesses answered their questions in a methodical way, using the interrogation to adroitly interfere with the investigation. For example, when asked if they knew Morales was a curandero, none of the witnesses answered directly, offering instead detailed narratives of the suffering their loved ones had endured. Additionally, almost every one of them included the failures of certified doctors to heal them. Impressively, they were able to answer the questions without contributing any incriminating evidence against the healer.

The police had no trouble finding witnesses to depose, as they seemed eager to share their experiences of the healer with the police in a way that emphasized his charitable nature and his lack of profiteering from his gift. According to the testimonies, his remedies consisted of a very precise combination of water and faith. For example, Antonio Sánchez, a Spanish-born forty-year-old farmer with twenty-five years in the country, shared the story of his ten-year-old daughter, Isabel, who was forced to constantly travel to Buenos Aires for operations due to a severe throat condition. Instead, Morales recommended a treatment based on a succession of hot and cold baths throughout the week, which the father believed completely healed his daughter without any further surgical intervention. Witness after witness told how Morales would tell his patients "to have faith" as he worked to heal them; to constantly think about healing, until they eventually were. Morales's patients contrasted his success to the failures of local doctors, emphasizing how he had acted out of need—not an urgent need, but one nonetheless. They also made a point of highlighting how "Morales . . . did not charge for his services . . . he lets those with means support him if they want to." Supported by wealthy patrons, Morales was able to heal the poor members of his community without charging them.

Not all healers had such savvy followers, but even modest attempts by witnesses to refuse to cooperate with the investigation stalled it. Consider the case of Cornelio Goñi, a sixty-year-old Spanish butcher who arrived in the country at the age of twenty-one.[27] In 1935, following an anonymous tip that he had been illegally practicing medicine in San Antonio Oeste, the police arrested him after a few weeks without much trouble: he had a checkered past and the police constantly suspected him of illegal medical practices.[28] Despite a long list of witnesses, the police were unable to extract incriminating evidence from their testimonies, which painted Goñi as an unorthodox healer who combined common household items with intense prayer. For example, Silvana Paileman, a sixteen-year-old who was bedridden for over a week after a shelving unit collapsed on top of her at the school kitchen she worked in, causing her a painful "baseball-sized" lump on her torso. Goñi treated her for two days, massaging cooking oil on the injury with his right hand, while placing his left hand on her forehead and "praying quietly under his breath."

Similarly, a patient who was losing his eyesight, was healed when Goñi suggested that he place boiled egg-whites over his eyelids every night. A pair of widows received a "blessed water and prayer" treatment from the spiritual healer for their aching legs. None of the witnesses gave the police evidence of solicitation or payment, and they all agreed that he did not charge but he "would accept whatever [they] could afford." Convinced that there should be more witnesses, the investigator spent the next year and a half requesting nationwide reports for this case, hoping to depose more patients. Goñi had managed to forge strong connections with his patients, who stalled the investigation simply by refusing to talk. His redemption was not complete, however, as Goñi spent several weeks in jail, and continued to receive police suspicion until the case was ultimately dismissed two years later. More savvy followers could have attempted to delegitimize the investigation further, like Onofrio Morales's supporters did.

Before his arrest in 1934, Morales's patients had already been waging a campaign to protect the faith healer. For example, when "police harassment" forced him to move out of General Roca in November 1933 they sent a petition to Governor Adalberto Pagano demanding that the government stop persecuting the healer. One of the neighbors, Bernardo Santos, wrote the petition as a sort of legal brief which challenged the underlying assumptions of Art. 208, and wrestled with the moral merits of persecuting those that sought to help their communities. In the opening paragraphs of the petition, Santos contended that "to advise a desperate or disillusioned patient on ways to mitigate physical pain is not quackery . . . to morally and financially help those in need is not illicit trade, nor does it invade the jurisdiction of the sciences."[29] Conscious of the subtle points of the law, he claimed that Morales not only refused to charge his patients but he gave them money when he thought they needed it more than him. The petition reflected a careful understanding of how the law was being applied in northern Patagonia, but it is unclear if the author had legal training, was himself in any way related to the police, or was simply a canny observer.

The letter aimed to present Morales as a selfless servant of the community. since "patients that appeal to Morales not only bring to him their ailments, but also bring their saving faith in this humanitarian man who knows nothing of selfish calculations, nor cares for profit . . . he does not advertise, and never charges, accepting only the complete gratitude of those that are helped or saved by their faith." The letter also attempted to add a precedent to his makeshift legal brief by referencing the "well-known case" of Yrina Silva de Figueredo, a widowed faith healer from a nearby town in Avellaneda County. The police had detained Silva de Figueredo for suspicion of practicing medicine illegally but were forced to free her from custody soon after, admitting publicly that her activities did not violate Art. 208. The petition concluded with twenty pages of tightly packed signatures—a staggering almost five hundred names from all walks of life—who supported the work that Morales had done in their community. The letter succeeded in forcing the governor to investigate the police's actions, and conditioned how the subsequent police inquiry into Morales was handled.

These kinds of letter were not always effective, especially when the police believed the healer to be a threat. For example, the followers of Felix Susso, a Spanish immigrant who combined spiritual work with animal sacrifices to heal, mobilized to his defense in the hamlet of Colonia Frías, near the beet-sugar mill of San Lorenzo.[30] The neighbors sent a letter to the judge requesting the dismissal of all charges against Susso, since they considered him a communal "treasure." They argued that he should not suffer unjust persecution for "his gift," insisting that he was not a quack or a charlatan. The seven-page letter was tightly packed with the signatures of merchants, day laborers, homemakers, peons, and everyone in between. Despite the community's support, the police pursued the case relentlessly, believing he had been "openly treating patients" in the entire region, moving from town to town periodically to avoid detection. After a futile four-day manhunt in San Lorenzo, Colonia Frías, and nearby Cubanea, the police requested a nationwide search for Susso after reports that he had left the region altogether for Bahía Blanca, in southern Buenos Aires. When the police finally captured him on his way upriver from Colonia Frías to Choele Choel, the slippery healer surrendered peacefully.

Without a confession or material evidence, the police needed witnesses to collaborate with the investigation, but they refused. Susso himself claimed not to be a doctor, or a practitioner of any kind of medicine, and identified himself as "someone attuned to the spiritual world." He explained that he did not charge for his services because he believed that charging for healing would result in the loss of his powers, a punishment for "not sharing his gift." Witnesses similarly stalled the investigation by refusing to add any incriminating evidence. For example, Leopoldo Linares, a neighbor, explained that he had visited Susso extensively while the healer stayed in San Javier, but he had done so in search of friendship, not treatment. Cleverly, he claimed that he had never "seen" Susso treat anyone. This seemed to have been an orchestrated effort. Other witnesses refused to comment on secondhand stories ("have you heard about Felix Susso's treatments?") or on his reputation ("is it true that it is public and notorious that Felix Susso heals people?"). The person responsible for transporting patients to see Susso declined to add anything useful to the investigation, steadfastly responding that he had never "seen" Susso doing anything illegal since he "always waited outside." A particularly effective strategy was to resort to vague and unrevealing answers—for example, when asked how long they had known Susso they coyly answered "for some years" or "since I moved here."

One particularly clever piece of obstructionism deserves special attention. When pressed by the investigator to name any "strangers" (*personas extrañas*) seen around Núñez's house, every single one of the witnesses denied knowing anyone that fit that description. Although it is possible that the witnesses all decided to lie to the police, another possibility offers a more compelling interpretation. In a small town like San Javier no one would be a "stranger," making their statement true, if misleading. These strategies were "weapons of the weak," to borrow James C. Scott's term for everyday forms of peasant resistance.[31] They were small ways in which common people attempted to modify and condition the state's monopoly on how legitimacy was determined. This kind of folk challenge to how the state applied the law recalls the efforts by indigenous people and their advocates to reframe the ways in which the law applied to their families and traditions, discussed in chapter 2. None of healers in this chapter identified as indigenous, but alternative legal cultures continued to survive in northern Patagonia half a century into the colonial rule by Argentina. The broad coalition of settlers in tiny agricultural villages that made up these faith healers' social network felt emboldened enough to challenge the investigation in formal letters, demanding a different application of the law for their healers.

While not as impressive as those built by vecinos, these networks of loyalties were formidable and managed to limit the scope of the state's efforts to eradicate nonscientific forms of healing. If not based on political or economic power, how were these networks sustained? The outpouring of public support for Susso and Morales suggests a deeper affinity between these healers and the population they served. They provided a service in the absence of more established medical options—though the continued police attention that some of these men encountered suggests that someone was unhappy with their activities, possibly the accredited doctors. By refusing to charge a standard fee these healers not only made their services available to the poorer people in their towns but also avoided conviction. Even when they avoided conviction, the healers could still face informal punishments. For example, though Susso was not convicted, the prosecutor kept the case file for two years without offering an opinion for the judge to rule on, and citing flight risk, the judge forbade him from leaving the territory without written permission between 1936 and 1938.

Although they represented the antiscientific social type that Ramos Mejía had imagined when crafting Art. 208, they seemed to operate beyond the reach of the law, as part of the community and not as outsiders. In many ways, it was their informal, familiar manner that made them so accessible to settlers and so slippery for law enforcement agents. Regardless, at the national level, critics continued to denounce these kinds of healers, demanding stiffer sentencing and believing that the "insignificant punishments" levied against them nationwide had failed to stymie this "plague."[32] The mounting attack, at a national level, on esoteric healers through the 1930s increasingly reflected the medical establishment's concern with shoring up its own "scientific authority."[33] In Patagonia, these broader concerns by the medical community ran into the complexities of the frontier, where legitimacy from a title and state institutions could not easily overcome the legitimacy of popular support.

Conflict at the Edges of Medicine:
Medical Professionals Negotiate the Law

One of the key provisions of Art. 208 punished individuals "who exceeded the limits of their authorization" to practice medicine. This particular restriction was strategically used by doctors in northern Patagonian to fend off rivals and settle scores with other certified professionals. The scarcity of doctors forced settlers to rely not only on curanderos and faith healers for medical advice and treatment, but also on pharmacists and other health professionals who were on the margins of the restrictions of Art. 208.

Consider that, in a 1909 survey of the territories, the government could only identify one medical professional in the entire Neuquén Territory, and six in the Río Negro Territory (one medic, two pharmacists, and three midwives).[34] By 1940, a similar survey revealed that Neuquén boasted fifteen medical professionals and Río Negro fifty, but in the interceding years, certified doctors and other medical professionals worked alongside one another in a symbiotic and uneasy relationship.[35] Occasionally, when disputes arose, rival legitimacies of community and title came into sharp focus, showing the police and the health provider exactly how much respect and standing they had in town. In these cases, Art. 208 was not so much an instrument by state authorities to rationalize and make medical practices legible, but a tool for rivals to secure their practices and settle scores. The cases in this section underscore the power of seemingly vulnerable practitioners to avoid conviction—usually because of their deep local ties, and the lack of comparable relationships for the certified doctors.

Pharmacists, in particular, served a dual role in the towns in which they operated. Not only were they in charge of selling over-the-counter medicines, supplies, and filling prescriptions, but they also offered their customers rudimentary medical advice and first aid. This second role got Francisco Pagano Vivancio, the apothecary in the town of General Roca in the early 1920s, into trouble for constant *curanderismo*. Vivancio's activities had been common knowledge to the four certified doctors in General Roca: Álvaro Sellanos (a thirty-six-year-old Uruguayan surgeon), Isaac Auday (a twenty-eight-year-old surgeon), Félix Navarre (a thirty-two-year-old surgeon) and a person referred to in the documents simply as "Dr. Dengler." Álvaro Sellanos, who had arrived in General Roca in 1923, had developed a "personal enmity" with the pharmacist, leading the two men to "barely talk to each other" by mid-1924 after a complaint by the doctor against Vivancio had been ignored by the police. Early in 1925, Sellanos closed his practice and moved his family to the town of Tres Arroyos in southern Buenos Aires province—but before leaving he tried once more to bring Vivancio to justice, this time accusing him of contributing to a patient's death.[36]

Sellanos's accusation was serious. He claimed that "in the two years since I have been practicing here, I have been able to ascertain, based on the testimony of patients, that many of them had previously followed a treatment ordered by the pharmacist. Due to professional courtesy, I have not tried to control these irregularities."[37] The "irregularities" had resulted, in his opinion, in a tragedy: Julio Mardones, a Chilean day laborer, died shortly after taking a purgative sold to his brother Herminio Mardones by Vivancio. Julio Mardones had returned from the countryside indisposed and his wife tried to treat him at home, eventually asking Herminio (a thirty-two-year-old Chilean mechanic) to get her a purgative from Vivancio, her "trusted pharmacist." The purgative did not seem to improve the condition, and the next morning Dr. Dengler was called in, but he could not diagnose the patient. The family called Dr. Navarre, who became worried upon discovering that the patient had taken the purgative as it was contraindicated and potentially deadly. When Sellanos heard from Navarre about Mardones's death he filed a complaint against the pharmacist, claiming that he had "illegally prescribed" the over-the-counter purgative. Sellanos was unable to recall the names of any of the patients alluded to in his complaint, so the police could not follow up the allegation to corroborate it.

The doctor's testimony, though brief, provides some key details of the dynamics in General Roca at the time. First, Sellano's inability to recall any of the names of the patients he had treated suggests that he had not established particularly meaningful relationships with them, and other cases in the archive provide similar indications.[38] As far as the poorer residents of General Roca were concerned, the local doctors did not care for them and only treated them begrudgingly, if at all. The second detail pertains to how long Sellanos had been turning a blind eye to the pharmacist's activities. When the doctor arrived in General Roca, he stepped into a situation where Vivancio was already embedded in the community as a reliable source of medical information, supplies, and services, making it difficult to establish his practice in the crowded town. Finally, Sellanos's choice of words—"professional courtesy"—when explaining why he allowed Vivancio's illegal activities to continue, hint at the working understanding in the town, with synergy between some of the doctors and the pharmacist. These arrangements allowed people other than doctors to provide some medical assistance, but they also reinforced their dependency on the goodwill of certified doctors.

This precarity had far-reaching consequences, particularly when the more vulnerable party relied on the more established doctor for patients and resources. Consider the example of Carlos María Sánchez Antelo, a thirty-two-year-old Argentine-born dental surgeon based in San Antonio Oeste, who sent a telegram to the National Hygiene Department denouncing the illegal practice of dentistry by José Brogstein.[39] Brogstein had been seeing patients in the towns of Maquinchao, Ingeniero Jacobacci, and Pilcaniyeu, which Sánchez Antelo claimed were under his jurisdiction. Since the case came to implicate the local police chief and his concubine, a local medic, and one of the justices of the peace, the inquiry required an outside investigator. The witnesses, from a Greek merchant (Jorge Calamara) to a surgeon (José Esteban Novoa García), the pharmacy attendant (Severo La Canale), and even the justice of the peace (Enrique Hansen Seler), all testified that José Brogstein (a thirty-four-year-old Russian dentist, in the country for over a decade) had not technically performed any dental work on them. What he had done, the witnesses confirmed, was repair molar crowns, fix dental bridges, and other assorted "mechanical" tasks.

The difference between medical care—on the one hand—and craft work that supplemented medical care—on the other—was not lost on the witnesses who carefully parsed both activities in their depositions, exculpating the Russian dentist. For example, one of the patients, justice Hansen Seler, claimed that he had paid Brogstein for "mechanical [dental] work" without thinking twice about it since Sánchez Antelo had previously asked Brogstein to take care of such work for all his patients in town. The partnership between the two men had not been disclosed in the initial complaint. Brogstein confirmed the ill-fated partnership when he was finally deposed after fleeing the region south to the Territory of Chubut to avoid conflict. Echoing the friendly witnesses, he explained that he had "performed much mechanical work," not actual dental work, and that the work he had done "was referred to him by the dentist . . . in the towns." He had trained as a dentist in his native Russia, but he turned to craft work in the region while waiting for proper accreditation.

Sánchez Antelo's complaint did not lead to a conviction against Brogstein, but the investigation snowballed as other people with gripes against him volunteered their testimonies to the police. One witness in particular, Rafael Ana, suggested that the Russian dentist had indeed violated Art. 208. Ana was also an immigrant, from Italy, and he owned the hotel in Maquinchao which Brogstein had used as an office. Ana recalled being treated by the Russian, who not only claimed to be a certified dentist but also charged him for the examination and a tooth extraction. His testimony depicted a highly damning, straightforward case of "illegal practice of medicine": Brogstein misrepresented himself, executed a medical procedure, and charged for it, breaking all the provisions in Art. 208. The Russian dentist suggested that Ana's testimony was influenced by a recent squabble between them. The two men had had a public disagreement over rent money shortly before Brogstein left the region, and Ana approached the police investigation without being summoned to add incriminating evidence and, perhaps, settle the score. Because Brogstein operated in a gray area on the edges of medicine and made a living under the patronage of the accredited local practitioner, his position was weaker than the pharmacist Vivancio's had been as he was forced to abandon his fledging practice and relocate to avoid further problems.

Even modest social networks could help shore up the defense of beloved but unlicensed practitioners. On the island of Choele Choel, a physician, Dr. Vieroni, filed a complaint against Ralph George Jolliffe, an English-born fifty-year-old pharmacist, who had sold homemade capsules to a longtime friend whose condition deteriorated quickly.[40] When the out-of-town doctor arrived to stabilize the patient, he noticed the capsules and proceeded to lodge a complaint against Jolliffe. The case quickly got tangled up in a series of political disagreements: a key witness was the brother of the town's police chief, who in turn was a "sworn enemy" of Jolliffe, and the doctor who initiated the complaint shared an office in town with the justice of the peace. Despite these complications, the investigation was unable to establish Jolliffe's "habit of quackery" and the prosecutor recommended the dismissal of the case. Crucial to that determination was the testimony of two separate character witnesses for the pharmacist, who insisted on the Englishman's unimpeachable reputation in town since opening the pharmacy two years earlier. They articulated for the police the specific role played by the pharmacist in their town, as a stop-gap solution in between visits from Vieroni's roaming practice.

The law was as effective a tool in clearing out competitors as the local police allowed it to be. Since the police were not terribly enthusiastic about pursuing the case against Vivancio, they did not arrest him or confiscate his possessions during the investigation as some police did. Consider, for example, the case that upended the livelihoods of the pharmacists in General Conesa and the nearby sugar-beet mill, Ingenio San Lorenzo, when a conflict between two unlicensed doctors engulfed the region in 1934. When the investigation tried to determine how Abraham Feintuch (a thirty-four-year-old recently immigrated Polish surgeon) was able to operate on patients illegally, his rival Arnaldo Dobrenky (a thirty-one-year-old Russian doctor who had been living in Argentina for twenty-two years) pointed out that he had been using ill-gotten surgical supplies from the hospital staff and the local pharmacist, Eduardo Leiva, who was warned to stop supplying them.[41]

A second pharmacist, Manuel Palmeiro, was inculpated after a series of prescriptions signed by Feintuch were found in the pharmacy he owned in the Ingenio San Lorenzo, about ten miles downriver.[42] The police deposed Palmeiro (a thirty-two-year-old Spaniard, who had lived in Argentina since age eleven) and, after finding some irregularities, sequestered his prescription logbook. The police discovered that Palmeiro's logbook was registered to a different pharmacist (a Mr. Tomasini) and had been extensively filled out by yet another pharmacist (Carlos Nozzi), with names appearing "altered"—written over or smudged. Palmeiro claimed that the damage to the logbook was due to a "lemonade-related incident," which the police deemed suspicious, and took the logbook as evidence, ultimately keeping it for nine months. Without having access to the logbook Palmeiro was forced to cease operations: it was a critical component of how pharmacies operated by recording the movement of inventory and serving as a cross-reference for the prescriptions being filled. These actions short-circuited the ability of Feintuch to operate at the margins but completely ruined Palmeiro, who was unable to operate his business for the better part of a year.

As these cases suggest, local networks were easily entangled, as family and professional relationships, feuds, and interests warped the way justice was administered in these small frontier towns. Recall that when Sellanos filed his complaint against Vivancio he was unable to provide the investigation with the names of the patients who he believed had visited the pharmacist. Had he provided a list, the police would have had to question those witnesses and could have begun to establish whether the pharmacist was a "repeat offender." A more zealous police investigation could have found patients willing to corroborate Vivancio's habitual practice, especially if the pharmacist was as active as Sellanos and Navarre suspected. Sellanos said as much in a letter, bemoaning that the "police authorities, either for lack of competence, negligence, or in order not to compromise those people who are practicing quackery, have not fulfilled their duties." The informal arrangements of vecino-led politics frayed as new arrivals contested their legitimacy, but even frayed, they endured.

Even when complaints did not lead to convictions, they still disrupted the lives of the accused and their allies while enabling the resolution of underlying, simmering social conflicts. The success of the state's coercive apparatus preceded the resolution of the case itself; simply by investigating a complaint, the police made the legitimizing presence of the state felt in these small towns. Ultimately, cases brought by doctors against pharmacists and dentists had straightforward solutions—as long as the accused could prove that their role was ancillary and had some allies, they could avoid conviction. As a case in point, both Feintuch and Dobrenky appear to have arrived in the region at the same time, and their local support networks were equally established. How would this kind of conflict play out when one of the two rivals had deep roots in the community and a massive support network to summon in an effort to stop the judicial process and delegitimize his accuser?

The Fight for a Trusted Doctor:
The Endurance of Pioneer Networks

The case that opened the chapter, between the newly arrived doctor, Núñez, and his older counterpart, Koessler, offers a clear example of the ways in which mature social networks operated on the frontier to establish legitimacy. As noted, this case showcased how entire communities came together to challenge the ways in which the state attempted to legitimize medical care on the frontier. Unlike the previous cases in this chapter, this complaint hinged on the "exceeding their authorization" provision of Art. 208—when a town doctor trespassed on to another's territory.[43] These professional rivalries divided entire communities, forcing everyone to take sides and leaving behind a long trail of disruption. Issues such as personal animosities, prior working arrangements, control of rural areas, private contracts with *estancias* and government agencies, as well as the often-impossible distinction between domestic and professional space, made these cases deeply personal for those involved.

Rodolfo Koessler had been practicing medicine in San Martín de los Andes, a small town in a remote Andean valley deep in the lake country, almost since the town had been established, following familiar patterns as other immigrants.

Rodolfo Koessler and his wife, Bertha Igl, met in their native Bavaria and were married soon after in Geneva.[44] He had studied medicine in Germany, while his wife worked as a nurse for the Red Cross. After the Great War, they migrated to Argentina to fill a job opening in the German hospital in Buenos Aires. In 1920, the Koessler family moved to San Martín de los Andes (at the time a logging town of merely two hundred people) at the insistence of Enrique Schroeder, a German-born administrator for one of the large estancias in the area. Schroeder was concerned with the lack of medical options in the southern half of Neuquén and recruited the young couple to settle there. Koessler was professionally trained as a surgeon and quickly became an all-around town doctor, serving as the region's dentist, obstetrician, pediatrician, ophthalmologist, and pharmacist, often traveling on horseback for days to reach the more isolated ranches. In her biography of her husband, Bertha artfully illustrated the couple's adoption of their new environment with her nickname for Rodolfo: the "witchdoctor" of the Lanín ("Medizinmann am Lanín" in German, and "El Machi del Lanín" in Spanish).[45] He built a reputation as a public servant, treating patients even if they could not afford his services.

Besides developing his medical practice, the couple became deeply intertwined with the broader frontier community. They slowly transformed an abandoned country store building on the edge of town into an eighteen-bedroom practice, with several specialized clinics and boarding rooms for patients from out of town. Bertha used her training as a nurse to help with the patients, and in her spare time she collected stories from their indigenous patients, eventually publishing a well-known ethnography of the Mapuche people in the region (*Cuentos Mapuches de la cordillera*).[46] Koessler actively participated in the town's public life; he served on the municipal council at least three different times, even serving as the vice president for a two-year period. In many ways, the couple embodied the emblematic, archetypical immigrant "pioneer" of the early period of Patagonian settlement. They were the kind of pioneers who dominated their towns with their can-do attitude, resourcefulness, and ability to generate social capital through their wealth and charity (much like Primo Capraro, discussed in chapter 5). Unbeknownst to these pioneers, the world they had built was coming to an end as the Great Depression coincided with a period of heightened state presence in the early 1930s, and the arrival of new settlers (people like Núñez) began to transform the Patagonian frontier, bringing with them a different set of ways to garner and deploy social capital.

The complaint by Núñez portrayed himself a young physician struggling to establish his practice in town because an older doctor continued treating patients, refusing to abide by the directives of the Hygiene Department and constantly undermined his authority with the patients. Núñez, a thirty-one-year-old surgeon, made sure to frame Koessler as a "foreign national" that practiced medicine in the town without proper accreditation. Núñez set up the core of the complaint in a letter to the police: "as the comisario is well aware, [Koessler] has been appropriately notified that he is forbidden from practicing medicine since the town has received a nationally certified doctor on 15 February 1932, . . . and that the authorization that he had expired . . . in January of 1932." In the note Núñez provided a staggering amount of evidence for the police to start their case against Koessler: from the names of patients and potential witnesses, to the treatments and procedures performed, as well as the dates on which the transgressions occurred. As we have seen in previous examples, Núñez made sure not to give the police any reason to stall their investigation. The police responded swiftly to the direct complaint by the newly arrived doctor, and within a week they had deposed the people mentioned in the complaint.

Koessler's own testimony attempted to reframe the investigation from whether he saw any of the patients to why he did. He attempted to recast Núñez as an uncaring, unprepared, and petty urbanite, ill-suited for the life of a frontier-town doctor. Koessler not only corroborated Núñez's accusation—admitting to having treated each of the people in the list—but volunteered additional names of patients whom he treated in the months since Núñez's arrival. Koessler presented himself as someone who "the people in this county, regardless of social status, know me as an utterly selfless doctor who attends to the well-being of the entire population, to which I have provided my professional services for over ten years." Koessler's justifications for his continued practice of medicine in San Martín were threefold: sick people were going untreated due to Núñez's lack of flexibility; the new doctor had asked him to help out with some patients he himself was unqualified to assist; and some patients' care in the frontier transcended the artificial jurisdictions and limits imposed by the Hygiene Department.

Koessler argued that Núñez was known to regularly "deny assistance to sick people without resources." To make matters worse, he even denied assistance to people with "serious cases that required immediate action." Consider how Tomasa Catalán de Pelletieri, the forty-year-old widow who had jammed a needle in her finger while sewing characterized her interactions with Dr. Núñez. She recalled that he took ten hours to come see her, and that as soon as he walked through the door he proclaimed, "I'm here unwillingly," and appeared to be "annoyed" by her.[47] She recalled his rude curses as he cured her, and how he showed "a cruelty that knows no boundaries"—particularly since he refused to see her again without receiving payment upfront. Although Tomasa's case was the most dramatic, she was not the only poor patient that Núñez either refused to treat or treated unkindly. For example, Apolinario Vera, a Chilean farmer who moved to the region at the age of ten and had lived there for over three decades, testified that his pregnant wife, too sick to leave her bed, had needed medical treatment but Núñez had refused to provide a house call for free. Vera then appealed to Dr. Koessler, who attended his wife at home without charging the couple due to their "extreme poverty." Similarly, Victor Marangelo (a Chilean cattle-breeder from the edge of town, and a resident of Argentina for thirty-two years) fell off a wagon badly spraining his shoulder. When Núñez realized he would not be able to pay him, he began inquiring "without much tact" about what goods, or livestock he would be willing to part with in exchange for medical treatment. Marangelo got permission from Núñez to seek help from Koessler, who treated him free of charge. Ultimately, Koessler framed his actions in moral terms, claiming "it is understandable that . . . I would not refuse a friend, a patient, or especially a poor person who—as is publicly known—would not be attended to by the town's new doctor."[48]

Beyond establishing his "charitable" work, Koessler provided the investigation with cases in which he assisted people either in collaboration with Núñez or after a referral from him. The most significant of these cases was that of the infant Gabriela González, who was treated by Núñez for about four days, according to her father Juan González (a fifty-eight-year-old farmer from Chile, living on the impoverished outskirts of San Martín). Núñez diagnosed her with an infected kidney and possible appendicitis. He decided the girl needed an operation, but he did not have the required equipment. The family asked Dr. Koessler to come to their house from his office in Junín de los Andes, and he offered a different diagnosis. After treating the child for severe indigestion, she was completely recovered six months later.

Koessler also claimed that Núñez would refer patients to him when the new physician seemed unsure of the treatment or when the logistics of a case exceeded the new doctor's practice. For example, since Núñez did not have the instruments to perform dental extractions, he routinely sent those cases to Koessler's house to be treated. Similarly, when Daniel Sandoval (a forty-seven-year-old Chilean farmer, from the agricultural hamlet of Vega de Maipú on the edge of town) fell off a wagon and dislocated his left hip, he asked Núñez to call in Koessler, saying that he "trusted him more" ("tenía más confianza con el Dr. Koessler"). Working together, the physicians proceeded to push Sandoval's hip back into place, an excruciatingly painful treatment. Koessler personally took over Sandoval's care for about five weeks, as he recovered from his procedure.

Koessler established that he treated anyone needing care throughout March 1932, since Dr. Núñez was out of town—he was in Buenos Aires "for the season." Núñez confirmed that "during March [1932] I was indeed in Buenos Aires, and as for any patients that Dr. Koessler treated, I do not know, nor do I care, about them." Núñez's absence for a whole month in early fall (the beginning of the rainy season) a couple of weeks after starting his practice in San Martín was framed interestingly by the police investigator, who used the word "temporada" to refer to the absence—though the word literally means "season" it can also be understood as a "vacation." During that time Koessler treated the unnamed child of Belicario Troncoso, a thirty-seven-year-old Chilean contractor working as a wire-fence installer for the Sociedad Ganadera Gente Grande, who had lived in the region for over two decades.[49] While Belicario was away on a job, his wife called Koessler, who intervened immediately since the child had an "urgent pulmonary issue" and could not wait for Núñez's return. He also treated Bautista Pacheco, who received a stab wound to his abdomen while in a bar fight that had punctured his intestines, causing the police to fear he would bleed to death while in custody. The German doctor surgically treated the patient in his home and also lodged him there for fifteen days so that Bertha could monitor his recovery—without charging the state or the patient for the treatment or the care.

Another contentious issue between the two physicians was Koessler's new practice in a neighboring town, specifically how to handle his long-term relationships, existing contracts, and other personal arrangements in the broader region. He presented himself to the police investigator as "the certified doctor for the town of Junín de los Andes," a scant twenty-seven miles north, just over the county line. He was forced to commute a couple of times a week between the two towns since he still resided in San Martín, where his wife, home, and other interests remained.[50] Koessler argued that "having been the doctor of the people of San Martín de los Andes since 1920 and having earned the trust of the community" he could not simply extirpate himself from their lives because of a bureaucratic decision. For example, he treated Enrique Schroeder's wife, a compatriot and friend to the

German doctor. She had come to visit the Koessler family in San Martín de los Andes from their home in the countryside, and while there asked the doctor to follow up on a cure he had performed earlier in his office in Junín. Similarly, the case of Luis Castillo, a peon from the Establecimiento Ganadero Gente Grande, who was brought to Koessler's home to be treated for an emergency since the German doctor had a contract to treat all the workers from that company. The jurisdictions were not clear, and as the examples suggest, the patients moved freely between Junín and San Martín.

Likewise, after his establishment as the official doctor of Junín de los Andes Koessler became the default physician for the police force in that town, assisting them and their family members free of charge. In some cases, those family members lived in San Martín de los Andes, creating an additional jurisdictional problem. Additionally, as Núñez began as part of his regular rotation to tour the remote hamlets in his district he would absent himself from San Martín, leaving the town in need of a competent backup for emergencies and unexpected patients. For example, Koessler treated Juan Mestritua, who was gravely ill and needed emergency treatment, but Dr. Núñez was absent for the better part of the week, since he was "doing professional work in the hamlet of Lolog." Ironically, the more Núñez established himself in the frontier region, the less he was available to treat people in his urban practice (when Koessler made similar journeys on horseback in the previous decade, his wife Bertha acted as his backup).

Like the faith healers and the pharmacists, Koessler tried to claim legitimacy from performing a social good, which he considered superior to the legitimacy conferred by the state. He argued that he practiced medicine according to the dictates of his conscience, performing "what would be legally considered acts of humanity, since there would have been personal tragedies to lament without my attention in certain cases, especially among the needy, who are the worthiest of attention." Unlike the curanderos, faith healers, and pharmacists discussed earlier, Koessler was an elite male, a trained doctor who until recently had had permission to work in the area, and a respected vecino with deep ties to the police in the community, which made his claim to popular legitimacy harder for the police to reject.

Núñez, unsurprisingly, did not agree and offered the police a final, voluntary deposition at the end of the investigation restating the particulars of case and mocking his older rival's "holistic link to the population." He reminded the investigator that Koessler "openly admitted to treating patients, and that doing so in the name of some holistic link to the population which makes it impossible to refuse, does not exempt him from the crime of illegal practice of medicine . . . [and] the law is clear in this matter." The police were in the unenviable position of deciding if they ought to detain the only doctor the town had ever known, and a member of the town government, because he helped some patients in their moment of need. Of course, having Koessler arrested was not Núñez's endgame. Rather, it was a warning shot, fired across the prow of an older warship in lieu of an open battle.

The representatives of the state understood this well. The judicial system in Neuquén opted to steer clear of the squabble between the doctors, hoping that the situation would eventually settle itself—which it apparently did. After three years of depositions, investigations, and objections, the prosecutor determined that there was not enough evidence of a crime, finally recommending the dismissal of the case in September 1935. Núñez became the Director de la Asistencia Pública in 1934, and later that year established an urgent care center (Sala de Primeros Auxilios) replacing Koessler's house.[51] The *sala* cemented the institutionalization of health care in the region, serving as the county's health-care center (Delegación Sanitaria del Departamento). Núñez continued to run the *asistencia pública* until his retirement in 1954. Koessler retired in 1955, having outlasted his challenger. To commemorate his "relentless work toward the public good," the "people of San Martín de los Andes and the surrounding area" gave Koessler a certificate with over five hundred signatures—San Martín had only two hundred residents when he first arrived, and he attended over three thousand births in his thirty-three years there—which the German doctor proudly displayed in his house until his death.[52]

Conclusion

Cases against illegal practitioners of medicine progressed through the judicial process in a haphazard manner without much of a pattern as to how they were adjudicated. The conflicts between doctors, patients, curanderos, pharmacists, "quacks," and the state representatives obscure where exactly power and legitimacy resided in these frontier towns. Seemingly powerful people on respectable rungs of society were unable to compel the police to pay attention to their complaints, as in Dr. Sellano's complaints against the pharmacist Vivancio, for example. However, poor folk were not immune from police attention, as the case of María Guzmán illustrated. What can appear as state independence—state agents that were not beholden to any particular social class—was instead a complicated alchemy of judicial flexibility (as the outward expression of incompetence and scarcity) and dependence by state agents on different members of society.

The representatives of the state in small northern Patagonian towns had to interpret Art. 208's vague passages to establish if particular interventions fell within criminal parameters, while also collecting evidence to back that interpretation. That process allowed for two human moments to alter the way the rule of law was maintained in the frontier. First, the state agents' own relationship with the accused—either positive or negative—influenced how likely they were to have latitude in their interpretations of the law and the events. We saw how an outsider like Leopoldo de la Place received swift and violent attention from the police. Second, the accused's extended social network could attempt to deflect the state's attention by reframing the events in a benign light, or by refusing to add anything of value to the investigation. Recall how the newcomer Álvaro Sellano struggled to mount a crusade against the pharmacist in town. The tension between these two interlocking networks—networks of patronage and friendship between settlers and state agents, and networks of loyalty and reputation between settlers—dictated how effective the state was at responding to complaints by doctors, and by extension how successful it was at making the practice of medicine legible.

The police played a central role in how the state's coercive power was ultimately deployed, especially since judges and prosecutors tended to follow their lead. This made the establishment and maintenance of good relationships with local police an imperative for accused *and* accusers. When the accuser (sometimes anonymously) got to establish the narrative at the onset of the investigation with help from a sympathetic police force, as in the cases against María Guzmán, Filomena Salvo, and Abraham Feintuch, the accused had an uphill battle in their struggle to acquit themselves. With the police (and by extension the state) working against them, the only chance these healers had to avoid a conviction came from their social network's efforts to recast the investigation or to stall it.

Often avoiding a conviction was not enough, as the investigation could mete out informal punishments (not dissimilar to how the confiscation of hides was used by police to "punish" merchants during investigations). The deliberate pace of the investigations often penalized suspects before the judge even reviewed the case, detaining them, sequestering their belongings as evidence, and scaring off their allies. These byproducts of a police investigation not only forced the offending party to cease, they also frightened potential patients and reinforced the state-sanctioned legitimacy of the accuser. Some witnesses in the Koessler case mention how, *now that they were aware* that Núñez was the official town doctor, they would call on him when in need. The pharmacist in Conesa, Leiva, similarly expressed that the investigation had clarified Feintuch's illegitimacy for him. The investigations laid bare the social relationship and allegiances in a particular town, as witnesses testified in favor of one party or the other. The majority of these cases mimicked those explored in previous chapters, as agreements between prominent neighbors and police prevailed, while judges and prosecutors prioritized the rule of law over social harmony, and investigations served as de facto tools of social control.

On the few occasions when the authorities in Viedma reversed the investigator's recommendation in a case, the common denominator was a concerted popular outpouring of support for the accused. The mobilization in support of people perceived as "public servants," like Felix Susso, Onofrio Morales, and Rodolfo Koessler, appear to have made an impression on the prosecutors and judges. These cases bucked the trend, as the judicial authorities acted in a manner that made allowances for (apparent) violations of the law in order to maintain the peace, and to preserve the "public welfare" by not incarcerating people who improved their neighbors' lives. The level of success enjoyed by these popular fronts against the state depended on the legal understanding of the people mounting the resistance. The wide range of actions—from merely refusing to contribute to the investigation to openly contesting the finer points of the law—required courage in the face of a police inquisition, as well as some degree of coordination, and even a ringleader. The accused in these cases were in a disadvantaged position in relation to their accusers (either impoverished rural dwellers or doctors without the appropriate backing from the state-regulatory body) as their support networks were drawn primarily from the poorer segments of society.

This active, ongoing social dimension to the development of an increasingly robust state presence in Patagonia underscores the contingent nature of state formation. The creation and maintenance of frontier order required the careful interplay of social networks, patronage networks, and state action over thousands of individual, and highly personal, encounters.

Nationalism, Development,
and the End of the Frontier

Between 1885 and 1940, the national territories of northern Patagonia operated under a system that I have called *frontier justice*, characterized by informal arrangements channeled through formal avenues. In using this term, I mean to conjure up the image of a skeletal state, in most ways lacking resources to govern effectively, but one that could be built upon by settlers and made to serve their interests. This kind of arrangement proved surprisingly flexible—partially the result of incompetence, but also because state representatives had an interest in both following the spirit if not the letter of the law and in maintaining harmony. Settlers learned to turn the limitations of that "skeletal state" to their advantage, alternately cooperating, co-opting, or clashing with local police, mobilizing wide social networks to appeal to regional authorities, and using connections at the national level to pressure political appointees into action. Through these maneuvers, northern Patagonian settlers became active stakeholders in the success of the frontier state, exercising citizenship and establishing alternative sources of legitimacy based on perceived service to the community. The case of northern Patagonia shows that despite its shortcomings, and sometimes because of them, a weak state can create strong citizens.

Governing northern Patagonia required surprisingly little coercion, outside of the ongoing expropriation and criminalization of indigenous groups. Settlers in Río Negro and Neuquén had no experience equivalent to the brutal repression of strikers in Patagonia's far south that marred the 1920s. To maintain peace and order on the northern Patagonian frontier, Argentine government representatives relied on practices and mechanisms commonly associated with Latin America's colonial era. Since Patagonia had never truly fallen under Spanish rule these were not *continuities* but, rather, *re-creations* of colonial practices, borrowed liberally to supplement the shortcomings of the liberal order imposed on the region after military conquest.

In the aftermath of the Conquest of the Desert, state agents at the regional and local levels combined as creatively as they could an array of strategies to keep settlers from rebelling. Settlers, in turn, devised mechanisms to control or at least curb their unelected government officials. This complex dynamic of negotiated governance was the result of a layered process in which institutions, practices, people, and traditions took hold in northern Patagonia. In a sense it appears like an organic process that resulted in an arrangement that was both flexible and predictable. Still, like the colonial regime of old, Patagonia's twentieth-century regime of frontier justice only claimed to have found equilibrium.

Inferences about the Relationship between State and Society

The example of northern Patagonia offers some striking, interrelated takeaways. First, the absence of democratic institutions and practices at the regional level did not result in the establishment of authoritarian rule. This is particularly remarkable because the heavy restrictions placed on the political life of the national territories were much more onerous than in the western territories of the United States, for example, where settlers still elected legislatures and had local political rights. The two federal appointees to each national territory (governor and judge) learned how to limit their own power and actions in order to remain legitimate, often accommodating and compromising to ensure compliance from subalterns and from the general population.

Unchecked by regional legislatures, northern Patagonian governors could have become authoritarian figures, but they did not. The appointment of disinterested "political hacks," former military men, and people without a vested interest in the region's welfare did not make the office of the governor a "fictional government," as feared by one early governor. Paradoxically, ineffective and underfunded, regional governments failed to develop infrastructure and nurture civic institutions, but their futility did not lead to lawlessness or insurrection. On the contrary, the power vacuum enabled the strengthening of civil society because their government weakness gave civil society more importance. Judges similarly avoided the "judicial dictatorship" that critics feared when the system was established. Rather than rule in draconian fashion from their isolated perches in the regional capitals, federal judges managed, and sifted through the opinions and suggestions of, a disparate set of advisers—from local police injecting local sensibilities into investigations to ambitious prosecutors offering creative interpretations of the evidence.

Scholars have noted the centrality of the judiciary in Argentine political life, especially its stabilizing influence in times when democratic principles were abridged and subverted. The prominent role given to the judiciary by the framers of Law 1532 set northern Patagonia apart from similar territorial administrations in the hemisphere, for example, the US Southwest, whose notoriously weak and incompetent judiciary was embodied by the beleaguered office of US Marshal. That Argentine lawmakers allowed frontier judges such a central governing role signified a quiet preference by national elites, not for the development of a recognizably urbane political life on the frontier, but for the establishment of the rule of law and thus a private property regime.

Second, maintaining the rule of law on the frontier turned out to be a collaborative effort—not only between different rungs of the state but also between the state and society. Each case entailed a contested negotiation between the letter of the law and the particular specificity of each community. From that dialectic a significant civic identity developed—what this book has called *vecinos*. Vecinos were formally disenfranchised from local, regional, and national political life, but found informal political roles as the patrons of the police, which they conceptualized as *their* police. Vecinos also signaled through their collaboration, or by malingering, their expectations for the police in any given investigation. If the police were unable to get supplies for any given mission, it meant that the local elite opposed it. Similarly, if the police fabricated fines, arrested suspects on spurious charges, or compelled individuals to comply with arcane processes, the local elite surely desired them to punish someone informally. These avenues were also available to non-elites, like jóvenes seeking to overturn parental rights or abused wives looking to escape their tormentors. Local state representatives were available for capture by settlers if their reputations in town allowed them to.

Third, the importance of municipally based political life for the stability of the undemocratic political arrangement in northern Patagonia offers a glimpse into the ways power and legitimacy operated away from the regional capitals. The active role settlers played in maintaining order in the communities—alternately working with and resisting the actions of local-level state representatives—offers a lesson in the ways in which state legitimacy was maintained without the resources of a large-scale military occupation. The successful ways in which healers and noncertified medical practitioners parried accusations of illegal practice of medicine underscore how legitimacy based on community reputation counterweighed the legitimacy conferred by the state.

Although historical studies of urban life—its vibrancy, its political fervor, and its byzantine social orders—exist for Buenos Aires and other large cities in the Argentine interior, small towns remain poorly understood. Between 1895 and 1947, the proportion of Argentina's urban population (those living in towns with at least five hunderd people) skyrocketed from 37 percent to 62 percent, according to the 1947 census. Given that a majority of Argentines lived in the kinds of municipalities typical of northern Patagonia in the first half of the twentieth century, studies like this one can shed light on how informal political networks came to dictate many people's lives.

Some Thoughts on the Closing of the Frontier

Two interrelated developments changed the nature of the frontier in the late 1930s, fundamentally altering political life in northern Patagonian communities. First was a demographic transformation, followed by an institutional revolution. The demographic transformation included the arrival of a new generation of settlers, like Dr. Núñez or the Liga Patriótica–affiliated newcomers in Bariloche, as well as a "second generation" of settlers born on the frontier. The result was an increase, in both absolute and relative terms, of the Argentine-born population on the frontier. After a high-water mark in the 1910s, the decline of the foreign-born as a share of the region's total population was steady, reaching less than one in six Patagonians by the time of the 1947 census. In the territory of Neuquén about 12,000 of the 86,000 residents identified as "foreign-born" (less than 15 percent).

FIGURE 19. (*opposite*) "Ferrocarril del Estado en construcción en el ramal de Ingeniero Jacobacci sobre el Rio Chico, 1939" (AGN-Ddf, Inventario #144968). The longest single-span suspension bridge in Argentina showcases how the expansion of expensive infrastructure to better integrate the more remote areas of the plateau continued throughout the 1930s.

The Territory of Río Negro had a similar proportion, with about 22,500 foreigners out of a population totaling 134,000.

This demographic shift toward creolization, plus the rise of nationalism during the "Infamous Decade," encouraged immigrant groups either to embrace Argentine identities or risk becoming marginalized, as discussed in chapter 5. Additionally, the new generation of settlers reconceptualized northern Patagonia's earlier mélange of Chilean, indigenous, and immigrant inhabitants as a homogenous *primeros pobladores* ("first settlers"), flattening their own past, and in the processes disarticulating the kind of spaces available for local authorities to deploy frontier justice. Still more outsiders moved to Patagonia in the 1940s and 1950s, in part because infrastructure improvements made the region more accessible and settlement less daunting.

Related to demographic change, growing state intervention in the economy at the national level during the 1930s resulted in a deep transformation of the nature of the state presence in the region. The worldwide economic crisis shined an unflattering light on the agro-export model of economic development that had fueled liberal Argentina's meteoric expansion. The Conservative regimes of the 1930–1943 period responded to the crisis by strengthening the role of the state in several key areas, including setting currency exchange rates, negotiating labor relations, reordering industrial production, and manipulating trade in key raw materials. As we have seen, there was also a massive expansion of infrastructure. The total length of roadways in Argentina jumped from 2,000 km to 30,000 km between 1932 and 1944, for example.[1] All these policies together aimed to strengthen internal markets and reduce export dependency.

And all these developments affected northern Patagonia, none more so than the expansion of infrastructure. In the fifteen years between 1930 and 1945, Patagonia was "blanketed with national parks" as new roadways carved up the landscape, bridges replaced barges in the main cities, military bases sprung up along borders and other strategic locations, oil and gas fields multiplied, and mining for coal and iron also expanded.[2] Post offices flourished, and the state built newly staffed border posts in several Andean valleys to further institutionalize its presence there. The period after 1930 also saw an explosion in the construction of monuments. The sixtieth anniversary of the Conquest of the Desert in 1939 included commissioning of statues of General Julio Argentino Roca to adorn town plazas in Choele Choel, Bariloche, and Río Gallegos.

FIGURE 20. "Balnearios de Nahuel Huapi, 1936" (AGN-Ddf, Inventario #415072). The image shows "Señores Alberto Ruiz and Carlos Angeletti with their respective wives" illustrating how the establishment of the national park on the western shores of the great lake, and the extension of the railroad to the national park opened up the region to elite tourists.

Following the roadmap of the United States, the Argentine government in the 1930s promoted integration through tourism.[3] The Agriculture Ministry declared 1937 as "The Year of Patagonia," prompting journalists, tourists, senators, and other statesmen to visit the region in droves. A certain synergy emerged between the expansion of roadways—as well as the ancillary expansion of Argentina's main car-enthusiast club, the ACA (Automovil Club Argentino), the development of the state-owned oil company (YPF), and the growth of national parks. The ACA published maps and eventually opened service stations and hotels along the highways. YPF provided the gasoline for the service stations and the tax revenue for the roadways. And the national parks provided the impetus to see the countryside as part of the nation.

This new tourist-infrastructure complex stimulated the economy, in particular the extraction and processing of hydrocarbons, but also construction of roads, bridges, and hotels. Perhaps the clearest example of this synergy was the construction of two parallel north–south national highways on either side of Patagonia (Route 3 hugging the coast, and Route 40 abutting the Andes). These and other roads sutured the region to the rest of the country. To boot, the state finally completed the long-delayed transcontinental railroad joining Nahuel Huapi Lake with the Atlantic Coast, thus integrating the region in an east–west fashion.

The tourist-infrastructure complex created by the Conservative regimes effectively made "the road, the hotel, and the tourist the tip of the nationalizing effort" on the Patagonian frontier, as Ernesto Bohoslavsky aptly phrases it.[4] What had been an exclusively elite clientele in the first couple of decades of state-sponsored tourism became socialized and popularized in the Peronist era, when it served a dual purpose. It rewarded union voters and it educated Argentine citizens. Union-supported hotels, which multiplied in the Andean region slightly later than they had along the Atlantic Coast of Buenos Aires and the hills of Córdoba, offered a democratized sense of social well-being for the working class, while simultaneously underscoring the "need for a broader knowledge of the country's geography."[5] In the populist state, tourism became more than a well-earned right; it became a national duty.

By the end of the 1930s, state agencies were managing entire communities in Patagonia. The National Park Administration (NPA) designed and built most of Bariloche's iconic downtown, including the civic center, the promenade, and the cathedral, turning the former agricultural hamlet into the centerpiece of Nahuel Huapi National Park. The same architect designed a monumental hotel, Hotel Llao Llao, just outside town, and the state-built roadways to connect Bariloche to the park's attractions, physically reorienting the town plan.

Bariloche was the model, but the NPA also administered the land, roads, and urban development of San Martín de los Andes, which bordered the newly created Lanín National Park not far to the north. The state-owned oil company, YPF (Yacimientos Petrolíferos Fiscales), built and maintained worker housing in Plaza Huincul, Cutral-Có, and Comodoro Rivadavia, cementing and deepening its role elsewhere in Patagonia. Military garrisons in towns like General Roca, Chos Malal, and Zapala similarly distorted traditional town politics, and thus their economies, as new businesses proliferated to supply soldiers with food, goods, and entertainment. Several state agencies stepped into the institutional vacuum typical of these towns. Most had, in the previous decades, been too small to elect their own city council to manage more than minimal governance.[6]

FIGURE 21. "Road to Traful, along the Limay River in Neuquén, 1930" (AGN-Ddf, Inventario #183073). Although the picture is probably mislabeled and was taken in the 1950s, it features the single-width gravel road typical of the main access roads to the Andean Valleys.

Northern Patagonia's Continued Exceptionalism

In 2016, Argentina's Minister of Education, Esteban Bullrich, inaugurated a veterinary school in Choele Choel, near the site where the campaign to subdue Patagonia had been launched. In a speech on the national holiday with which that campaign got underway, Bullrich grandiosely proclaimed a "Second Conquest of the Desert," but this time using "books instead of rifles." The speech set off a public opinion firestorm.[7] Seizing the modest occasion to make a grand statement about more than a century of Argentine administration and control of Patagonia, Bullrich observed that even at this late date, state institutions, infrastructure investments, and steady demographic growth had not succeeded in "populating this desert." Bullrich's comments expressed Argentina's muted anxiety about Patagonia, and perfectly illustrated the two narratives that Argentines tell themselves about the region.

The first narrative depicts Patagonia as a place possessing an untapped, protean power to radically transform Argentina. The minister tried to turn the opening of the veterinary school into another chapter in this story. Education, he argued, was the last piece in that puzzle that would finally unleash Patagonia's productive potential. The second narrative, dating back to the middle of the nineteenth century, holds that Patagonia's incomplete incorporation—the persistence of "the desert"—threatened Argentina's claim to it, demanding yet another attempt to "conquer" the region. The sense that Patagonia—its landscape, its people—remains not only alien to the rest of Argentina but is also an adversary to be subdued has fueled the government's haphazard policy toward the region since it was annexed.

These competing narratives underscore the tension between Patagonia's central importance to Argentina and the way in which the region has been treated as inescapably marginal. For some, the incorporation, colonization, and Argentinization of Patagonia was the resolution of the nation's founding tension between barbarism and civilization.[8] This was wishful thinking, since the region, as we have seen, was incorporated in name only. Patagonia was colonized by subjects of dubious allegiance, and its Argentinization was never completed.

The limits of the state's reach into Patagonia before 1940 created a space for a dynamic civil society to develop, mostly independent from national elites. Their independence meant that when national authorities invested in the region's economy, they did so without being able fully to count on the regional elite and without needing to politically co-opt it first. This independence forced the national authorities to invest in developing the region's economy without the ability to completely integrate the region's political elite. Patagonia's independence and self-reliance for over half a century of neglect made the region *appear* fragile to the authorities in Buenos Aires, who continued to operate under the dual narratives of incomplete incorporation and unfulfilled potential. Much like Minister Bullrich's impromptu speech when launching a veterinary school, national authorities continued to view Patagonia as precariously Argentinized and requiring more investment to fully unlock the economic potential of the region. In the eyes of the national elite, the Conquest begun in 1878—the closing of the last internal frontier—has not ended, for they continued to see Patagonia as an incomplete promise rather than a unique experiment.

Frontier Isolation: Towns and Geography

Patagonia's "sterile plains" and "silent mountains," as Lady Florence Dixie remarked, shaped how human development in northern Patagonia took shape.[1] Isolated by vast distances and by the government's "precarious reach" into the frontier, settlers in northern Patagonia also experienced uneven access to infrastructure and newspapers. How well a town was connected—by roads, rails, and press—to the rest of the country dictated how much local conflict there was, or at least, how much of the local conflict reached the outside world.

The Physical World of Northern Patagonia

Northern Patagonia can be divided broadly into three separate geographic regions, with radical differences in political economy, settlement, and access to water. The Andean region is defined by a long north–south mountain range, punctuated by the occasional volcano. Transversal valleys and lakes, evidence of the last glaciation, cut the landscape between the mountains, facilitating east–west communication in a way that is not possible farther to the north along the Andes.

On the eastern edge of this mountainous area, a fifty-mile-wide zone made up of smaller hills (known as the *precordillera*) eases the transition into the plateau. Some Andean valleys grow dense, humid forests (part of the Valdivian temperate rainforest), while in others, ancient araucaria conifers dominate. The Andean peaks create a "rain shadow" effect, which condenses most of the moisture from the westerly winds over the mountains, leaving dry winds to sweep the plateau, leading to staggeringly different rainfall totals in relatively close areas. For example, some parts of the Valdivian rainforest in the western Andean valleys receive as much as 4,500 millimeters (about 178 inches) of rainfall each year, while areas in the Somún Curá volcanic plateau receive around 200 millimeters (less than 8 inches) of rain per year, making access to water precarious.

The volcanic plateau, known simply as the Meseta Patagónica, is the second region. Characterized by staggered plateaus (*mesetas escalonadas*) that descend toward the ocean, the *meseta* covers most of the surface area of northern Patagonia. Seasonal runoff creeks dot the plateaus, carving steep canyons and ravines in the volcanic soil, scarring the landscape. These creeks empty into a series of wide, land-locked basins known locally as *bajos* (low-lying depressions), most notably the salt ponds of Bajo del Gualicho, which sit seventy-two meters below sea level, the second-lowest point in the Southern Hemisphere. An array of sturdy shrubs and bushy grasses, such as the thorny *neneo* or the tall *coirón*, thrive in this steppe landscape, as they are especially adept at surviving in the clayey, sandy, and salty ground. The plateau ends abruptly in the Gulf of San Matías, in a long, sparsely populated coastline defined by sheer cliffs and cold, almost constant easterly winds that bring some Atlantic moisture and winter rains.

The third region of northern Patagonia is the fertile river valleys. Patagonian rivers, fed mostly by snowmelt, begin as turbulent whitewater brooks as they descend the Andes, adding tributaries from different valleys before slowing down into meandering, navigable waterways in the plateau. As the rivers slow down, they deposit sediments that provide the distinctive colors of the main rivers: Río Negro has a muddy chocolate color, while Río Colorado carries clay from northern Neuquén and southern Mendoza, making its waters notoriously reddish.

Following the confluence of the Neuquén and Limay rivers, the meandering Río Negro valley traverses the width of the continent, carving a ten-kilometer-wide fertile floodplain through the steppe. Before the construction of a series of dams along its tributaries, the Río Negro experienced periodic flooding on an apocalyptic scale; in 1899 the waters washed away many of the settlements in the lower valley, and in 1903 most of the towns in the upper valley suffered almost complete destruction. The varied weather and terrain of the Comahue region had important consequences for human settlement. Despite the potential and promise of some areas of Patagonia in the eyes of the statesmen and travelers, the vastness of the region routinely thwarted any attempts to integrate and develop it in a consistent, coherent fashion. Paradoxically, this tension between the possibilities of the enticing areas and the pitfalls of the less hospitable ones fueled the debates around the importance of the region.

Towns and Settlements in Northern Patagonia

Settlements in northern Patagonia developed quickly and chaotically, even though most districts remained primarily rural well into the twentieth century. Official creation of towns had "little connection to reality," representing instead an after-the-fact acknowledgment of a settlement's existence or a manifestation of a desire for the existence of a settlement there.[2] Ley 1532 established that settlements with at least a thousand residents would elect their own municipal councils, en route to formally becoming independent towns.

This process usually played out very differently. For example, the presidential decree recognizing Cutral-Có as a town in 1933 noted that the settlement already had 2,000 residents, merely legalizing and regularizing an ad hoc community that had emerged on the edge of the oil fields there (previously known simply and ominously as "Barrio Peligroso," the dangerous neighborhood). On the other hand, in 1908 the government established a sprawling "shepherd's colony" ("Colonia Pastoril Coronel Mariano Chilavert") in southeastern Río Negro, which remained little more than a "paper town" until the 1970s, when an iron mine was established nearby in Sierra Grande. The vibrancy of a community, official recognition of a town, and the conferral of local political rights rarely correlated during the period.

Access to the region's infrastructure fueled the emergence and growth of settlements throughout northern Patagonia. Two railroads (one owned by British interests, and the other funded entirely by the Argentine state) connected many of the settlements to one another and to the rest of the country, but an expansion of those lines to cover the region more comprehensively never materialized. The state-owned line was designed to cross the plateau, linking the Andes Mountains and the Atlantic Ocean. Work on the line begun in 1908 and advanced slowly, only reaching its terminus at Nahuel Huapi Lake in 1934 but establishing a series of towns along the rails during the 1910s and 1920s. In 1896, the British-owned Ferrocarriles del Sud (which operated throughout Buenos Aires province) built a line from Bahía Blanca to the Río Negro valley, reaching Choele Choel in 1898, the eastern shore of the Confluence in 1899, and the western shore in 1902, the present site of the city of Neuquén. A decade later the line was extended into the heart of the Neuquén territory in a failed effort to extend it across the Andes, with the railhead in present-day Zapala. Some settlements deep in the Andean valleys remained ill-connected to infrastructure, but developed nonetheless, tapping into centuries-old trading networks with Chile. The reach of the state into those isolated towns and rugged valleys depended, in great part, on how much the settlers *needed* the state for their livelihood.

Settlements coalesced in apparently idiosyncratic patterns, but responded to one of three impetuses: military connections, state planning, or international commerce. The main settlements in the Andean range region were established to support military bases or sprouted up to take advantage of trade with Chile through the mountain passes. For example, Neuquén's first governor, Col. Olascoaga, founded Chos Malal in the place where the fort for the Fourth Division had been, to control a key waypoint in the cattle trade between Chile and the Pampas region. Chos Malal served as the seat of government for the Neuquén Territory following its founding in 1887 until the capital moved to the more accessible location in the confluence of the Limay and Neuquén rivers. Similarly, Junín de los Andes sprouted in 1883 to support the military detachment there (Fuerte Junín), but was only officially recognized as a town in 1958. About thirty miles to the south, San Martín de los Andes was established in 1898 on the site of the Fuerte Maipú, by order of the military commander, who wanted a forward military presence on the shore of Lake Lácar to strengthen the Argentine presence in a contested area. The town remained under military governorship until 1911, when its primary economic activity turned to lumber and cattle, taking advantage that the waters of the lake flowed to the Pacific, integrating it with Chile.

The rest of the towns in the Andean area had an economy that, at least at first, depended on commerce for their survival. Las Lajas, along the Agrio River, served as a commercial hub for standing cattle between Chos Malal and Neuquén, but lost prominence when the British-owned railroad reached Zapala in 1913. Zapala itself grew out of the railroad construction, as workers, contractors, and those supplying them settled in the railhead area, quickly becoming a significant "dry dock" and transportation hub for the entire territory.[3] San Carlos de Bariloche, and its neighboring agricultural colony of Nahuel Huapi, benefited from an accessible mountain pass along the great Nahuel Huapi Lake, receiving heavy inflows of population and investment from Chile. In a long valley, roughly eighty miles to the south of the Nahuel Huapi region, the village of El Bolsón similarly developed as an isolated agricultural community with commercial links across the Andes. The Welsh colonies in Esquel and Trevelin, on either side of the longitudinal "16 de octubre" valley, also developed primarily as agricultural producers.

The main settlements in the central plateau only appeared after the state-owned railroad had created stations along its path, often in places with seasonal creeks. The main population centers in this region were, from east to west, San Antonio Oeste, Valcheta, Sierra Colorada, Maquinchao, Los Menucos, Ingeniero Jacobacci, Comallo, and Pilcaniyeu (collectively known as the "Línea Sur"). The towns of Cutral-Có and Plaza Huincul in Neuquén are not *physically* in the central plateau, but share similar physical characteristics and also emerged as a result of state-investment in infrastructure, in this case oil extraction. The primary economic activity in the towns of the Línea Sur was sheep-raising and, to a lesser degree, mineral extraction. The town of Maquinchao, for example, grew to supply and support the large sheep-raising estancia on the edge of town operated by the British-owned Argentine Southern Land Company (A.S.L.Co., for short), which also operated other estancias throughout Patagonia.

Immigrants were slow to move to these towns, given the isolation and harshness of the terrain, and the majority of the population in some Línea Sur towns remained primarily indigenous until well into the twentieth century. Throughout the period, the Argentine government struggled with how to economically develop and make its presence felt in the rugged plateau, experimenting with the land-reform initiatives of the 1908 Ley de Fomento, the state-owned railroad line, and later with a variety of massive infrastructure projects, including a series of monumental police stations intended to project state power in these remote rural districts.

The Río Negro valley region was the area of earliest settlement after the military occupation, and the one which received the most significant commercial and productive investment. The Río Negro valley is currently characterized by dense population spread out into several towns webbed together by roadways and irrigation canals. The upper Río Negro valley has the highest population concentration of the region, clustered around two urban centers: the Neuquén-Cipolleti-Plottier metropolitan area (straddling the confluence of the Neuquén and Limay rivers) and the General Roca-Villa Regina-Allen metropolitan area farther downriver. The most important settlement of the middle Río Negro valley is the archipelago where the town of Choele Choel was established, which is surrounded by smaller settlements like Fray Luis Beltrán, Lamarque, and Pomona. Finally, the lower Río Negro valley comprises a less densely populated stretch of the valley, roughly from the town of General Consea to the Viedma-Carmen de Patagones metropolitan area close to the river's mouth, and including San Lorenzo (with its famous beet-sugar mill) and Guardia Mitre between them.

The growth of these villages, towns, and cities dictated the rate and intensity of conflict with state authorities. The rapid arrival of immigrants after the expansion of a rail line, for example, tended to create conflict with local authorities who either resented or sought to benefit from the newcomers (for example, the immigrant merchants turned virulent vecinos in Maquinchao, featured in chapter 5). Access to printed media, both locally and nationally, modulated the intensity and tenor of the conflicts in these isolated outposts.

Notes

Introduction

1. Theroux, *Old Patagonian Express*, 377.

2. The original reads: "Hacete amigo del Juez / y no le des de qué quejarse . . . / siempre es bueno tener palenque 'ande ir a rascarse." Hernandez, *Martín Fierro*, ll. 2319–24

3. "Gómez, Pedro—homicidio, lesiones, robo, incendio, rapto, violación y estupro," Leg #1921-1299, f.742 (Archivo de la Justicia Letrada, Territorio del Neuquén, hereafter AJL, TN).

4. Abrams, "Notes on the Difficulty of Studying the State," 82.

5. Pérez, "Cuatreros, comerciantes, comisarios," 12.

6. Vita, "El Concepto 'Estado.'"

7. Hämäläinen and Truett, "On Borderlands," 348.

8. Turner, *Frontier in American History*; Weber, "Turner, the Boltonians, and the Borderlands"; DeLay, *War of a Thousand Deserts*; Langfur, "Frontier/Fronteira"; Slatta, "Comparing and Exploring Frontier Myth and Reality"; Prado, "Fringes of Empires"; Jones, "Civilization and Barbarism"; Sarmiento, *Facundo*.

9. Noel, *Debating American Identity*; Meeks, *Border Citizens*; Benton-Cohen, *Borderline Americans*; Gordon, *Great Arizona Orphan Abduction*.

10. For the South Africa example, see Christopher Saunders's piece in Thompson and Lamar, *Frontier in History*, 123–48. For the Yucatan example, see Karen Deborah Caplan, *Indigenous Citizens*; Clendinnen, *Ambivalent Conquests*; Dumond, *Machete and the Cross*; Sullivan, *Unfinished Conversations*. For the Russian example, see Yuri Slezkine, *Arctic Mirrors*; and Crews, *For Prophet and Tsar*.

11. Silver, *Our Savage Neighbors*; Aron, *American Confluence*; Aron, *How the West Was Lost*.

12. Lamar, *Far Southwest*.

13. Adapted from Gutiérrez and Romero's characterization of citizenship "from below" in their reinterpretation of political citizenship in pre-Peronist Argentina; Gutiérrez and Romero, *Sectores populares, cultura y política*, 155–56.

14. These historiographic debates actually underscore the multifaceted nature of citizenship and the many avenues open for people without political rights to actively participate in the construction of "the political," broadly defined, even if the authors disagree

on precisely when these practices of citizenship began. At the heart of it, the debate about rights centers on the nature of the liberal state, and the relative value of non-institutional political participation in the liberal regime underpins much of the conversation on the nature of citizenship in this period. For example, for popular participation in groups opposed to the liberal state, see De la Fuente, *Children of Facundo*, for a view that highlights the "electoral practices and participation in the public sphere" of plebeian porteños as early as 1870, see Sábato, *Many and the Few*; for an interpretation based on how "popular politics remained dormant until the 1890s," given the "exceptionally elitist" nature of the liberal project, see Rock, *State Building and Political Movements in Argentina* 216–231; for a look at the advance of social rights as political rights retreated in the 1930s, see Lobato, "El estado en los años treinta," 42–43.

15. For example, Lobato, "El Estado en los años treinta," 49–55, looks at the expansion of maternity rights for workers in the mid-1930s, a paradoxical expansion of social rights in a period of receding political rights. Similarly, Quijada, "Nación y territorio" looks at the expansion and support for Afro-Argentine ethnic and political rights even as the state curtailed and homogenized indigenous identities in the second half of the nineteenth century; and, to a lesser degree, so does Quijada, "Hijos de los barcos." Interestingly, Bertoni, *Patriotas, cosmopolitas y nacionalistas* teases out the complex and changing attitudes between cosmopolitanism and nationalism surrounding the rights and expectations for the mass of immigrants arriving to Argentina in the last two decades of the nineteenth century. The debates around citizenship at the time blended national and class-based concerns with strictly political considerations.

16. Fischer, *A Poverty of Rights*, for example, argues that even at a time of broad expansions of citizenship rights in Brazil during the 1930s and 1940s, the poorest urban residents of Rio faced institutional and structural limits to accessing those rights. Guardino, *Time of Liberty*. Caplan, *Indigenous Citizens*, for example shows how citizenship was not only locally negotiated but also had far-reaching consequences for regional stability and subaltern incorporation. For a frontier outlook, see Valerio-Jiménez, "Neglected Citizens and Willing Traders." Bloemraad, *Becoming a Citizen*, for example, shows how the rates of naturalization (that is, of acquiring citizenship) in early twentieth-century America followed local patterns of "openness" as well as local political mobilization of immigrants. See also Bloemraad, "Citizenship Lessons from the Past." Drake, *Between Tyranny and Anarchy*.

17. Classic accounts of the liberal project in northern Patagonia and its intellectual underpinnings include Schoo Lastra, *El indio del desierto*; Walther, *La conquista del desierto*; Yunque, *Calfucurá*; Zeballos, *Callvucurá y la dinastía de los Piedra;* Rojas Lagarde, *"Viejito porteño"*; Trímboli, *"1979."*

18. Weber, *Peasants into Frenchmen.*

19. Rafart, *Tiempo de violencia en la Patagonia*; Ernesto Lázaro Bohoslavsky, *El Complot Patagónico*; Casullo and Perren, "'Cierta imponente majestad'"; Casullo, "'El Estado mira al sur'"; Ruffini, *La pervivencia de la República Posible*; Masés, *Estado y cuestión indígena*; Masés, *Un siglo al servicio*; Maggiori, *Historias de frontera.*

20. Sellers-García, *Woman on the Windowsill.*

21. Piccato, *City of Suspects*; Piccato, *History of Infamy*; Buffington and Piccato, *True Stories of Crime in Modern Mexico*; Salvatore et al., *Crime and Punishment in Latin America.*

22. Even though *Patagonia* appears in academic literature as a shared area of both Argentina and Chile, within local understandings the limits of the region vary widely. In Chile, the term *Patagonia* is used to describe the rugged "Magallanes region," in the far south edge of the continental mass between the Pacific Ocean and the Andes range and wedged between the island of Chiloe (to the north) and the Diego Ramirez islands to the south. Bohoslavsky, *El Complot Patagónico*, 30–31; Navarro Floria, *Historia de la Patagonia*, 19.

23. Bandieri, *Historia de la Patagonia*, 20; Borrero, *La Patagonia trágica*; Torres, "Two Oil Company Towns in Patagonia"; Harambour-Ross, "Borderland Sovereignties"; Bohoslavsky, "Clase y ciudadanía."

Chapter One

1. The original reads: "Que el territorio rionegrino se mantiene inculto es una verdad; el estado nada hizo por él jamás . . . Nada se hizo para impulsar hacia el progreso a esa rica zona de la república y el alcanzado lo debe, repetimos, al esfuerzo aislado de sus habitantes." Quoted from Casullo, "Las pujas por la Justicia Letrada," 38.

2. The original reads: "La ley me coloca como guardián de la humanidad entera" in "Cifuentes, José Luis—infanticido," Leg #1917-177, f.915" (Archivo de la Justicia Letrada del Territorio de Neuquén, administered by the GEHiSo, in the UNCo, hereafter AJL-TN).

3. "La Municipalidad de General Roca—queja contra el Juez de Paz de General Roca," Leg #43-1653 (Archivo Histórico Provincia de Río Negro, Justicia Letrada, hereafter AHP-RN, JL).

4. Manuel Lainez (Senator from Buenos Aires) in a speech against a spending bill for infrastructure in Patagonia. Taken from "Diario de Sesiones del Senado, 1907," 533–535.

5. Casullo and Perren, "Cierta imponente majestad," 16.

6. Quoted in Ruffini, *La pervivencia de la República Posible*, 210.

7. "Juzgado de Paz de Patagones. Pobreza Franciscana," *La Nueva Era*, 29 March 1908—quoted in Casullo and Perren, "Cierta imponente majestad."

8. Bohoslavsky and Casullo, "Sobre los límites del castigo en la Argentina periférica," 53–56.

9. Lamar, *Far Southwest*, 9–11; Wilson, "Government and Law in the American West," 503.

10. Ruffini, "La consolidación inconclusa del Estado," 96.

11. Sábato, *Many and the Few*, 5.

12. Alberdi, *Bases y puntos de partida*, 60 (section XV).

13. Alberdi, *Bases y puntos de partida*, 59; the original reads: "La planta de la civilización no se propaga de semilla. Es como la viña: prende de gajo."

14. Moya, *Cousins and Strangers*, 48–50.

15. Ramón J. Cárcano, a national representative from Córdoba province, authored much of the law and famously declared that the national territories were "completamente despoblados"; Gallucci, "El espejismo de la República posible," 69.

16. Ruffini, "La consolidación inconclusa del Estado," 97.

17. Ruffini, "Ecos del centenario," 3–5.

18. Ruffini, *La pervivencia de la República Posible*, 79–84.

19. "Memorias del Gobernador de la Pampa" for 1911; quoted in Zink, "La política territoriana pampeana," 2.

20. Ruffini, "El tránsito trunco hacia la 'República verdadera,'" 99.

21. Ruffini, *La pervivencia de la República Posible*, 78, 88, 112–115.

22. Quoted in Ruffini, "'Hay que argentinizar la Patagonia,'" 665.

23. Navarro Floria, "La nacionalización fallida de la Patagonia Norte."

24. Gallucci, "El espejismo de la República posible," 71–72.

25. Ruffini, "Ciudadanía y Territorios Nacionales," 3.

26. Gallucci, "Las prácticas electorales," 3.

27. Gallucci, "Las prácticas electorales," 6–8.

28. The Liga and their popular supporters had not managed to dislodge Cháneton's Unión Vecinal from power, but had shown resilient growth, challenging their long-standing grip on power. At the same time, the other newspaper in the capital, *La Cordillera*, defended the Liga, claiming that the incumbents had purposely mishandled the electoral rolls.

29. Ruffini, *La pervivencia de la República Posible*, 194–207; Bandieri, "La masonería en la Patagonia," 28.

30. From the "Memoria presentada al Congreso Nacional por el Ministro del Interior, 1899: Vol. 1," 228.

31. Ruffini, "Ciudadania y Territorios Nacionales," 3–6.

32. Bandieri, "La masonería en la Patagonia," 33.

33. Ruffini, "El tránsito trunco hacia la 'República verdadera,'" 107.

34. For a short biographic note on Viera, see Ruffini and Masera, *Horizontes en perspectiva*, 421.

35. Ruffini, *La pervivencia de la República Posible*, 238–40.

36. For an excellent study of the justices of the peace in southern Buenos Aires, see Palacio, *La paz del trigo*. For the national territory of La Pampa, see Diez, "Instituciones territoriales, orden público"; Diez, "Justicia y policía"; Moroni, "La construcción de un espacio institucional"; Moroni, "Cattle Raiding, State Control." For a summary of the deployment of judicial institutions in northern Patagonia, see Casullo, "'El Estado mira al sur.'"

37. "Memorias del Ministro de Justicia, Culto e Instrucción Pública presentadas al Congreso Nacional de 1891," quoted from Rafart's *Tiempo de Violencia en la Patagonia*, 140.

38. Varela, "Estado y Territorios Nacionales," n.p. (n. 109).

39. Ball, *United States Marshals*, 241.

40. "Carlos Vivoni—queja contra el Juez de Paz de General Roca," Leg #xx, 23811 (AHP-RN, JL).

41. Casullo, "El Estado mira al sur," 342–44.

42. For a few examples, see Leg# 191-7617; 209-8299; 216-8600; 229-9170; 233-9313; 238-9543/4; 241-9599; 242-9619; 253-10069; 264-10464; 268-10649; 269-10690; 908-39189 (AHP-RN, JL), and 1900-581, f.1; 1903-293, f.267; 1917-74, f.211; 1917-361, f.250; 1918-152, f.273; 1920-6, f.398; 1924-391, f.230; 1924-721, f.292 (from AJL-TN).

43. Rafart, *Tiempo de violencia en la Patagonia*, 146; Rafart and Debattista, "El nacimiento de una alquimia imperfecta."

44. Palacio, *La paz del trigo*.

45. Argeri, *De guerreros a delincuentes*, 202.

46. Argeri, *De guerreros a delincuentes*, 271.

47. See, for example, the biographies of the first few governors in Martha Ruffini, "Anexo: Figuras relevantes de Río Negro entre 1878–1908," in Ruffini and Masera, *Horizontes en perspectiva*, 406–14.

48. Lamar, *Far Southwest*, 13.

49. Taken from: "Memoria presentada ante el Congreso Nacional de 1899," as quoted in Ruffini, *Pervivencia de la República posible*, 210.

50. Ruffini, *La pervivencia de la República Posible*, 259–62.

51. For example, in the "Memorias anuales del Gobernador de Río Negro, 1929," 1930, Caja 16, documento #7006 (AGN-AI), the acting governor concluded his otherwise glowing cover letter to the Minister of the Interior with the remark that postal and judicial data were missing in the final report because the postal administration and the judge refused to send their reports to him.

52. "Memorias anuales del Gobernador, 1918," 1919, Caja 13, documento #3611 ("Colección del Ministerio del Interior, comunicación con Territorios Nacionales," Archivo General de la Nación-Archivo Intermedio, hereafter AGN-AI).

53. For example, in 1929, Governor Quaglia of Río Negro insisted that the palace of justice planned for Lamarque was "grotesque," while asking the minister to push for irrigation canals for the town instead. In "Memorias anuales del Gobernador de Río Negro, 1928," 1929, caja 21, documento #8382 (AGN-AI).

54. Ruffini, *La pervivencia de la República Posible*, 169–70.

55. Ruffini and Masera, *Horizontes en perspectiva*, 407–8.

56. Ruffini and Masera, *Horizontes en perspectiva*, 408.

57. The powers and limits of the governor's office are laid out masterfully in Ruffini, *La pervivencia de la República Posible*, 172–77, 222–29.

58. Ruffini, *La pervivencia de la República Posible*, 191–207, 245–55.

59. "José M. Lerman, querella criminal contra Don Fracisco R. Denis por usurpación y abuso de autoridad," Leg #1922-204-f. 807 (Archivo de la Justicia Letrada del Territorio de Neuquén, administered by the GEHiSo, in the UNCo, hereafter AJL-TN).

60. Fischer, *Poverty of Rights*, 91–93.

61. In his farewell memorandum to his supervisor, Río Negro's governor León Quaglia dedicated significant time to trying to appeal, in no uncertain terms, for more funding for police officers. Arguing that they risked backsliding into chaos unless more funds were secured for salaries and furniture for rural police. "Memorias anuales, 1928" (AGN-AI). Quaglia's report differed very little from the pleas for better funding to train and retain police officers issued by the governor of Río Negro ten years earlier. "Memorias anuales del Gobernador, 1918"—AGN-AI.

62. Rafart, *Tiempo de violencia en la Patagonia*, 169–89.

63. Rafart, *Tiempo de violencia en la Patagonia*, 170.

64. Suárez, "La Policia en la Región Andina Rionegrina," 235.

65. Rafart, *Tiempo de violencia en la Patagonia*, 185; Masés, *El mundo del trabajo*, 17.

66. Rafart, *Tiempo de violencia en la Patagonia*, 182.

67. Gayol, "Sargentos, cabos y vigilantes," 139; as a matter of fact, a lot of the problems in the police force in northern Patagonia seem to mirror the issues in the Buenos Aires

of 1860–1880, including absenteeism in times of harvest, poor pay, and lack of troop cohesion.

68. Rafart, *Tiempo de violencia en la Patagonia*, 183–86.

69. Bohoslavsky, "El brazo armado de la improvisación," 220–21; Rafart, *Tiempo de violencia en la Patagonia*, 178.

70. The cases of Eduardo Talero and Juan Francisco Palermo stand out as competent exceptions. Talero, a renowned Colombian intellectual and politician, exiled by the violence in his homeland, served as police chief for the territory of Neuquén. Palermo, on the other hand, received an appointment as Río Negro's police chief after years of well-known work as a police and crime reporter for the national daily *Crítica*; Rafart, *Tiempo de violencia en la Patagonia*, 172–73. For more information on the role of *Crítica* and other popular urban dailies in making crime and police activity a central social issue in the 1920s, see Lila Caimari's brilliant *Apenas un Delincuente* (specially pp. 199–230).

71. Rafart, *Tiempo de violencia en la Patagonia*, 177; Rafart notes that the figure misrepresents the situation slightly, as fifteen of the appointments were made for long-term solutions; and of the substitutes, three of them acted as chief a dozen times each, and another one an additional seven times. But the instability and constant acephaly at the highest territorial office prevented coherent guidelines or sustained reform. See Bohoslavsky, "El brazo armado de la improvisación," 234–38, for an in-depth analysis of the changing length in service years of the police in Neuquén.

72. Rafart quotes (176) Oscar Fermin Lapalma's *Leyendas del Río Negro* (1933): "Aparte de la escasez del personal de policía, los hombres de tropa son, por lo común, individuos ineptos, sin arraigo en el territorio, desconocedores del medio y con escasa noción de la función que desempeñan. En homenaje a la verdad, esto no reza hoy para *el personal superior, que constituye todo un ejemplo de probidad y competencia*" (p. 105 in the original; emphasis added).

73. Rafart, *Tiempo de violencia en la Patagonia*, 173.

74. Suárez, "La Policia en la región Andina," 238.

75. See, for example, "Gamboa, Mariano—abuso de autoridad," Leg#279-11070 (AHP-RN, JL); or "Minayo, Cándido—queja contra José García," Leg#690-27934 (AHP-RN, JL).

76. Suárez, "La Policia en la región Andina," 244.

77. Some examples of this can be found in "Martínez, Ángel E.—abuso de autoridad," Leg. #618-25266, AHP-RN, JL; similarly, see "Sánchez, Faustino—denuncia contra el sub-comisario," 1916-154, f.173 (AJL-TN); for an example of the *limits* of their power in the frontier despite their standing, see "Velázquez, José del Carmen y otros—cuatrería," Leg#418-16519, AHP-RN, JL.

Chapter Two

1. The original reads: "Destruyamos pues moralmente esa raza, aniquilemos sus resortes y organización política, desaparezca su orden de tribus y si es necesario divídase la familia. Esta raza así quebrada y dispersa, acabará por abrazar la causa de la civilización."

2. The original reads: "La Barbarie esta maldita y no quedan en el desierto ni los despojos de sus muertos." Zeballos, *Viaje al país de los araucanos*, 228.

3. "Nahuelcheo, Alejandro—rapto de su esposa," Leg #42-1608 (Archivo Histórico Provincial-Río Negro, Justicia Letrada, hereafter: AHP-RN, JL).

4. The original reads: "ofensas de esta magnitud merecen todo el castigo de las leyes, mucho más en el caso presente en que el ofendido es un indígena que sometido y sujeto a las disposiciones de la sociedad civilizadas y a las leyes del cristiano, ha contraído matrimonio regular . . . y que viviendo pacíficamente con el trabajo y la [illegible] formaban un hogar de tranquilidad, arrebatada todo en un instante por un malhechor audaz y atrevido."

5. Greenwald, "'Improve Their Condition.'"

6. Quijada, "'¿Hijos de los barcos,'" 471–72.

7. Moldes and Entraigas, "La población del Territorio Nacional del Río Negro," 4.

8. Moldes and Entraigas, "La población del Territorio Nacional del Río Negro," 12–13.

9. Argeri, *De guerreros a delincuentes*, 91–100.

10. Kerr, *Sex, Skulls, and Citizens*, 24–28.

11. Jones, "Calfucurá and Namuncurá," 182–83.

12. Delrio, *Memorias de expropiación*, 33–83, 92–112.

13. Kellogg, *Law and the Transformation of Aztec Culture*; Walker, "Crime in the Time of the Great Fear"; Boyer, "Honor among Plebeians"; Socolow, *Women of Colonial Latin America*, 49; Sloan, *Runaway Daughters*.

14. Larson, "Introduction," 10.

15. Lenton et al., "Argentina's Constituent Genocide," 69.

16. Kerr, "Progress at What Price?," 17.

17. Ruffini, *La pervivencia de la República Posible*, 33; Rock, *Argentina*, 96–98.

18. Goldney, *El cacique Namuncurá*, 249.

19. Marley, *Wars of the Americas*, 781.

20. Jones, "Warfare, Reorganization, and Readaptation," 181; Masés, *Estado y cuestión indígena*, 37; Bandieri, *Historia de la Patagonia*, 141; Delrio, "Indios Amigos, Salvajes o Argentinos," 211–15.

21. Jones, "Warfare, Reorganization, and Readaptation," 177.

22. Zeballos, *Callvucurá y la dinastía de los Piedra*, 10; Jones, "Calfucurá and Namuncurá," 178–79.

23. This is hardly a unique phenomenon to the Patagonian frontier. For the emblematic case of the US-Mexican border, see DeLay, *War of a Thousand Deserts*, 16–31.

24. Navarro Floria, *Historia de la Patagonia*, 104; Bandieri, *Historia de la Patagonia*, 143; Ruffini, *La pervivencia de la República Posible*, 52.

25. Wolfe, "Settler Colonialism and the Elimination of the Native," 387–88.

26. Masés, *Estado y cuestión indígena*, 12; 63–65.

27. Delrio and Ramos, "Genocidio como categoría analítica," 3–4.

28. Bandieri, *Historia de la Patagonia*, 142.

29. Vezub and Healey, "'Occupy Every Road,'" 49–51.

30. Larson, "Conquest of the Desert," 25–27.

31. Vezub and Healey, "Occupy Every Road," 50.

32. Bandieri, *Historia de la Patagonia*, 144; Navarro Floria, *Historia de la Patagonia*, 106.

33. Originally found in "Memorias del Departamento de Guerra y Marina, Año 1885" but quoted from Masés, *Estado y cuestión indígena*, 55.

34. Greenwald, "'Improve Their Condition,'" 104–5.

35. Masés, *Estado y cuestión indígena*, 12.

36. The original from *El Nacional* (Buenos Aires, 31 December 1878) reads: "ENTREGA DE INDIOS. Los miércoles y los viernes se efectuará la entrega de indios y chinas a las familias de esta ciudad, por medio de la Sociedad de Beneficencia."

37. From the same issue of *El Nacional*, 31 December 1878.

38. Masés, *Estado y cuestión indígena*, 88; the drop-off is actually quite staggering: 1878: 1,805 captives; 1879: 2,403 captives; 1880: 131 captives; 1881: 44 captives; 1882: 54 captives; 1883: 60 captives; 1884: 68 captives; 1885: 445 captives; Vezub and Healey, "Occupy Every Road," 50.

39. Vezub, *Valentín Saygüeque*, 65–66.

40. Masés, *Estado y cuestión indígena*, 128–30.

41. Bandieri, *Historia de la Patagonia*, 139–54; Navarro Floria, *Historia de la Patagonia*, 104–10; Masés, *Estado y cuestión indígena*, 47–48.

42. Delrio and Ramos, "Genocidio como categoría analítica," 13.

43. Evans, *John Daniel Evans "El molinero."*

44. Delrio, *Memorias de expropiación*, 87, 97, 105; Masés, *Estado y cuestión indígena*, 145–46.

45. Moldes and Entraigas, "La población rionegrina durante la época territorial," 12.

46. Masés, *Estado y cuestión indígena*, 145.

47. Delrio, *Memorias de expropiación*, 120–43.

48. Delrio, *Memorias de expropiación*, 132–47; Masés, *Estado y cuestión indígena*, 165–70.

49. Bandieri, *Historia de la Patagonia*, 146–54; Navarro Floria, *Historia de la Patagonia*, 110–22; For a detailed description of the evolving, disjointed and ambivalent policy of the Argentine government toward the conquered indigenous people (and how the government came to think about the "Indian problem" as part of a larger "social problem"), see Masés, *Estado y cuestión indígena*, 18–24, but entire work deals with the issue. For a detailed look at how the shifting "Indian policy" affected one particular rural community (Colonia Cushamen), see Delrio, *Memorias de expropiación*, 85–87; For a discussion of the ways in which Argentine statesmen struggled with different conceptualizations of citizenship and "otherness" regarding conquered indigenous groups, see Jong, "Indio, Nación y Soberanía," 172–91.

50. Larson, Introduction, 10.

51. Bohoslavsky and Casullo, "La cárcel de Neuquén," 297–99.

52. Nicoletti and Barelli, "La Virgen Auxiliadora, patrona de la Patagonia," 106–12.

53. Langer and Jackson, "Colonial and Republican Missions Compared," 288–89; Rausch, "Frontiers in Crisis," 342.

54. Langer, *Expecting Pears from an Elm Tree*, 277.

55. Masés, *Estado y cuestión indígena*, 70–80; the Salesian presence in the frontier was so widespread that in 1934 the church erected a diocese in Viedma and made the Virgin Maria Auxiliadora the patron saint of Patagonia.

56. Carrizo, "Hombres, soldados y mecánicos," 3.

57. *Memoria Del Ministerio Del Interior*, 116.

58. Consejo Nacional de Educación, *El monitor de la educación común*, 428–30.

59. Argeri, "Las niñas depositadas," 68n5.

60. Argeri, *De guerreros a delincuentes*, 246; for the colonial context, see J. M. Kobayashi's "La educacion como conquista."

61. Tortorici, "Agustina Ruiz."

62. The lack of basic government documents (like birth certificates) was a similar barrier for destitute people elsewhere in Latin America at the time. See, for example, Fischer, *Poverty of Rights*.

63. "Acosta, Marta—reclama su hija" Leg #7-204, AHP-RN, JL.

64. The original reads: "me concreto solamente a pedir a la autoridad me haga restituir una hija menor sustraída, sobre la que tengo con su padre, el derecho de patria potestad,

que las leyes legales, tanto naturales como civiles, nos las acuerdan como a otros padres respecto de sus hijos legítimos menores de edad."

65. *Fallos de la Corte Suprema de Justicia de la Nación: con la relación de sus respectivas causas . . .* , vol. 39, 1891, 257–65.

66. Stasiulis and Yuval-Davis, "Introduction," 3.

67. Jacobs, *White Mother to a Dark Race*, 3.

68. Wolfe, "Settler Colonialism and the Elimination of the Native," 387.

69. Jacobs, *White Mother to a Dark Race*, 4.

70. Delrio and Ramos, "Genocidio como categoría analítica," 16.

71. *Fallos de la Corte Suprema de Justicia de la Nación (1890)*, 39:261–62.

72. *Fallos de la Corte Suprema de Justicia de la Nación (1890)*, 39:261.

73. Originally quoted in "The Indian's Friend," 12, no. 2 (October 1889), 9; quoted in Jacobs, *White Mother to a Dark Race*, 40.

74. Argeri, *De guerreros a delincuentes*, 245.

75. The original reads: "irrognado (sic) perjuicios al Establecimiento que has (sic) no llenar sus fines que son los de dar una completa educación e instrucción a los hijos del pueblo y enseñarles alguna labor con la cual se puedan ganar honradamente la vida se ve privada del auxilio que le podría proporcionar con sus pequeños trabajos domésticos, aún antes de recompensar de alguna manera los beneficios que en él se le han prodigado . . . Y si V.E. considera que nuestros Establecimientos solo viven de la caridad pública y del trabajo manual de esas mismas huérfanas recogidas, bien podrá echar de ver cuán justo es que se provea de conformidad con lo pedido."

76. Ford, *Settler Sovereignty*, 2–3.

77. Ford, *Settler Sovereignty*, 12.

78. "Suárez, Martín—corrupción de menores" Leg# 40-1534, AHP-RN, JL. The original reads: "Martín Suárez ha *comprado* una indígena" (emphasis added here).

79. The original reads: "me la cedieron a mí para mujer mía y yo les di una recompensa a cambio, dos caballos y dos yeguas, y desde que me la cedieron la lleve y la tuve en mi casa a dicha menor haciendo vida marital con ella, como *Ley de Indio*" (emphasis added).

80. The original reads: "nos regaló en recompensa algunos animales como es costumbre entre Indios."

81. The original reads: "Me vi obligada a acceder a Suárez porque un gringo de la Aguada de los Loros llamado Antonio Pilla, valiéndose que estaba yo sola en un despoblado . . . me agarró y haciéndome fuerza me violó, hace diez meses: este hecho me decidió a acceder a la proposición de Suárez."

82. The original reads: "todos ellos son indígenas: como tales no hablan ni aun comprenden bien el castellano, así pues, no debe extrañar ni debe confundirse lo que Suárez en su declaración quiere decir 'que le fue entregada la menor y dio una recompensa.'"

83. The original reads: "Las costumbres de estos pobres seres son muy pocas las personas que las desconocen. Es sabido pues que *el Indio es altivo y orgulloso* que él no compra a la mujer que toma por compañera si no que está en sus hábitos puede decirse <u>es una ley propia de su raza</u> que al serle entregada la que va a ser su compañera tienen el deber de osequiar [sic] en el mismo acto a los padres y aun a los parientes con prendas y animales en cuya demostración prueban o manifiestan el estado de sus fortuna" (emphasis added).

84. Joseph, "Preface," xiv–xvi.

85. "Reuque, Leonarda—su desaparición," Leg. #33-1228 (AHP-RN, JL).

86. The original reads: "alguna persona mal intencionada oculta en el monte."

87. The original reads: "hablaba indígena con facilidad y poco el idioma nacional."

88. For example, Leg# 415-16398 ("Sandalio, Rolando—denuncia fuga del hogar conyugal de su esposa"), where the police investigator noted "the general negative opinion of the population toward Sandalio, as well as his involvement with illegal activities." Similarly, in Leg# 413-16348 ("Fornagueira, Ines—fuga del hogar de la menor María Domínguez"), the investigator added that "it is public knowledge that Maria Domínguez had been making marital life with low-lives, which leaves no doubt that she left Carro's house on her own initiative." Both cases came from the AHP-RN, JL.

89. The original reads: "por cuanto la imprudencia la motivó su grave estado y *la ignorancia de que esta embatado [sic] el indígena* la hizo cometer un desativo [sic], en la creencia que hacia un bien." (emphasis added).

90. Walker, "Crime in the Time of the Great Fear," 45–46.

91. "Sandalio, Rolando—denuncia fuga del hogar conyugal de su esposa," Leg. #415-16398 (AHP-RN, JL).

Chapter Three

1. The original reads: "El suscripto ignora hasta qué punto la Policía puede obligar a una mujer casada volver hacer vida marital con el esposo contra su voluntad." Found in "Rebolledo, Jesús Manuel—denuncia fuga de su esposa (Benita Barrios de Rebolledo)," Leg #463-18429 (Archivo Histórico Provincial de Rio Negro, Justicia Letrada, hereafter AHP-RN, JL).

2. "Anzini de Moriconi, María—su denuncia" 1924-218, f.845 (Archivo de la Justicia Letrada—Territorio de Neuquén, hereafter AJL-TN).

3. Gallucci, "Las prácticas electorales," 10.

4. Bennett, *History Matters*, 55.

5. Wiesner-Hanks, "Forum Introduction."

6. Dialeti, "Patriarchy as a Category of Historical Analysis," 331.

7. Hill Collins, *Intersectionality as Critical Social Theory*.

8. Amussen, "Contradictions of Patriarchy," 255.

9. Amussen, "Contradictions of Patriarchy," 350–51.

10. Tutino, "Revolution in Mexican Independence," 393–97.

11. Caulfield et al., "Introduction," 1–2.

12. Bates, "Unaccompanied Minors and Fraudulent Fathers," 99.

13. Alonso, *Thread of Blood*, 50.

14. Szuchman, *Order, Family, and Community*; Johnson, "Dangerous Words, Provocative Gestures."

15. Sloan, *Runaway Daughters*.

16. Guy, *Sex and Danger in Buenos Aires*; Szuchman, *Order, Family, and Community*; Guy, "Parents before the Tribunals"; Szuchman, "Challenge to the Patriarchs."

17. Shelton, *For Tranquility and Order*, 157.

18. Hunefeldt, *Liberalism in the Bedroom*; Christiansen, *Disobedience, Slander, Seduction, and Assault*.

19. Shumway, *Case of the Ugly Suitor*.

20. Chambers, *From Subjects to Citizens*, 104–5.

21. Lavrin, *Women, Feminism, and Social Change*, 206–11.

22. Guy, "Parents before the Tribunals," 181.

23. West, *Growing Up with the Country*, 248–49.

24. Levy, "At the Intersection of Intimacy and Care," 70.

25. Szuchman, *Order, Family, and Community*, 4–6.

26. "Molina, José de la Rosa—fuga del hogar," 1930-463, f.712 (AJL-TN).

27. Bates, "Unaccompanied Minors and Fraudulent Fathers," 117–18.

28. Bates, "Unaccompanied Minors and Fraudulent Fathers," 107.

29. Hunefeldt, *Liberalism in the Bedroom*, 206.

30. "Arraigada, Renulfo Cerceda—rapto de una menor," Leg #1930-1318, f.884 (AJL, TN).

31. Uribe-Urán, *Fatal Love*, 32–33.

32. Socolow, "Women of the Buenos Aires Frontier," 78–79.

33. Lavrin, *Women, Feminism, and Social Change*, 206–11; Lavrin notes that the period between 1915 and 1920 saw a series of changes in attitudes toward civil rights for women, stemming from the Pan-American Conference and jurists evolving their thinking on this issue.

34. "Sandalio Rolando—denuncia fuga del hogar conyugal de su esposa," Leg #415-16398 (AHP-RN, JL).

35. Guy, "Parents before the Tribunals."

36. Retrieved from the Argentine Ministry of Economy's InfoLEG initiative: http://www.infoleg.gov.ar/infolegInternet/anexos/45000-49999/48953/norma.htm (accessed on 25 February 2015). Law 2393 was further amended the following year, with Law 2681. The law was amended again in 1968 through a presidential decree, and again in 1987, with Law 23515, which greatly reformed civil marriage.

37. Emphasis added. The original reads: "Art. 53.—La mujer está obligada a habitar con su marido donde quiera que este fije su residencia. Si faltase a esa obligación, el marido puede pedir las medidas judiciales necesarias y tendrá derecho a negarle alimentos. Los tribunales, con conocimiento de causa, pueden eximir a la mujer de esta obligación cuando de su ejecución resulte peligro para su vida."

38. Interestingly, Law 2393 included similar but less onerous provisions for the male partner in Art. 51, which specified that the husband had to not only live with his wife (outlawing absenteeism) but also that he was required to provide for her. The courts were empowered to forcefully guarantee that this happened. This progressive imagining of marital responsibility and reciprocity was summarily repealed by Law 2681 eleven months after being enacted. The original text of Law 2393 reads: "Art. 51.—El marido está obligado a vivir en una misma casa con su mujer y a prestarle todos los recursos que sean necesarios. Faltando el marido a estas obligaciones, la mujer tiene derecho a pedir judicialmente que aquél le dé los alimentos necesarios. En este juicio podrá pedir las expensas que le fueren indispensables."

39. "Álvarez, Tránsito—solicita la restitución de su esposa al hogar," Leg#30-1131 (AHP-RN, JL).

40. Her testimony originally reads: "Que hace ocho años que son casados habiéndola Sandalio raptado de su hogar en Conesa, y casándose en Viedma, empezando por castigarla al mes de casados, impidiéndole en todas formas tener relaciones con los hermanos y la madre [de ella] y siendo en toda ocasión víctima de todo género de negaciones."

41. "Rebolledo, Jesús Manuel—denuncia fuga de su esposa (Benita Barrios de Rebolledo)," Leg #463-18429 (AHP-RN, JL).

42. Ley Nacional #11357-Sobre los derechos civiles de las mujeres.

43. "Galeano, Crescenia—fuga del hogar marital," Leg # 597-24453 (AHP-RN, JL).

44. "Carrasco, Benedicto—denuncia fuga del hogar de su esposa," Leg# 1930-221, f.973 (AJL-TN).

45. Guy, "Parents before the Tribunals," 176.

46. "Sinsky, Eloisa—fuga del hogar," Leg#462-18334 (AHP-RN, JL).

47. Guy, "Parents before the Tribunals," 178.

48. Davis, *Fiction in the Archives*, 24–25.

49. West, *Growing Up with the Country*, 147–49.

50. "Barrientos, Gregorio—denuncia fuga de su hija Delia del hogar paterno," Leg# 317-12474 (AHP-RN, JL).

51. "Rivero, Roberto y Flora (menores)— sus fugas del hogar," Leg #1933-127, f.763 (AJL-TN).

52. Guy, "Girls in Prison."

53. "Godoy, Juana—fuga del hogar de su guardador," Leg# 599-24542 (AHP-RN, JL).

54. "Parra, Segundo (menor)—su fuga," Leg#1116-49001 (AHP-RN, JL).

55. Hardwick, *Sex in an Old Regime City*, 172.

56. Alonso, "Rationalizing Patriarchy," 29, 42.

57. Slatta, *Gauchos and the Vanishing Frontier*, 67.

58. "Biorki, Lina—su denuncia," Leg #1913-175, f.711 (AJL-TN).

59. "Cifuentes, José Luis—infanticidio," Leg #1917-177, f.915 (AJL-TN).

60. "Carrasco, Benedicto—denuncia fuga del hogar de su esposa," Leg# 1930-221, f.973 (AJL-TN).

61. "Amador, Carmen—abandono de persona," Leg #1146-50307 (AHP-RN, JL).

62. Hardwick, *Sex in an Old Regime City*, 185.

63. Slatta, *Gauchos and the Vanishing Frontier*, 61.

64. "Contreras, Ramona—infanticidio," Leg #1924-595, f.270 (AJL-TN).

65. "Morón, Margarita—infanticidio," Leg #623-25456 (AHP-RN, JL).

66. "Rodriguez, Leonor ("La Ñata")—corrupción de menor," Leg #1107-39385 (AHP-RN, JL).

67. Shelton, *For Tranquility and Order*, 158.

68. Diaz, *Female Citizens, Patriarchs, and the Law*, 6.

Chapter Four

1. Mercedes Arraigada—su fuga del hogar con Yanino Ramírez, Leg #1922-571, f.880 (Archivo de la Justicia Letrada del Territorio de Neuquén, administered by the GEHiSo, in the Universidad Nacional del Comahue, hereafter AJL-TN).

2. Gentile, "Las Niñas Del Viento," 49.

3. Slatta, *Gauchos and the Vanishing Frontier*, 59.

4. In his deposition, Marcelino claimed that he *did* have sex with her, and because she did not bleed he took that as a sign that she had had sex in the past. Magdalena insisted that she fought him off, and the medical exam confirmed that she had not been "deflowered," though she had severe bruising on her inner thighs, probably from his errant thrusting that night ("femoral coitus," as the medical examiner called it).

5. "Yenkis, Eduardo—estupro," Leg #611-25024 (AHP-RN, JL).

6. Gentile, "Las Niñas Del Viento," 56.

7. "Sambueza, Dolores o María Trinidad—fuga del hogar," Leg #1933-746, f.915 (AJL, TN).

8. Gentile, "Las Niñas Del Viento," 51.

9. "Mariboli, Corina del Carmen—fuga del hogar," Leg #1289-56430 (AHP-RN, JL).

10. Gentile, "Las Niñas Del Viento," 58.

11. Miguel Esteban Walsh and his wife (Dora Gil) had welcomed their third child that January: Rodolfo Walsh, the famous Argentine journalist, author, and activist, who was disappeared and killed in 1975 by the military government. Rodolfo characterized his father as a "transculturado al que los peones mestizos de Rio Negro llamaban *Huelche*" (which roughly translates as "fearless and elusive" in the Araucanian language). He said that his father, who worked on the estancia until 1932 before trying his luck as an *arrendatario* on a farm in Buenos Aires, "tuvo tercer grado, pero sabía bolear avestruces y dejar el molde en las canchas de bochas." He described his mother tragically as a woman who "vivía en medio de cosas que no amaba: el campo, la pobreza." I want to thank Tomás Moller Poulsen, who first alerted me to this connection.

12. Sloan, *Runaway Daughters*, 32–61.

13. Sloan, *Runaway Daughters*, 34.

14. Socolow, "Women of the Buenos Aires Frontier," 80.

15. Davies Lenoble, "El impacto de la política cacical," 92–93.

16. "Pérez, Manuel—denuncia fuga de su hija (Camila) [originalmente caratulada como Rapto]," Leg#359-14104 (AHP-RN, JL).

17. Gentile, "Las Niñas Del Viento," 49–50.

18. Socolow, "Spanish Captives in Indian Societies," 86.

19. Shumway, *Case of the Ugly Suitor*, 97–114.

20. Edwards, *Hiding in Plain Sight*, 66–84; for the demographic data, see p. 18.

21. Shumway, "'Purity of My Blood,'" 203.

22. Shumway, "'Purity of My Blood,'" 214.

23. Bates, "Unaccompanied Minors and Fraudulent Fathers," 111–13.

24. Farnsworth-Alvear, *Dulcinea in the Factory*, 164–65.

25. Klubock, *Contested Communities*, 188.

26. Otovo, *Progressive Mothers, Better Babies*, 55–81.

27. Tossounian, *La Joven Moderna in Interwar Argentina*, 54–55, 61.

28. Miller, "Assent as Agency," 62.

29. "Arraigada, Renulfo Cerceda—rapto de una menor," Leg #1930-1318, f.884 (AJL, TN).

30. Gentile, "Las Niñas Del Viento," 55.

31. Guy, *Sex and Danger in Buenos Aires*, 42–43.

32. Sloan, *Runaway Daughters*, 54.

33. Socolow, "Women of the Buenos Aires Frontier," 75.

34. Slatta, *Gauchos and the Vanishing Frontier*, 59.

35. "Mases, Luis—rapto de la menor Mercedes Oliva," Leg #51-1965 (AHP-RN, JL).

36. "Soto, Margarita—denuncia por fuga de su hija Aida Cabrera y denuncia Alberto Álvarez por corrupción de menor," Leg# 1932-43, f.338 (Archivo de la Justicia Letrada del Territorio de Neuquén, administered by the GEHiSo, in the Universidad Nacional del Comahue, hereafter AJL-TN).

37. For another example, see "Oballe, Rómulo—denuncia la fuga del hogar de su hija Sara," Leg# 1084-47374 (AHP-RN, JL)—in that case the father consented to the marriage under protest, adding that he though they should wait since "creía oportuno que primero se buscase un trabajo o colocación fija, ya que *era un hombre que no posee ni lo más indispensable para la vida*" (emphasis added).

38. Hunefeldt, *Liberalism in the Bedroom*, 189.

39. Scott, "Gender," 45.

40. Szuchman, "Challenge to the Patriarchs," 141.

41. Haworth, "'To Do as I Will.'"

42. Haworth, "'To Do as I Will.'"

43. García, *El fracaso del amor*, 50.

44. None of the jóvenes I encountered in the archive challenged their assigned gender roles or even their gender expressions, but they asserted their right to marry whom they chose.

45. "Molleni, María Enriqueta ('Milonguita')—fuga del hogar," Leg #842-36026 (AHP-RN, JL).

46. Socolow, "Acceptable Partners," 226.

47. "Guillermo, Ángela—fuga del hogar," Leg # 646-26287 (AHP-RN, JL).

48. The original reads: "para *así obligar* a sus padres a que le dieran el consentimiento ... lo ha hecho con el sólo propósito *de obligar a sus padres* a que le den el consentimiento para casarse con su novio" (emphasis added). Elsewhere in the file, Manuel remarks: "y en esa forma sus padres se *verían obligados* a hacerlos casar."

49. "Guerra, Edubina—fuga del hogar," Leg #1914-595, f.950 (AJL, TN).

50. "Contreras, Robinson—rapto y estupro," Leg #1916-181, f.176 (AJL, TN).

51. Sloan, *Runaway Daughters*, 38.

52. Sloan, *Runaway Daughters*, 38.

53. Caulfield, *In Defense of Honor*, 105–9.

54. "Castillo, Pedro José—denuncia por fuga del hogar de su hija Humbertina," Leg #132-512, f.430 (AJL, TN).

55. Hunefeldt, *Liberalism in the Bedroom*, 188.

56. Hunefeldt, *Liberalism in the Bedroom*, 206.

57. Sloan, *Runaway Daughters*, 58.

58. Hunefeldt, *Liberalism in the Bedroom*, 180.

59. "Tejero, Juana—Fuga del hogar," Leg #653-26559 (AHP-RN, JL).

60. Hunefeldt, *Liberalism in the Bedroom*, 221.

61. "Vazquez, Marcelino—rapto de la menor Magdalena Vazquez," Leg #1930-260, f.983 (AJL-TN).

62. "Fornagueira, Inés—fuga del hogar de la menor María Domínguez," Leg #413-16348 (AHP-RN, JL).

63. I want to thank Denise Cikota for helping me interpret the garbled handwriting in this part of the document.

64. "Rial de Antemil, María—denuncia fuga del hogar de su hija (Paula)," Leg# 326-12851 (AHP-RN, JL). It should be noted that the case had an additional complaint attached. María Rial initiated a separate complaint against the lead police investigator claiming he had been incompetent. The police officer detailed his side of the story before sending the case to his supervisors, complaining in turn that María Rial was unreasonable ("antojosa"), and did not know how to read or write, which was making the investigation especially difficult. The complaint was acknowledged by the *fiscal*, but it did not ultimately affect the investigation.

65. The original reads: "pues concurría siempre de visita a la casa donde *tenía libertad amplia y oportunidad para usar de la honestidad de aquella* sin necesidad de sacarla de la casa, y más aún cuando en tiempo anterior el deponente hacia vida marital con la madre de Paula, María Rial" (emphasis added).

66. "Fuentes, Pedro Santos—violación y ultraje al pudor," Leg #1924-737, f.245 (AJL, TN).
67. Dialeti, "Patriarchy as a Category of Historical Analysis," 334–35.
68. Cowling and Martin, "Marx's 'Eighteenth Brumaire,'" 19.
69. Dialeti, "Patriarchy as a Category of Historical Analysis," 335.
70. Miller, "Assent as Agency," 49.
71. Gleason, "Avoiding the Agency Trap," 447.
72. Thomas, "Historicising Agency," 324–26.
73. Johnson, "On Agency," 115.
74. Scott, "Gender," 1067.
75. Sloan, *Runaway Daughters*, 33.
76. Townsend, *Malintzin's Choices*, 5.
77. Gentile, "Las Niñas Del Viento," 61.
78. Thomas, "Historicising Agency," 335.
79. Gleason, "Avoiding the Agency Trap," 458.
80. Proyecto de Ley (s-0297/12) Senado de la Nación, Ana M. Corradi de Beltrán.
81. Borrello, *La volvería a matar*.

Chapter Five

1. Taken from "Diario de sesiones del Senado, 1907," 533–535. The original reads: "*Los territorios no necesitan más que buena justicia y mucha policía.*"
2. As quoted in Méndez, *Estado, frontera y turismo*, 232–33.
3. "Gallardo, Evaristo—su denuncia contra el Comisario de Bariloche," Leg #803-34873 (Archivo Histórico Provincial – Rio Negro, Justicia Letrada, hereafter AHR-RN, JL).
4. The original reads: "la cultura del pueblo."
5. Ruffini, *La pervivencia de la República Posible*; Ruffini, "El tránsito trunco hacia la 'República verdadera'"; Ruffini, "Ciudadania y Territorios Nacionales"; Gallucci, "Las prácticas electorales"; Gallucci, "La vida política de los instrumentos"; Bandieri, "Asuntos de familia"; Bandieri, "Sociedad civil"; Kircher, "Miradas, relaciones y prácticas"; Prislei, "Imaginar la Nación, modelar el desierto.'"
6. Cikota, "Uncertain Flags."
7. Gallucci, "Ciudadanía y orden institucional," 305.
8. Baeza, *Fronteras e identidades en Patagonia central*, 144–46.
9. Pérez, "Cuatreros, comerciantes, comisarios," 2–3.
10. Adelman and Aron, "Trading Cultures," 2.

11. Privitellio, *Vecinos y ciudadanos*.

12. Gutiérrez and Romero, *Sectores populares, cultura y política*, 71–107.

13. For example, see Di Meglio, *¡Viva el Bajo Pueblo!*; Johnson, "Empire's Long Goodbye"; and the classic Salvatore, *Wandering Paysanos*.

14. Sábato, *Republics of the New World*; Johnson, *Workshop of Revolution*.

15. Sábato, *The Many and the Few*.

16. Gallucci, "El espejismo de la República posible," 71.

17. Sellers-García, *Woman on the Windowsill*, 213.

18. For some examples of this vast literature, see Guardino, *Time of Liberty*; Mallon, *Peasant and Nation*; Mallon, "Reflections on the Ruins." For a discussion on the role of vecinos in Mexico's besieged northern frontier, see DeLay, *War of a Thousand Deserts*, 2009; Shelton, *For Tranquility and Order*; Reséndez, *Changing National Identities at the Frontier*.

19. For example, in the context of the Mexican Revolution (1910–1940), "vecinos" were neighbors who actively participated in the construction of schools (Rockwell, "Schools of the Revolution"), town dwellers who had benefited from the privatization of indigenous land (Mallon, "Reflections on the Ruins"), or parishioners with an active hand in shaping religious institutions (Marjorie Becker, *Setting the Virgin on Fire*), or more broadly, politically active neighborhood liaisons (Lear, *Workers, Neighbors, and Citizens*).

20. Pérez, "Cuatreros, comerciantes, comisarios," 3.

21. Pérez, "Las policías fronterizas," 3.

22. "Bruce, Ricardo—denuncia ocultación de delito y abuso de autoridad contra sub-Comisario Servellon Ortellado," Leg# 648-26375 (AHP-RN, JL).

23. "Juzgado de Paz de Patagones. Pobreza Franciscana," *La Nueva Era*, 29 March 1908—quoted in Casullo and Perren, "Cierta imponente majestad," 15.

24. "Perelli, Francisco—abuso de autoridad," Leg. #43-1657 (AHP-RN, JL).

25. Rafart, *Tiempo de violencia en la Patagonia*, 182.

26. Casullo and Perren, "Cierta imponente majestad," 15–17.

27. Baeza, *Fronteras e identidades en Patagonia central*.

28. Palacio, *La paz del trigo*.

29. Rafart, *Tiempo de violencia en la Patagonia*, 146–47.

30. Muzzopappa et al., "Una Impronta Rionegrina," 2; the authors reference the work by "Gayol and Kessler (2002)" but it was not listed in their references.

31. "Comerciantes de 'Cinco Saltos'—pedido a favor de Segundo Ibarra," Leg# 706-28530 (AHP-RN, JL).

32. "Ramasco, Lorenzo—denuncia contra oficial Basualdo"—Leg# 789-33708 (AHP-RN, JL.)

33. The original reads: "Como podría matarte indio de mierda, ratero, hijo de puta."

34. The original reads: "tiene el mejor concepto público y de sus superiores, por la corrección y competencia en sus funciones como tal."

35. "Vecinos de Maquinchao, su queja contra la Policía (Almendra, Pedro; Rodríguez, Bernabé y Arrieta, Gregorio) sobre delito contra la libertad individual." Leg. #717- 28927 (AHP-RN, JL).

36. The original reads: "comerciantes industriales y vecinos más respetables."

37. The case was attached to a couple of earlier complaints by some of the individual merchants, which had gone unanswered until the joint complaint.

38. The police investigators used "árabe" and "turco" as umbrella terms to describe immigrants from the territories that had been part of the Ottoman Empire before 1919. It is unclear if the witnesses themselves identified that way, or if the police simplified their answers to a more familiar ethnic nomenclature.

39. "Los Vecinos de 'El Bolsón'—su queja contra la policía de esa localidad," Leg #810-35294 (AHP-RN, JL).

40. "Afione, Severino (y otros concejales)—denuncian abusos del comisario," Leg# 1927-140, f.36 (AJL, TN).

41. Walker, *German Home Towns*; see chapters 4 and 9, in particular.

42. "Fuentes, Arturo—denuncia oficial Libermann (de los Menucos), Leg# 814-34798 (AHP-RN, JL).

43. "Martínez, Ángel E. (gendarme)—abuso de autoridad (inc. Denuncia de la Liga de Defensa), Leg #618-25266 (AHP-RN, JL).

44. Bohoslavsky, *El Complot Patagónico*, 42 (emphasis added).

45. Bohoslavsky, *El Complot Patagónico*, 51.

46. Bohoslavsky, *El Complot Patagónico*, 40–44.

47. Quoted in Baeza, *Fronteras e identidades en Patagonia central*, 102.

48. Baeza, *Fronteras e identidades en Patagonia central*, 102–3.

49. McGee (Deutsch), "Visible and Invisible Liga Patriótica Argentina," 235–49; the statistical data are broken down in three tables on pp. 248 and 249.

50. Gallucci, "Nación, república y Constitución."

51. Méndez, *Estado, frontera y turismo*, 191–94.

52. Méndez, *Estado, frontera y turismo*, 211.

53. Méndez, *Estado, frontera y turismo*, 211–33.

54. Méndez, "'El león de la cordillera,'" 36–37.

55. Méndez, *Estado, frontera y turismo*, 218–20.

56. "Capraro, Primo (y otros)—contra Luis Pastor por calumnias e injurias," #705-28478/79/80 (AHP-RN, JL).

57. Méndez, *Estado, frontera y turismo*, 220–21.

58. Méndez, *Estado, frontera y turismo*, 224–26.

59. Méndez, *Estado, frontera y turismo*, 230.

60. Vallmitjana, *Bariloche, mi pueblo*, 105.

61. Cikota, "Uncertain Flags."

Chapter Six

1. Quoted from Mauricio Ernesto Macagno's *Salus Populi, Suprema Lex*. Originally from the memos and discussions around the 1906 project to reform the penal code. The original reads: "El curanderismo, en todas sus formas, es uno de los peores enemigos de la salud . . . que, desgraciadamente, se extiende en todas partes. No podíamos prescindir . . . ya que hacemos obra nacional, *del clamor público contra estos profesionales del engaño y de la mentira*; no podíamos, en fin, ser sordos a la protesta de todos los hombres cultos y de las corporaciones científicas más autorizadas . . . a fin de llegar a la extirpación completa de este reconocido mal." (emphasis added).

2. "Núñez, Ernesto—denuncia contra Doctor Rodolfo Koessler por ejercicio ilegal de la medicina." Leg# 1932-1309, f.630 (AJL-TN).

3. Ruggiero, *Modernity in the Flesh*; Bohoslavsky and Di Liscia, "La profilaxis del viento"; Macagno, "Salus populi, suprema lex"; Di Liscia, "Cifras y problemas"; Di Liscia, "Imaginarios y derroteros"; Salvatore, "Sobre el Surgimiento del Estado Médico Legal." The classic text for this subject is Foucault, *Birth of the Clinic*.

4. Macagno, "Salus populi, suprema lex," 2. The reform of the penal code was delayed by a decade and a half as the ruling elite coalition splintered on the eve of the electoral reform of 1914, and legislative consensus was not marshalled again until 1921. Although the delay may seem remarkable, it was not unusual: the original penal code was first drafted in 1867, and was not promulgated until 1886. For an in-depth analysis of the evolution of criminal and legal thinking, see Duve, "¿Del Absolutismo Ilustrado al Liberalismo Reformista?," 144–55.

5. The actual text of the law reads as follows:

> Art. 208: Será reprimido con prisión de quince días a un año:
> 1° El que, sin título ni autorización para el ejercicio de un arte de curar
> o excediendo los límites de su autorización, anunciare, prescribiere,
> administrare o aplicare habitualmente medicamentos, aguas, electricidad,

hipnotismo o cualquier medio destinado al tratamiento de las enfermedades de las personas, aun a título gratuito;

2° El que, con título o autorización para el ejercicio de un arte de curar, anunciare o prometiere la curación de enfermedades a término fijo o por medios secretos o infalibles;

3° El que, con título o autorización para el ejercicio de un arte de curar, prestare su nombre a otro que no tuviere título o autorización, para que ejerza los actos a que se refiere el inciso 1° de este artículo.

6. Bubello, *Historia del esoterismo en la Argentina*, 100.

7. Belmartino, *La atención médica argentina*, 61.

8. There are some interesting tendencies evidenced in the cases found in the archives. I counted 5 cases in the Neuquén Territory between 1921 and 1940, compared with 43 in the Río Negro Territory. Higher population in Río Negro—estimated at 115,380 in 1933, according to Moldes and Entraigas, "La población del Territorio Nacional del Río Negro," compared with just 42,241 in Neuquén, according to Mases, *El mundo del trabajo, 15*— explains some of the discrepancy, but not all of it. Other reasons for this disparity include: (a) the lower population density in Neuquén—still 74 percent rural in 1920, according to Rafart, *Tiempo de violencia en la Patagonia*, compared with a low-water mark of 51 percent for Río Negro that same year, according to Moldes and Entraigas, "La población del Territorio Nacional del Río Negro"; (b) the higher concentration of people of indigenous descent in Neuquén, as well as; (c) the greater integration of northeastern Río Negro with the province of Buenos Aires. The combination of these factors could explain why there was less police attention to these kinds of crimes in the hinterlands of Neuquén, where certified doctors arrived years later (and in smaller numbers) than in the midsize towns of the Río Negro valley and the central plateau. A less disarticulated indigenous culture in the remote Andean valleys of western Neuquén similarly suggests less of a police presence in that area as well as less reliance by those settlers on the state to mediate disputes arising from medical irregularities.

9. Belmartino, *La atención médica argentina*, 86–95.

10. Based on the data presented in the "Boletin Sanitario" of 1940. The data were gathered, secondhand from Bohoslavsky and Di Liscia, "La profilaxis del viento," 198; Di Liscia, "Cifras y problemas," 262.

11. Slatta, *Gauchos and the Vanishing Frontier*, 68.

12. Bohoslavsky and Di Liscia, "La profilaxis del viento," 195.

13. Di Liscia, "Cifras y problemas," 271.

14. Weber, *Peasants into Frenchmen*, 58.

15. Weber, *Peasants into Frenchmen*, 496.

16. Di Liscia, "Imaginarios y derroteros de la salud," 57.

17. Bohoslavsky and Di Liscia, "La profilaxis del viento," 189.

18. "Della Place, Leopoldo—ejercicio ilegal de la medicina," Leg #874-37459 (AHP-RN, JL). There were a series of nicknames for Leopoldo de la Place in this case, many of them alluding to his "exoticness": *El Príncipe Indú, el Heredero de Abyssinia, el Maestro*. When prompted during his deposition, he denied having any aliases.

19. The original reads: "sin plata, no podía trabajar."

20. Bohoslavsky and Di Liscia, "La profilaxis del viento."

21. The original reads: "se lo acomodó . . . haciéndole una *untura* de huevos de gallina y un poco de harina [?] se la puso encima de la herida."

22. "Joaquín Spuch denuncia contra Filomena Salvo por ejercicio ilegal de la medicina," Leg #642-26165 (Archivo Histórico Provincial de Río Negro, Justicia Letrada, hereafter AHP-RN, JL).

23. Strangely, none of the cases found in the archives was against an indigenous healer (*machi* or "witch-doctor"). One possible explanation for this is temporal: most of the cases hail from the late 1920s and early 1930s— almost fifty years after the beginning of the military occupation of the region, suggesting a certain level of success in disarticulating indigenous societies' social and cultural practices. Another explanation is spatial: most of these types of cases took place in rural areas with a high proportion of settlers from European descent—urban areas tended not to offer fertile ground for spiritual healers, and rural areas with high concentration of people of indigenous descent often did not turn to the state to mediate their disputes. See Bubello, *Historia del esoterismo en la Argentina*, 21, which argues very effectively for the amalgamation by the end of the colonial period of the homegrown and transnational esoteric fields in present-day Argentina.

24. Some had powerful patrons, like Pancho Sierra in Buenos Aires, who used his close relationship with President Julio Roca to secure an office close to the presidential palace and immunity from the police. For other examples, see Bubello, *Historia del esoterismo en la Argentina*, 61.

25. Bubello, *Historia del esoterismo en la Argentina*, 123; in his study of similar cases in Buenos Aires, Bubello notes the widespread popular support for some of these esoteric healers, but he focuses more on the extralegal avenues taken by them to circumvent the legal process entirely.

26. "Morales, Onofre s/ ejercicio ilegal de la medicina" (and other attached documents), Leg #1075-46881 (AHP-RN, JL).

27. Quoted from Cornelio Goñi's deposition in "Goñi, Cornelio ("El Curandero") s/ ejercicio ilegal de la medicina" Leg #1240-53138 (AHP-RN, JL).

28. In 1927 Cornelio Goñi, a widower, was found guilty of robbery in the town of Nahuel Niyeo (in the central plateau of Río Negro) and ordered to spend four years in prison. He was released after serving only eighteen months in June 1928, and spent the next seven years bouncing between San Antonio Oeste and Viedma. The San Antonio Oeste police had detained him twice in the early 1930s over his suspected illegal practice of medicine without charges being filed.

29. The original quote reads: "dar consejo a un paciente decepcionado o desesperado sobre modo de mitigar los dolores ficicos (sic), no es ser curandero. . . . Ayudar moral y pecuniariamente al que nececita (sic), ni es egercer (sic) un comercio prohibido, ni con ello invade jurisdicción en el campo de la ciencia."

30. "Susso, Felix, s/ ejercicio ilegal de la medicina," Leg #1367-61263 (AHP-RN, JL).

31. Scott, *Weapons of the Weak*, 28–29.

32. Bubello, *Historia del esoterismo en la Argentina*, 129.

33. Bubello, *Historia del esoterismo en la Argentina*, 141.

34. Di Liscia, "Imaginarios y derroteros de la salud," 56, 65.

35. Di Liscia, "Cifras y problemas," 262.

36. "Sellanos, Álvaro, denuncia contra Francisco Pagano Vivancio, por ejercicio ilegal de la medicina." Leg. #872-37352 (AHP-RN, JL).

37. The original reads: "en los dos años que llevo ejerciendo mi profesión, he podido observar, por manifestaciones hechas por enfermos que concurrieron a mi consultorio, que *muchos de ellos habían seguido previamente un tratamiento indicado por el farmacéutico . . .* no he querido controlar esa irregularidad por delicadeza profesional" (emphasis added).

38. For example, there is an additional case (#35732, in the AHP-RN, JL) against Francisco Pagano Vivancio, in which he provided first aid to a day laborer, Juan Maldonado, who had been injured while working on the pharmacist's property. During the course of the investigation Maldonado told the police that he had previously been denied attention, due to his extreme poverty, by all the local doctors: they only assisted him after being compelled by the authorities. Maldonado speculated that the resentment built up from that previous experience surely contributed to doctors' desire to punish him (and Vivancio) in this case.

39. "Sánchez Antelo, Carlos María—denuncia contra José Brogtein/Bronstein su ejercicio ilegal de la medicina," Leg #1283-56179 (AHP-RN, JL). Note: the name of the defendant is changed repeatedly in the file from Brogtein to Bronstein, but since he identified himself with the former spelling, that is the one that will be used here.

40. "Jolliffe, Ralph George—ejercicio ilegal de la medicina," Leg. #803-34354 (AHP-RN, JL).

41. "Abraham Feintuch—ejercicio ilegal de la medicina (Art. 208-Inc.1ro Código Penal)," Leg. #775-32778 (AHP-RN, JL).

42. The "Ingenio San Lorenzo" was a bold attempt by Benito Lorenzo Raggio—a young entrepreneur from a wealthy Buenos Aires trading family, with a business background in Switzerland and Italy—to bring agro-industrial development to the lower Río Negro valley, centered on sugar beet cultivation and refinement. It was part of the Compañía Industrial y Agrícola San Lorenzo Limitada. The project included expansive beet plantations throughout the valley, the installation of Mercedes-Benz–powered water pumps for irrigation, the extension of the railroad line to better serve the Ingenio, even importing from Canada prefabricated housing for the workers of the company. The Ingenio was inaugurated, with much fanfare in 1929, and operated until 1941, when it closed down for good. The end had seemed imminent after an unknown plague ravaged the beet plantations throughout the valley and, following health concerns, Raggio was forced to sell the complex and the new owners dismantled the whole operation. The national government, owing to pressure from sugar cane producers in the northern provinces of Tucuman and Salta, placed severe production quotas throughout the 1930s, dooming this unique attempt to create a labor-intensive industrial center in the central Patagonian plateau. Within a few short years, the beet fields were completely replaced with alfalfa and hay, returning the region to an extensive crop with low-labor requirements, instead of the labor-intensive and much more technical industry built around beets. For more on the "Ingenio San Lorenzo," see the articles Pedro Pesatti, "El ingenio de Conesa," *Rio Negro*, May 2009, and Héctor Pérez Morando, "Hacia 80 años nacia el Ingenio San Lorenzo en General Conesa, *Rio Negro*, May 2009.

43. "Núñez, Ernesto—denuncia contra Doctor Rodolfo Koessler por ejercicio ilegal de la medicina." Leg# 1932-1309, f.630 (AJL-TN).

44. The wedding was held in secrecy, since she was of noble birth, Lutheran and older, while he was a young Catholic, of common birth.

45. Lanín is the name of a massive volcano that dominates the area's landscape. Koessler-Ilg, *El machi del Lanín*.

46. Kössler-Ilg, *Cuentos mapuches de la cordillera.*

47. The actual quote reads: "concurrió a su casa el nombrado facultativo quien al ver a la diciente le expresó estas textuales palabras '*vengo de mala voluntad*' sin antes haber saludado ni propuesto palabra alguna."

48. The original quote reads: "Siendo el que suscribe médico de la población de San Martín de los Andes desde el año 1920 y actuando como profesional de la confianza de los vecinos es comprensible que aun autorizado para el ejercicio de la medicina legal en Junin de los Andes un pueda negarse de veces de ver a un amigo, un enfermo y *principalmente a un pobre que—como es sabido y público—no se ve atendido de veces por el médico de la localidad por no poder recompensarle en el acto sus servicios."*

49. One of the largest cattle companies in Patagonia, operating in both Chile and Argentina, with a presence as far south as Tierra del Fuego and as far north as northern Neuquén Territory. It was formerly known as the Sociedad Ganadera Chile-Argentina. For further information, see Blanco, "Las sociedades anónimas cruzan los Andes," 123–24.

50. Interestingly enough, today the access road between these two cities—Highway 234—is named "Avenida Koessler" as it enters San Martín de los Andes.

51. Comisión del Centenario y Fundación de San Martín de los Andes, *El Libro de los 100 años*, 261.

52. The certificate reads: "Al Doctor Rodolfo Koessler, en Prueba de reconocimiento y Gratitud por su abnegada labor de Bien Social en 33 años de Ejercicio de la Medicina entre Nosotros, el Pueblo de San Martín de los Andes y sus Alrededores// 27 de diciembre de 1953," and was signed by over five hundred people. I was unable to find out anything else about Koessler's later life, but in a separate deposition, taken during July 1933, he spoke of the period of time when he was the official medic of Junín in the past tense, suggesting that the situation had changed.

Conclusion

1. Ballent, "Kilómetro cero," 107.

2. Bohoslavsky, *El Complot Patagónico*, 213–17; Navarro Floria, *Historia de la Patagonia*, 208–13.

3. Pastoriza, *Las puertas al mar*, 21–27.

4. Bohoslavsky, *El Complot Patagónico*, 217.

5. Pastoriza, *Las puertas al mar*, 89–106. For an interesting treatment of how tourism was perceived by workers as a "type" of land reform, see James, *Doña María's Story*, 71–74.

6. Bohoslavsky, *El Complot Patagónico*, 216; Bandieri, *Historia de la Patagonia*, 315; For an in-depth study of the role of these state agencies in transforming Bariloche into a tourist center, see Méndez, *Estado, frontera y turismo*, 190–98, 239–50; Méndez solemnly summarizes: "the crisis of the '30s concluded a long political transformation . . . the nation became the owner of the city [Bariloche], while the members of renown porteño families, reaped the benefits" (250). For a study on the role of YPF as a key broker in the development

of oil towns (and for a comparison with how a "private" town fared), see Torres, "Two Oil Company Towns in Patagonia." See also chapter 2 of Shever, "Powerful Motors," for a look at how these developments in the 1930s greatly shaped the towns and the people living in them for the remaining decade.

7. "Esteban Bullrich,'" *La Nación*.

8. Prado, "Fringes of Empires."

Appendix

1. Penaloza, "Sublime Journey to the Barren Plains," 87.

2. Vapnarsky, *Pueblos del norte de la Patagonia*, 44–46.

3. The first ever successful airplane flight over the Andes range took off from Zapala in 1918. After about two and a half hours, the eighty-horsepower airplane and its pilot, Luis Cenobio Candelaria, landed safely in a makeshift landing strip in Cunco, Chile. The plane flew at an estimated 4,000 meters above the sea level, more than enough to safely clear the mountain peaks.

Bibliography

Manuscript Sources

Archivo de la Justicia Letrada, Territorio del Neuquén
Archivo Histórico Provincia de Río Negro, Justicia Letrada
Archivo General de la Nación Argentina–Archivo Intermedio

Printed and Online Primary Sources

Argentina. *Diario de sesiones de la Cámara de Senadores: 1907:1.* N.P.,1907.
Argentina. *Memoria del Ministerio del Interior (1900).* Buenos Aires: Impr. de El Siglo, n.d.
Argentina: Ministerio del Interior. *Memoria presentada al Congreso Nacional de . . . por el Ministro del Interior: v. 3 (1899) (instruccion).* Vol. 3. Buenos Aires: n.p., 1899.
Argentina, Suprema Corte de Justicia de la Nación. *Fallos de la Corte Suprema de Justicia de la Nación: con la relación de sus respectivas causas . . .* Vol. 39. Buenos Aires: n.p., 1890.
Comisión del Centenario y Fundación de San Martín de los Andes. *El Libro de los 100 años: 1898–1998.* Buenos Aires: Editorial S.A., 1999.
Consejo Nacional de Educación (Argentina), ed. *El monitor de la educación común.* Vol. 8. Buenos Aires: Consejo Nacional de Educación, 1890.
"Esteban Bullrich: 'Esta es la nueva Campaña del Desierto, pero no con la espada sino con la educación.'" *La Nación.* 16 September 2016, sec. Política. www.lanacion.com. ar/politica/esteban-bullrich-esta-es-la-nueva-campana-del-desierto-pero-no-con-la-espada-sino-con-la-educacion-nid1938454/.
Ley Nacional #11357-Sobre los derechos civiles de las mujeres. Argentina.gob.ar. Accessed 4 March 2024. www.argentina.gob.ar/normativa/nacional/ley-11357-232934/ texto.

Secondary Sources

Abrams, Philip. "Notes on the Difficulty of Studying the State (1977)." *Journal of Histori-cal Sociology* 1, no. 1 (1 March 1988): 58–89.

Adelman, Jeremy, and Stephen Aron. "Trading Cultures: The Worlds of Western Merchants." In *Trading Cultures: The Worlds of Western Merchants: Essays on Authority, Objectivity, and Evidence,* edited by Jeremy Adelman and Stephen Aron, 1–6. Turnhout, Belgium: Brepols, 2001.

Alberdi, Juan Bautista. *Bases y puntos de partida para la organización política de la República Argentina.* Buenos Aires: Ed. Libertador, 2005.

Alonso, Ana María. "Rationalizing Patriarchy: Gender, Domestic Violence, and Law in Mexico." *Identities* 2, nos. 1–2 (1 January 1995): 29–47.

———. *Thread of Blood: Colonialism, Revolution, and Gender on Mexico's Northern Frontier.* Tucson: University of Arizona Press, 1995.

Amussen, Susan D. "The Contradictions of Patriarchy in Early Modern England." *Gender and History* 30, no. 2 (2018): 343–53.

Argeri, María E. *De guerreros a delincuentes: la desarticulación de las jefaturas indí-genas y el poder judicial: Norpatagonia, 1880–1930.* Madrid: Consejo Superior de Investigaciones Científicas, Instituto de Historia, Departamento de Historia de América, 2005.

———. "Las niñas depositadas, el destino de la mano de obra femenina infantil en Río Negro a principios del siglo XX." *Boletín americanista,* no. 49 (1999): 31–43.

Aron, Stephen. *American Confluence: The Missouri Frontier from Borderland to Border State.* Bloomington: Indiana University Press, 2009.

———. *How the West Was Lost: The Transformation of Kentucky from Daniel Boone to Henry Clay.* Baltimore: Johns Hopkins University Press, 1999.

Baeza, Brígida Norma. *Fronteras e identidades en Patagonia central (1885–2007).* Rosario: Prohistoria, 2009.

Ball, Larry D. *The United States Marshals of New Mexico and Arizona Territories, 1846–1912.* Albuquerque: University of New Mexico Press, 1978.

Ballent, Anahí. "Kilómetro cero: la construcción del universo simbólico del camino en la Argentina de los años treinta." *Boletín del Instituto de Historia Argentina y Americana Dr. Emilio Ravignani,* no. 27 (June 2005): 107–36.

Bandieri, Susana. "Asuntos de familia: la construcción del poder en la patagonia: el caso de Neuquén." *Boletín del Instituto de Historia Argentina y Americana Dr. Emilio Ravignani,* no. 28 (2005): 65–94.

———. *Historia de la Patagonia*. Buenos Aires: Editorial Sudamericana, 2005.

———. "La masonería en la Patagonia. Modernidad liberal y asociacionismo masón en Neuquén (1884–1907)." *Estudios Sociales* 38, no. 1 (2010): 9–38.

———. "Sociedad civil y redes de poder social en los Territorios Nacionales del Sur: Neuquén, Patagonia argentina, 1880–1907." *Boletín americanista*, no. 57 (2007): 53–67.

Bates, Juandrea M. "Unaccompanied Minors and Fraudulent Fathers: Civil Law in the Unmaking of Immigrant Family in Buenos Aires, 1869–1920." *Hispanic American Historical Review* 102, no. 1 (1 February 2022): 95–126.

Becker, Marjorie. *Setting the Virgin on Fire: Lázaro Cárdenas, Michoacán Peasants, and the Redemption of the Mexican Revolution*. Berkeley: University of California Press, 1996.

Belmartino, Susana. *La atención médica argentina en el siglo XX: instituciones y procesos*. Colección Historia y cultura. Buenos Aires: Siglo Veintiuno Editores Argentina, 2005.

Bennett, Judith M. *History Matters: Patriarchy and the Challenge of Feminism*. Philadelphia: University of Pennsylvania Press, 2007.

Benton-Cohen, Katherine. *Borderline Americans: Racial Division and Labor War in the Arizona Borderlands*. Cambridge, MA: Harvard University Press, 2011.

Bertoni, Lilia Ana. *Patriotas, cosmopolitas y nacionalistas: la construcción de la nacionalidad Argentina a fines del siglo XIX*. Sección de obras de historia. Buenos Aires: Fondo de cultura económica, 2001.

Blanco, Graciela. "Las sociedades anónimas cruzan los Andes: los inversores chilenos en Nuequén al comenzar el siglo XX." *América Latina en la Historia Económica: Revista de Investigación* 19, no. 2 (May 2012): 107–30.

Bloemraad, Irene. *Becoming a Citizen: Incorporating Immigrants and Refugees in the United States and Canada*. Berkeley: University of California Press, 2006.

———. "Citizenship Lessons from the Past: The Contours of Immigrant Naturalization in the Early 20th Century." *Social Science Quarterly* 87, no. 5 (1 December 2006): 927–53.

Bohoslavsky, Ernesto, and Fernando Casullo. "La cárcel de Neuquén y la política penitenciaria argentina en la primera mitad del siglo XX." *Nueva Doctrina Penal*, 2008, 295–314.

———. "Sobre los límites del castigo en la Argentina periférica. La cárcel de Neuquén (1904–1945)." *Quinto Sol* 7 (2013): 37–59.

Bohoslavsky, Ernesto, and María Silvia Di Liscia. "La profilaxis del viento. Instituciones represivas y sanitarias en la Patagonia argentina, 1880–1940." *Asclepio* 60, no. 2 (5 December 2008): 187–206.

Bohoslavsky, Ernesto Lázaro. "Clase y ciudadanía en los conflictos sociales y políticos en el extremo sur de la Argentina y de Chile a principios del Siglo XX." In *Construcción estatal, órden oligárquico y respuestas sociales: Argentina y Chile, 1840–1930*, edited by Ernesto Bohoslavsky and Milton Godoy Orellana. Buenos Aires: Prometeo Libros, 2010.

———. "El brazo armado de la improvisación. Aportes para una historia social de los policías patagónicos (1880–1946)." In *Un Estado con Rostro Humano. Funcionarios e instituciones estatales en Argentina (desde 1880 a la actualidad)*, edited by Ernesto Lázaro Bohoslavsky and Germán Soprano, 215–42. Buenos Aires: Prometeo Libros; Universidad Nacional de General Sarmiento, 2010.

———. *El Complot Patagónico: nación, conspiracionismo y violencia en el sur de Argentina y Chile (siglos XIX Y XX)*. Buenos Aires: Prometeo, 2009.

Borrello, Andrés. *La volvería a matar. El feminicidio de Carla Figueroa a manos de Marcelo Tomaselli y los crímenes de poder*. 2nd ed. Buenos Aires: 7 Sellos, 2020.

Borrero, José María. *La Patagonia trágica*. Buenos Aires: Editorial Americana, 1957.

Boyer, Richard. "Honor among Plebeians: Mala Sangre and Social Reputation." In *The Faces of Honor: Sex, Shame, and Violence in Colonial Latin America*, edited by Lyman L. Johnson and Sonya Lipsett-Rivera, 152–79. Albuquerque: University of New Mexico Press, 1998.

Bubello, Juan. *Historia del esoterismo en la Argentina: prácticas, representaciones y persecuciones de curanderos, espiritistas, astrólogos y otros esoteristas*. Historia. Buenos Aires: Editorial Biblos, 2010.

Buffington, Robert, and Pablo Piccato, eds. *True Stories of Crime in Modern Mexico*. Diálogos Series. Albuquerque: University of New Mexico Press, 2009.

Caimari, Lila M. *Apenas un delincuente: crimen, castigo y cultura en la Argentina, 1880–1955*. Buenos Aires: Siglo Veintiuno Editores, 2004.

Caplan, Karen Deborah. *Indigenous Citizens: Local Liberalism in Early National Oaxaca and Yucatán*. Stanford, CA: Stanford University Press, 2010.

Carrizo, Gabriel. "Hombres, soldados y mecánicos de la patria. La construcción de una identidad masculina en el Colegio Salesiano Deán Funes." In *Relaciones de género en la Patagonia*, edited by Edda Lía Crespo and Myriam Susana González, 177–89. Comodoro Rivadavia: Vela al Viento Ediciones Patagónicas, 2010.

Casullo, Fernando. "'El Estado mira al sur.' Administración de justicia en los Territorios Nacionales de Río Negro y del Neuquén (1884–1920)." In *Un Estado con Rostro Humano. Funcionarios e instituciones estatales en Argentina (desde 1880 a la actualidad)*, edited by Ernesto Lázaro Bohoslavsky and Germán Soprano, 333–58. Buenos Aires: Prometeo Libros; Universidad Nacional de General Sarmiento, 2010.

———. "Las pujas por la Justicia Letrada en Río Negro, 1884–1916. Una clave para entender a los territorios nacionales en el roquismo." In *Justicia, seguridad y castigo: concepciones y prácticas cotidianas en Patagonia (1884-1955)*, edited by Gabriel Carrizo, Fernando Casullo, and Marisa A. Moroni, 31–59. Rosario: Prohistoria; EdUNLPam, 2018.

Casullo, Fernando Hugo, and Joaquín Perren. "'Cierta imponente majestad': en torno a la administración de la justicia en el Territorio Nacional de Río Negro a partir de las fuentes cuantitativas (1884–1920)." In *Los estados del Estado: instituciones y agentes estatales en la Patagonia, 1880–1940*, edited by Fernando Hugo Casullo, Lisandro Gallucci, and Joaquín Perren, 15–42. Rosario, Argentina: Prohistoria Ediciones, 2013.

Caulfield, Sueann. *In Defense of Honor: Sexual Morality, Modernity, and Nation in Early-Twentieth-Century Brazil.* Durham, NC: Duke University Press, 2000.

Caulfield, Sueann, Sarah C. Chambers, and Lara Putnam. "Introduction: Transformations in Honor, Status, and Law over the Long Nineteenth Century." In *Honor, Status, and Law in Modern Latin America*, edited by Sueann Caulfield, Sarah C. Chambers, and Lara Putnam, 1–26. Durham, NC: Duke University Press, 2005.

Chambers, Sarah C. *From Subjects to Citizens: Honor, Gender, and Politics in Arequipa, Peru, 1780–1854.* University Park: Penn State University Press, 1999.

Christiansen, Tanja Katherine. *Disobedience, Slander, Seduction, and Assault: Women and Men in Cajamarca, Peru, 1862–1900.* Austin: University of Texas Press, 2004.

Cikota, Javier. "Uncertain Flags: Immigrant Colonies and Frontier Anxieties in Northern Patagonia (1890–1930)." *Latin Americanist* 64, no. 3 (September 2020): 305–33.

Clendinnen, Inga. *Ambivalent Conquests: Maya and Spaniard in Yucatan, 1517–1570.* 2nd ed. Cambridge: Cambridge University Press, 2003.

Cowling, Mark, and James Martin. *Marx's "Eighteenth Brumaire": (Post)Modern Interpretations.* London: Pluto Press, 2002.

Crews, Robert D. *For Prophet and Tsar: Islam and Empire in Russia and Central Asia.* Cambridge, MA: Harvard University Press, 2009.

Davies Lenoble, Geraldine. "El impacto de la política cacical en la frontera: las redes de parentesco y la estructura social de Carmen de Patagones, 1856–1879." *Boletín del Instituto de Historia argentina y americana Doctor Emilio Ravignani*, no. 46 (2019): 75–109.

Davis, Natalie Zemon. *Fiction in the Archives: Pardon Tales and Their Tellers in Six-teenth-Century France*. Stanford, CA: Stanford University Press, 1987.

DeLay, Brian. *War of a Thousand Deserts: Indian Raids and the U.S.-Mexican War*. New Haven, CT: Yale University Press, 2009.

Delrio, Walter Mario. "Indios Amigos, Salvajes o Argentinos. Procesos de construcción de categorías sociales en la incorporación de los pueblos originarios al estado-na-cion (1870–1885)." In *Funcionarios, diplomáticos, guerreros: miradas hacia el otro en las fronteras de pampa y patagonia (Siglos XVIII y XIX)*, edited by Lidia Rosa Nacuzzi, , 203–45. Buenos Aires: Sociedad Argentina de Antropología, 2002.

——. *Memorias de expropiación: sometimiento e incorporación indígena en la Patago-nia (1872–1943)*. Buenos Aires: Universidad Nacional de Quílmes Editorial, 2005.

Delrio, Walter, and Ana Ramos. "Genocidio como categoría analítica: memoria social y marcos alternativos." *Corpus. Archivos virtuales de la alteridad americana* 1, no. 2 (2011). https://journals.openedition.org/corpusarchivos/1129.

Delrio, Walter, and Pilar Pérez. "Beyond the 'Desert': Indigenous Genocide as a Structuring Event in Northern Patagonia." In *The Conquest of the Desert: Argentina's Indigenous Peoples and the Battle for History*, edited by Carolyne R. Larson, 122–45. Diálogos Series. Albuquerque: University of New Mexico, 2020.

De la Fuente, Ariel. *Children of Facundo: Caudillo and Gaucho Insurgency During the Argentine State-Formation Process (La Rioja, 1853–1870)*. Durham, NC: Duke University Press, 2000.

Di Liscia, Maria Silvia. "Cifras y problemas. Las estadísticas y la salud en los Territorios Nacionales (1880–1940)." *Salud Colectiva* 5, no. 2 (August 2009): 259–78.

——. "Imaginarios y derroteros de la salud en el interior argentino. Los Territorios Nacionales (fines del XIX y principios del XX)." *Revista de Historia Entrepasados* 18, no. 33 (2008): 46–69.

Di Meglio, Gabriel. *¡Viva el Bajo Pueblo!: La plebe urbana de Buenos Aires y la política entre la Revolución de Mayo y el rosismo, 1810–1829*. Buenos Aires: Prometeo Libros, 2006.

Dialeti, Androniki. "Patriarchy as a Category of Historical Analysis and the Dynamics of Power: The Example of Early Modern Italy." *Gender and History* 30, no. 2 (2018): 331–42.

Diaz, Arlene J. *Female Citizens, Patriarchs, and the Law in Venezuela, 1786–1904*. Lincoln: University of Nebraska Press, 2004.

Diez, María Angélica. "Instituciones territoriales, orden público y una ciudadanía en construcción: El Estado nacional y la formación de la Pampa Central (1884–1922)." PhD diss., Universidad Nacional de La Plata, 2002.

———. "Justicia y policía: formas de castigo a detenidos y presos en el Territorio Nacional de La Pampa a fines del siglo XIX y primeras décadas del XX." Paper presented in the V jornadas de Sociología de la UNLP, La Plata, December 2008.

Drake, Paul W. *Between Tyranny and Anarchy: A History of Democracy in Latin America, 1800–2006.* Social Science History. Stanford, CA: Stanford University Press, 2009.

Dumond, Don E. *The Machete and the Cross: Campesino Rebellion in Yucatan.* Lincoln: University of Nebraska Press, 1997.

Duve, Thomas. "¿Del Absolutismo Ilustrado al Liberalismo Reformista? La Recepción Del Código Penal Bávaro de 1813 de Paul JA von Feuerbach En Argentina y El Debate Sobre La Reforma Del Derecho Penal Hasta 1921." *Revista de Historia Del Derecho* 27 (1999): 125–52.

Edwards, Erika Denise. *Hiding in Plain Sight: Black Women, the Law, and the Making of a White Argentine Republic.* Tuscaloosa: University of Alabama Press, 2020.

Evans, John Daniel. *John Daniel Evans "El molinero": una historia entre Gales y la Colonia 16 de Octubre.* Edited by Clery A. Evans. 3rd ed. Grandes hombres de la Patagonia. Buenos Aires: C. A. Evans, 1994.

Farnsworth-Alvear, Ann. *Dulcinea in the Factory: Myths, Morals, Men, and Women in Colombia's Industrial Experiment, 1905–1960.* Durham, NC: Duke University Press, 2000.

Fischer, Brodwyn M. *A Poverty of Rights: Citizenship and Inequality in Twentieth-Century Rio de Janeiro.* Stanford, CA: Stanford University Press, 2008.

Ford, Lisa. *Settler Sovereignty: Jurisdiction and Indigenous People in America and Australia, 1788–1836.* Harvard Historical Studies 166. Cambridge, MA: Harvard University Press, 2010.

Foucault, Michel. *The Birth of the Clinic: An Archaeology of Medical Perception.* New York: Vintage, 1994.

Gallucci, Lisandro. "Ciudadanía y orden institucional en la Patagonia Norte. Notables y subalternos en Neuquén durante las primeras décadas del siglo XX." In *Construcción estatal, orden oligárquico y respuestas sociales: Argentina y Chile, 1840–1930,* edited by Ernesto Lázaro Bohoslavsky and Milton Godoy Orellana, 291–319. Buenos Aires: Prometeo Libros, 2010.

———. "El espejismo de la República posible. La cuestión de la ciudadanía política y la organización institucional de los Territorios Nacionales en Argentina (siglo XIX)." *Historia Crítica*, no. 60 (2016): 61–80.

———. "La vida política de los instrumentos: Imágenes y prácticas de los sectores subalternos en el Neuquén de la primera mitad del siglo XX." *Quinto sol*, no. 12 (December 2008): 151–74.

———. "Las prácticas electorales en un municipio patagónico: Neuquén, 1904–1916." *Revista Pilquen*, no. 7 (2005).

———. "Nación, república y Constitución. La Liga Patriótica Argentina y su Congreso General de Territorios Nacionales." *Anuario de Historia de América Latina* 54 (2017): 306–37.

García, Ana Lidia. *El fracaso del amor: género e individualismo en el siglo XIX mexicano*. Mexico City: Colegio de México, 2006.

Gayol, Sandra. "Sargentos, cabos y vigilantes: perfil de un plantel inestable en el Buenos Aires de la segunda mitad del siglo XIX." *Boletín americanista* 46 (1996): 133–51.

Gentile, María Beatríz. "Las Niñas Del Viento: Sexualidad, Delito y Justicia En El Territorio de Neuquén." In *Historia social y política del delito en la Patagonia*, edited by Gabriel Rafart, 49–65. Colección GEHiSo. Neuquén: EDUCO—Universidad Nacional del Comahue, 2010.

Gleason, Mona. "Avoiding the Agency Trap: Caveats for Historians of Children, Youth, and Education." *History of Education* 45, no. 4 (3 July 2016): 446–59.

Goldney, Adalberto A. Clifton. *El cacique Namuncurá: último soberano de la Pampa*. Buenos Aires: Librería Huemul, 1956.

Gordon, Linda. *The Great Arizona Orphan Abduction*. Cambridge, MA: Harvard University Press, 2001.

Greenwald, Hannah. "'Improve Their Condition While Making Them Useful': Colonia General Conesa and the Dynamics of Settler Colonialism in Nineteenth-Century Argentina." *Hispanic American Historical Review* 103, no. 1 (1 February 2023): 101–37.

Guardino, Peter F. *The Time of Liberty: Popular Political Culture in Oaxaca, 1750–1850*. Durham, NC: Duke University Press, 2005.

Gutiérrez, Leandro H., and Luis Alberto Romero. *Sectores populares, cultura y política: Buenos Aires en la entreguerra*. Buenos Aires: Editorial Sudamericana, 1995.

Guy, Donna J. "Girls in Prison: The Role of the Buenos Aires Casa Correccional de Mujeres as an Institution for Child Rescue, 1890–1940." In *Crime and Punishment in Latin America: Law and Society since Late Colonial Times*, edited by Ricardo

D. Salvatore, Carlos Aguirre, and Gilbert M. Joseph, 369–90. Durham, NC: Duke University Press, 2001.

———. "Parents before the Tribunals: The Legal Construction of Patriarchy in Argentina." In *Hidden Histories of Gender and the State in Latin America*, edited by Elizabeth Dore and Maxime Molyneaux, 172–93. Durham, NC: Duke University Press, 2000.

———. *Sex and Danger in Buenos Aires: Prostitution, Family, and Nation in Argentina*. Lincoln: University of Nebraska Press, 1991.

Hämäläinen, Pekka, and Samuel Truett. "On Borderlands." *Journal of American History* 98, no. 2 (1 September 2011): 338–61.

Harambour-Ross, Alberto. "Borderland Sovereignties: Postcolonial Colonialism and State Making in Patagonia, Argentina and Chile, 1840s–1922." PhD diss., State University of New York at Stony Brook, 2012.

Hardwick, Julie. *Sex in an Old Regime City: Young Workers and Intimacy in France, 1660–1789*. New York: Oxford University Press, 2020.

Haworth, Daniel S. "'To Do as I Will': Marriage Choice and the Social Construction of Female Individuality in Nineteenth-Century Guanajuato, Mexico." *Latin Americanist* 57, no. 3 (1 September 2013): 51–82.

Hernandez, José. *Martín Fierro*. Buenos Aires: Penguin Random House Grupo Editorial Argentina, 2018.

Hill Collins, Patricia. *Intersectionality as Critical Social Theory*. Durham, NC: Duke University Press, 2019.

Hunefeldt, Christine. *Liberalism in the Bedroom: Quarreling Spouses in Nineteenth-Century Lima*. University Park: Pennsylvania State University Press, 2000.

Jacobs, Margaret D. *White Mother to a Dark Race: Settler Colonialism, Maternalism, and the Removal of Indigenous Children in the American West and Australia, 1880–1940*. Lincoln: University of Nebraska Press, 2009.

James, Daniel. *Doña María's Story: Life History, Memory, and Political Identity*. Durham, NC: Duke University Press, 2000.

Johnson, Lyman. "Dangerous Words, Provocative Gestures, and Violent Acts: The Disputed Hierarchies of Plebian Life in Colonial Buenos Aires." In *The Faces of Honor: Sex, Shame, and Violence in Colonial Latin America*, edited by Lyman L. Johnson and Sonya Lipsett-Rivera, 127–52. Albuquerque: University of New Mexico Press, 1998.

———. "The Empire's Long Goodbye: Heroes, Crowds and the First Stage of Independence in Argentina." *History Compass* 10, no. 5 (2012): 386–98.

———. *Workshop of Revolution: Plebeian Buenos Aires and the Atlantic World, 1776-1810*. Durham, NC: Duke University Press, 2011.

Johnson, Walter. "On Agency." *Journal of Social History* 37, no. 1 (2003): 113–24.

Jones, Kristine L. "Calfucurá and Namuncurá: Nation Builders of the Pampas." In *The Human Tradition in Latin America: The Nineteenth Century*, edited by Judith Ewell and William H. Beezley, 2:175-86. Wilmington, DE: SR Books, 1989.

———. "Civilization and Barbarism and Sarmiento's Indian Policy." In *Sarmiento and His Argentina*, edited by Joseph T. Criscenti, 35–44. Boulder, CO: Rienner, 1993.

———. "Warfare, Reorganization, and Readaptation at the Margins of Spanish Rule: The Southern Margin (1573–1882)." In *The Cambridge History of the Native Peoples of the Americas*, edited by Bruce G. Trigger and Wilcomb E. Washburn, vol. 3, 138–87. Cambridge: Cambridge University Press, 1996.

Jong, Ingrid de. "Indio, Nación y Soberanía en la Cordillera Norpatagónica: fronteras de la inclusión y exclusión en el discusrso de Manuel José Olascoaga." In *Funcionarios, diplomáticos, guerreros: miradas hacia el otro en las fronteras de pampa y patagonia (Siglos XVIII y XIX)*, edited by Lidia Rosa Nacuzzi, 159–201. Buenos Aires: Sociedad Argentina de Antropología, 2002.

Joseph, Gilbert M. "Preface." In *Crime and Punishment in Latin America: Law and Society Since Late Colonial Times*, edited by Ricardo D. Salvatore, Carlos Aguirre, and Gilbert M. Joseph, ix-xxi. Durham NC: Duke University Press, 2001.

Kellogg, Susan. *Law and the Transformation of Aztec Culture, 1500–1700*. Norman: University of Oklahoma Press, 1995.

Kerr, Ashley. "Progress at What Price? Defenses of Indigenous Peoples in Argentine Writing about Patagonia (1894–1904)." *Decimonónica* 16 (2019): 17–33.

———. *Sex, Skulls, and Citizens: Gender and Racial Science in Argentina (1860–1910)*. Nashville: Vanderbilt University Press, 2020.

Kircher, Mirta. "Miradas, relaciones y prácticas: la construcción de la política en Neuquén (1884–1904)." In *Pasiones sureñas: prensa, cultura y política en la frontera norpatagonica, 1884–1946*, edited by Leticia Prislei, 1–20. Buenos Aires: Prometeo Libros, 2001.

Klubock, Thomas Miller. *Contested Communities: Class, Gender, and Politics in Chile's El Teniente Copper Mine, 1904–1951*. Durham NC: Duke University Press, 1998.

Köessler-Ilg, Bertha. *El machi del Lanín: un médico alemán en la cordillera patagónica*. Buenos Aires: El Elefante Blanco, 2003.

———. *Cuentos mapuches de la cordillera*. 2nd ed. Santiago: Ediciones Mundo, 1997.

Kobayashi, José María. *La educación como conquista: empresa franciscana en México*. México: El Colegio de México, 1974.

Lamar, Howard Roberts. *The Far Southwest, 1846–1912: A Territorial History*. New Haven, CT: Yale University Press, 1966.

Langer, Erick D. *Expecting Pears from an Elm Tree: Franciscan Missions on the Chiriguano Frontier in the Heart of South America, 1830–1949*. Durham, NC: Duke University Press, 2009.

Langer, Erick D., and Robert H. Jackson. "Colonial and Republican Missions Compared: The Cases of Alta California and Southeastern Bolivia." *Comparative Studies in Society and History* 30, no. 2 (April 1988): 286–311.

Langfur, Hal. "Frontier/Fronteira: A Transnational Reframing of Brazil's Inland Colonization." *History Compass* 12, no. 11 (2014): 843–52.

Lapalma, Oscar Fermín. *La leyenda del Limay: impresiones de un raid náutico por los ríos Limay y Negro*. Buenos Aires: Talleres Gráficos Porter, 1934.

Larson, Carolyne R. "Introduction: Tracing the Battle for History." In *The Conquest of the Desert: Argentina's Indigenous Peoples and the Battle for History*, edited by Carolyne R. Larson, 1–16. Diálogos Series. Albuquerque: University of New Mexico, 2020.

——. "The Conquest of the Desert: The Official Story." In *The Conquest of the Desert: Argentina's Indigenous Peoples and the Battle for History*, edited by Carolyne R. Larson, 17–42. Diálogos Series. Albuquerque: University of New Mexico, 2020.

Lavrin, Asunción. *Women, Feminism, and Social Change in Argentina, Chile and Uruguay, 1890–1940*. Lincoln: University of Nebraska Press, 1998.

Lear, John. *Workers, Neighbors, and Citizens: The Revolution in Mexico City*. Lincoln: University of Nebraska Press, 2001.

Lenton, Diana, Walter Delrio, Pilar Pérez, Alexis Papazian, Mariano Nagy, and Marcelo Musante. "Argentina's Constituent Genocide: Challenging the Hegemonic National Narrative and Laying the Foundation for Reparations to Indigenous Peoples." *Armenian Review* 53, nos. 1–4 (22 March 2012): 63–85.

Levy, Traci M. "At the Intersection of Intimacy and Care: Redefining 'Family' through the Lens of a Public Ethic of Care." *Politics and Gender* 1, no. 1 (March 2005): 65–95.

Lobato, Mirta Zaida. "El Estado en los años treinta y el avance desigual de los derechos y la ciudadanía." *Estudios Sociales* 12, no. 1 (2005): 41–58.

Macagno, Mauricio Ernesto. "Salus populi, suprema lex: control de la medicina y el arte de curar en Argentina y el monopolio de la corporación médica. Un ensayo acerca de los antecedentes y motivos del delito de Ejercicio Ilegal de la Medicina, art. 208, Código Penal." *Revista Pensamiento Penal* 1, no. 135 (November 2011).

Maggiori, Ernesto. *Historias de frontera: policías, bandidos, baqueanos, arrieros, comerciantes, peones y troperos: Patagonia.* Chubut, Argentina: Imprenta Gráfica de Armando E Andrade, 2004.

Mallon, Florencia. "Reflections on the Ruins: Everyday Forms of State Formation in Nineteenth-Century Mexico." In *Everyday Forms of State Formation: Revolution and the Negotiation of Rule in Modern Mexico,* edited by Gilbert Michael Joseph and Daniel Nugent, 69–106. Durham, NC: Duke University Press, 1994.

———. *Peasant and Nation: The Making of Postcolonial Mexico and Peru.* Berkeley: University of California Press, 1995.

Marley, David. *Wars of the Americas: A Chronology of Armed Conflict in the Western Hemisphere, 1492 to the Present.* Santa Barbara, CA: ABC-CLIO, 2008.

Masés, Enrique. *Estado y cuestión indígena: El destino final de los indios sometidos en el sur del territorio (1878–1910).* Buenos Aires: Prometeo Libros, 2002.

———, ed. *El mundo del trabajo: Neuquén, 1884–1930.* Neuquén: G. E. Hi. So, 1994.

———, ed. *Un siglo al servicio de la salud pública: la historia del Hospital Castro Roldán.* Neuquén: EDUCO—Universidad Nacional del Comahue, 2015.

McGee (Deutsch), Sandra F. "The Visible and Invisible Liga Patriótica Argentina, 1919–28: Gender Roles and the Right Wing." *Hispanic American Historical Review* 64, no. 2 (1984): 233–58.

Meeks, Eric V. *Border Citizens: The Making of Indians, Mexicans, and Anglos in Arizona.* Austin: University of Texas Press, 2007.

Méndez, Laura. "'El león de la cordillera.' Primo Capraro y el desempeño empresario en la región del Nahuel Huapi, 1902–1932." *Boletín americanista,* no. 59 (2009): 29–46.

———. *Estado, frontera y turismo: historia de San Carlos de Bariloche.* Buenos Aires: Prometeo Libros, 2010.

Miller, Susan. "Assent as Agency in the Early Years of the Children of the American Revolution." *Journal of the History of Childhood and Youth* 9 (1 December 2016): 48–65.

Moldes, Beatriz, and Jorge R. Entraigas. "La población del Territorio Nacional del Río Negro. Un aporte al conocimiento de sus principales características demográficas (1884–1955)." Paper presented in the IX Jornadas Argentinas de Estudios de Población, Huerta Grande (Córdoba), 2007.

———. "La población rionegrina durante la época territorial. Un aporte al cono-cimiento de las principales características demográficas: 1884–1955." In *Horizontes en perspectiva. Contribuciones para la historia de Río Negro, 1884–1955*, edited by Ricardo Freddy Masera and Martha Ruffini, vol. 1, 71–122. Viedma: Fundación Ameghino- Legislatura de Río Negro, n.d.

Moroni, Marisa. "Cattle Raiding, State Control, and Power Relations in the National Territory of La Pampa during the First Decades of the 20th Century." *Historia Crítica*, no. 51 (September 2013): 97–119.

———. "La construcción de un espacio institucional desde una perspectiva regional. La organización y administración de justicia en el Territorio Nacional de la Pampa a Fines del siglo XIX." *Estudios Sociales* 32, no. 1 (2007): 129–42.

Moya, Jose C. *Cousins and Strangers: Spanish Immigrants in Buenos Aires, 1850–1930.* Berkeley: University of California Press, 1998.

Muzzopappa, Eva, Pilar Pérez, Melisa Fernández Marrón, Walter Puebla Marón, Rubén Suárez, and Juan José Guidi. "Una Impronta Rionegrina: Prácticas, Saberes y Formación En Una Policía Patagónica." Paper presented in the I jornadas de Estudios Sociales Sobre Delito, Violencia y Policía, La Plata and Quilmes (Argentina), April, 2017.

Navarro Floria, Pedro. *Historia de la Patagonia.* Buenos Aires: Ciudad Argentina, 1999.

———. "La nacionalización fallida de la Patagonia Norte, 1862–1904." *Quinto Sol* 7 (2013): 61–91.

Nicoletti, María Andrea, and Ana Inés Barelli. "La Virgen Auxiliadora, patrona de la Patagonia y la Virgen Misionera, patrona de la provincia de Río Negro: construcción identitaria y territorial en el espacio rionegrino." *Sociedad y Religión: Sociología, Antropología e Historia de la Religión en el Cono Sur* 22, no. 38 (2012): 107–40.

Noel, Linda C. *Debating American Identity: Southwestern Statehood and Mexican Immigration.* 2nd ed. Tucson: University of Arizona Press, 2014.

Otovo, Okezi T. *Progressive Mothers, Better Babies: Race, Public Health, and the State in Brazil, 1850/1945.* Austin: University of Texas Press, 2016.

Palacio, Juan Manuel. *La paz del trigo: cultura legal y sociedad local en el desarrollo agropecuario pampeano, 1890–1945.* Buenos Aires: Edhasa, 2004.

Pastoriza, Elisa, ed. *Las puertas al mar: consumo, ocio y política en Mar del Plata, Montevideo y Viña del Mar.* Buenos Aires: Editorial Biblos, 2002.

Penaloza, Fernanda. "A Sublime Journey to the Barren Plains: Lady Florence Dixie's 'Across Patagonia' (1880)." *Limina* 10 (January 2004): 81–97.

Pérez, Pilar. "Cuatreros, comerciantes, comisarios. Poder y capital en las primeras décadas del siglo XX en Río Negro." Paper presented in Mesa #10: El mundo de los delitos, justicias y la Historia Social en Patagonia, Santa Rosa, La Pampa, 2011.

————. "Las policías fronterizas: mecanismos de control y espacialización en los territorios nacionales del sur a principios del siglo XX." Paper presented in *Actas XII Jornadas Interescuelas de Historia*, San Carlos de Bariloche (Argentina), 2009.

Piccato, Pablo. *A History of Infamy: Crime, Truth, and Justice in Mexico*. Oakland, CA: University of California Press, 2017.

————. *City of Suspects: Crime in Mexico City, 1900–1931*. Durham, NC: Duke University Press, 2001.

Prado, Fabricio. "The Fringes of Empires: Recent Scholarship on Colonial Frontiers and Borderlands in Latin America." *History Compass* 10, no. 4 (April 2012): 318–33.

Prislei, Leticia. "Imaginar la Nación, modelar el desierto: los '20 en tierras del 'Neuquén.'" In *Pasiones sureñas: prensa, cultura y política en la frontera norpatagonica, 1884–1946*. Buenos Aires: Prometeo Libros, 2001.

Privitellio, Luciano de. *Vecinos y ciudadanos: política y sociedad en la Buenos Aires de entreguerras*. Historia y cultura. Buenos Aires: Siglo Veintiuno, 2003.

Quijada, Mónica. "¿'Hijos de los barcos' o diversidad invisibilizada? La articulación de la población indígena en la construcción nacional argentina (siglo XIX)." *Historia Mexicana* 53, no. 2 (1 October 2003): 469–510.

————. "Nación y territorio: la dimensión simbólica del espacio en la construcción nacional argentina. Siglo XIX." *Revista de Indias* 60, no. 219 (2000): 373–94.

Rafart, Gabriel. *Tiempo de violencia en la Patagonia: bandidos, policías y jueces: 1890–1940*. Buenos Aires: Prometeo Libros, 2008.

Rafart, Gabriel, and Susana Debattista. "El nacimiento de una alquimia imperfecta: justicia, jueces y condenados." In *Pobres, marginados y peligrosos*, edited by Jorge A. Trujillo and Juan Quintar. Guadalajara: Universidad de Guadalajara 2003.

Rausch, Jane M. "Frontiers in Crisis: The Breakdown of the Missions in Far Northern Mexico and New Granada, 1821–1849." *Comparative Studies in Society and History* 29, no. 2 (1987): 340–59.

Reséndez, Andrés. *Changing National Identities at the Frontier: Texas and New Mexico, 1800–1850*. New York: Cambridge University Press, 2004.

Rock, David. *Argentina, 1516–1987: From Spanish Colonization to the Falklands War*. 2nd ed. Berkeley: University of California Press, 1987.

————. *State Building and Political Movements in Argentina, 1860–1916*. Stanford, CA: Stanford University Press, 2002.

Rockwell, Elsie. "Schools of the Revolution: Enacting and Contesting State Forms in Tlaxcala, 1910–1930." In *Everyday Forms of State Formation: Revolution and the*

Negotiation of Rule in Modern Mexico, edited by Gilbert Michael Joseph and Daniel Nugent, 170–208. Durham, NC: Duke University Press, 1994.

Rojas Lagarde, Jorge Luis. *"Viejito porteño": un maestro en el toldo de Calfucurá*. Buenos Aires: El Elefante Blanco, 2007.

Ruffini, Martha. "Ciudadanía y Territorios Nacionales. El ejercicio del poder político en los Concejos Municipales del Territorio Nacional de Río Negro (1886–1908)." *Revista Digital Escuela de Historia* 1, no. 3 (2004): 1–16.

———. "Ecos del centenario. La apertura de un espacio de deliberación para los territorios nacionales: la primera conferencia de gobernadores (1913)." *Revista Pilquén*, no. 12 (2010): 1–12.

———. "El tránsito trunco hacia la 'República verdadera.' Yrigoyenismo, ciudadanía política y territorios nacionales." *Estudios Sociales* 19, no. 36 (2009): 91–115.

———. "'Hay que argentinizar la Patagonia.' Miradas sobre la nación y la ciudadanía en tiempos de cambio (1916–1930)." *Anuario de Estudios Americanos* 68, no. 2 (30 December 2011): 649–72. https://doi.org/10.3989/aeamer.2011.v68.i2.553.

———. *La pervivencia de la República Posible en los Territorios Nacionales: poder y ciudadanía en Río Negro*. Buenos Aires: Universidad Nacional de Quílmes Editorial, 2007.

———. "La consolidación inconclusa del Estado: los Territorios Nacionales, gobernaciones de provisionalidad permanente y ciudadanía política restringida (1884–1955)." *Revista SAAP. Publicación de Ciencia Política de la Sociedad Argentina de Análisis Político* 3, no. 1 (2007): 81–101.

Ruffini, Martha, and Ricardo Freddy Masera, eds. *Horizontes en perspectiva: Contribuciones para la historia de Río Negro, 1884–1955*. Vol. 1. Viedma Fundación Ameghino- Legislatura de Río Negro, 2007.

Ruggiero, Kristin. *Modernity in the Flesh: Medicine, Law, and Society in Turn-of-the-Century Argentina*. Stanford, CA: Stanford University Press, 2004.

Sábato, Hilda. *Republics of the New World: The Revolutionary Political Experiment in Nineteenth-Century Latin America*. Princeton, NJ: Princeton University Press, 2018.

———. *The Many and the Few: Political Participation in Republican Buenos Aires*. Stanford, CA: Stanford University Press, 2001.

Salvatore, Ricardo. "Sobre el Surgimiento del Estado Médico Legal en la Argentina [1890–1940]." *Estudios sociales* 20, no. 1 (2005): 81–114.

———. *Wandering Paysanos: State Order and Subaltern Experience in Buenos Aires during the Rosas Era*. Durham, NC: Duke University Press, 2003.

Salvatore, Ricardo D., Carlos Aguirre, and Gilbert M. Joseph, eds. *Crime and Punishment in Latin America: Law and Society Since Late Colonial Times*. Durham, NC: Duke University Press, 2001.

Sarmiento, Domingo Faustino. *Facundo: Civilization and Barbarism*. Translated by Kathleen Ross. Berkeley: University of California Press, 2003.

Schoo Lastra, Dionisio. *El indio del desierto, 1535–1879*. Buenos Aires: Agencia general de libería y publicaciones, 1928.

Scott, James C. *Weapons of the Weak: Everyday Forms of Peasant Resistance*. New Haven: Yale University Press, 1985.

Scott, Joan Wallach. "Gender: A Useful Category of Historical Analysis." *American Historical Review* 91, no. 5 (1986): 1053–75.

Sellers-García, Sylvia. *The Woman on the Windowsill: A Tale of Mystery in Several Parts*. New Haven, CT: Yale University Press, 2020.

Shelton, Laura Marie. *For Tranquility and Order: Family and Community on Mexico's Northern Frontier, 1800–1850*. Tucson: University of Arizona Press, 2010.

Shever, Elana. "Powerful Motors: Kinship, Citizenship and the Transformation of the Argentine Oil Industry." PhD diss., University of California, Berkeley, 2008.

Shumway, Jeffrey M. *The Case of the Ugly Suitor and Other Histories of Love, Gender, and Nation in Buenos Aires, 1776–1870*. Lincoln: University of Nebraska Press, 2005.

———. "'The Purity of My Blood Cannot Put Food on My Table': Changing Attitudes Towards Interracial Marriage in Nineteenth-Century Buenos Aires." *Americas* 58, no. 2 (October 2001): 201–20.

Silver, Peter. *Our Savage Neighbors: How Indian War Transformed Early America*. Reprint ed. New York: Norton, 2009.

Slatta, Richard W. "Comparing and Exploring Frontier Myth and Reality in Latin America." *History Compass* 10, no. 5 (May 2012): 375–85.

———. *Gauchos and the Vanishing Frontier*. Lincoln: University of Nebraska Press, 1992.

Slezkine, Yuri. *Arctic Mirrors: Russia and the Small Peoples of the North*. Ithaca, NY: Cornell University Press, 1994.

Sloan, Kathryn A. *Runaway Daughters: Seduction, Elopement, and Honor in Nineteenth-Century Mexico*. Albuquerque: University of New Mexico Press, 2008.

Socolow, Susan Migden. "Acceptable Partners: Marriage Choice in Colonial Argentina, 1778–1810." In *Sexuality and Marriage in Colonial Latin America*, edited by Asunción Lavrin, 209–44. Lincoln: University of Nebraska Press, 1989.

———. "Spanish Captives in Indian Societies: Cultural Contact along the Argentine Frontier, 1600–1835." *Hispanic American Historical Review* 72, no. 1 (1992): 73–99.

———. *The Women of Colonial Latin America*. New York: Cambridge University Press, 2015.

———. "Women of the Buenos Aires Frontier, 1740–1810 (or the Gaucho Turned Upside Down)." In *Contested Ground: Comparative Frontiers on the Northern and Southern Edges of the Spanish Empire*, edited by Donna J. Guy and Thomas E. Sheridan, 67–82. Tucson: University of Arizona Press, 1998.

Stasiulis, Daiva, and Nira Yuval-Davis. "Introduction: Beyond Dichotomies—Gender, Race, Ethnicity and Class in Settler Societies." In *Unsettling Settler Societies: Articulations of Gender, Race, Ethnicity and Class*, 1–38. London: Sage, 1995.

Suárez, Graciela. "La Policía en la Región Andina Rionegrina, 1880–1920." *Revista Pilquén* 5 (2003): 225–46.

Sullivan, Paul. *Unfinished Conversations: Mayas and Foreigners between Two Wars*. Reprint ed. Berkeley: University of California Press, 1991.

Szuchman, Mark D. "A Challenge to the Patriarchs: Love among the Youth in Nineteenth-Century Argentina." In *The Middle Period in Latin America: Values and Attitudes in the 17th–19th Centuries*, edited by Mark D. Szuchman, 141–66. Boulder, CO: Lynne Rienner, 1989.

———. *Order, Family, and Community in Buenos Aires, 1810–1860*. Stanford, CA: Stanford University Press, 1988.

Theroux, Paul. *The Old Patagonian Express: By Train through the Americas*. Boston: Houghton Mifflin, 1979.

Thomas, Lynn M. "Historicising Agency." *Gender and History* 28, no. 2 (2016): 324–39.

Thompson, Leonard, and Howard Lamar. *The Frontier in History: North America and Southern Africa Compared*. New Haven: Yale University Press, 1981.

Torres, Susana Beatriz. "Two Oil Company Towns in Patagonia: European Immigrants, Class and Ethnicity (1907–1933)." PhD diss., Rutgers University, 1995.

Tortorici, Zeb. "Agustina Ruiz: Sexuality and Religiosity in Colonial Mexico." In *The Human Tradition in Colonial Latin America*, 2nd ed., edited by Kenneth J. Andrien, 117–31. Lanham, MD: Rowman and Littlefield, 2013.

Tossounian, Cecilia. *La Joven Moderna in Interwar Argentina: Gender, Nation, and Popular Culture*. Gainesville: University of Florida Press, 2020.

Townsend, Camilla. *Malintzin's Choices: An Indian Woman in the Conquest of Mexico*. Albuquerque: University of New Mexico Press, 2006.

Trímboli, Javier A. "1979. La larga celebración de la conquista del desierto." *Corpus. Archivos virtuales de la alteridad americana* 3, no. 2 (20 December 2013). https://journals.openedition.org/corpusarchivos/568.

Turner, Frederick Jackson. *The Frontier in American History.* New York: H. Holt, 1920.

Tutino, John. "The Revolution in Mexican Independence: Insurgency and the Renegotiation of Property, Production, and Patriarchy in the Bajío, 1800–1855." *Hispanic American Historical Review* 78, no. 3 (1998): 367–418.

Uribe-Urán, Victor. *Fatal Love: Spousal Killers, Law, and Punishment in the Late Colonial Spanish Atlantic.* Stanford, CA: Stanford University Press, 2016.

Valerio-Jiménez, Omar S. "Neglected Citizens and Willing Traders: The Villas Del Norte (Tamaulipas) in Mexico's Northern Borderlands, 1749–1846." *Mexican Studies/ Estudios Mexicanos* 18, no. 2 (2002): 251–96.

Vallmitjana, Ricardo. *Bariloche, mi pueblo.* Buenos Aires: Fundación Antorchas, 1989.

Vapnarsky, César A. *Pueblos del norte de la Patagonia, 1779–1957.* Buenos Aires: Centro de Estudios Urbanos y Regionales, 1983.

Varela, Maria Teresa. "Estado y Territorios Nacionales. Relaciones, tensiones y conflictos en la sociedad y política rionegrina (1916–1943)." PhD diss., Universidad Nacional de La Plata, Facultad de Humanidades y Ciencias de la Educación, 2015.

Vezub, Julio Esteban. *Valentín Saygüeque y la "gobernación indígena de las Manzanas": poder y etnicidad en la Patagonia septentrional (1860–1881).* Buenos Aires: Prometeo Libros, 2009.

Vezub, Julio Esteban, and Mark A. Healey. "'Occupy Every Road and Prepare for Combat': Mapuche and Tehuelche Leaders Face the War in Patagonia." In *The Conquest of the Desert: Argentina's Indigenous Peoples and the Battle for History,* edited by Carolyne R. Larson, 43–70. Diálogos Series. Albuquerque: University of New Mexico, 2020.

Vita, Leticia. "El Concepto 'Estado' en la Ciencia Política Moderna." *Revista Electrónica Instituto de Investigaciones Jurídicas y Sociales A. L. Gioja,* no. 3 (25 October 2016): 99–112.

Walker, Charles. "Crime in the Time of the Great Fear: Indians and the State in the Peruvian Southern Andes, 1780–1820." In *Crime and Punishment in Latin America: Law and Society Since Late Colonial Times,* edited by Ricardo D. Salvatore, Carlos Aguirre, and Gilbert M. Joseph, 35–55. Durham, NC: Duke University Press, 2001.

Walker, Mack. *German Home Towns: Community, State, and General Estate, 1648–1871.* Ithaca, NY: Cornell University Press, 1971.

Walther, Juan Carlos. *La conquista del desierto: síntesis historica de los principales sucesos ocurridos y operaciones militares realizadas en La Pampa y Patagonia, contra los indios (años 1527–1885).* 3rd ed. Buenos Aires: Editorial Universitaria de Buenos Aires, 1970.

Weber, David J. "Turner, the Boltonians, and the Borderlands." *American Historical Review* 91, no. 1 (1986): 66–81.

Weber, Eugen. *Peasants into Frenchmen: The Modernization of Rural France, 1870–1914.* Stanford, CA: Stanford University Press, 1976.

West, Elliott. *Growing Up with the Country: Childhood on the Far Western Frontier.* Histories of the American Frontier. Albuquerque: University of New Mexico Press, 1989.

Wiesner-Hanks, Merry. "Forum Introduction: Reconsidering Patriarchy in Early Modern Europe and the Middle East." *Gender and History* 30, no. 2 (2018): 320–30.

Wilson, Aaron Steven. "Government and Law in the American West." In *The World of the American West*, edited by Gordon Morris Bakken, 492–530. New York: Routledge, 2010.

Wolfe, Patrick. "Settler Colonialism and the Elimination of the Native." *Journal of Genocide Research* 8, no. 4 (1 December 2006): 387–409.

Yunque, Alvaro. *Calfucurá; la conquista de las pampas.* Buenos Aires: Ediciones A. Zamora, 1956.

Zeballos, Estanislao Severo. *Callvucurá y la dinastía de los Piedra.* Biblioteca argentina fundamental. Buenos Aires: Centro Editor de América Latina, 1981.

———. *Viaje al país de los araucanos.* Buenos Aires: El Elefante Blanco, 2002.

Zink, Mirta. "La política territoriana pampeana en los años 30 e inicios de los 40." Paper presented in the XI Jornadas Interescuelas, Departamentos de Historia, Tucuman, September 2007.